The WO[...]
Thirty-
CHAPT[...]
DR JOHNSON'S
Guide to Life

Henry Hitchings was born in 1974. He has written mainly about language and history, starting in 2005 with *Dr Johnson's Dictionary*. *The Secret Life of Words* (2008) won the John Llewellyn Rhys Prize and a Somerset Maugham Award, as well as seeing him shortlisted for the title of *Sunday Times* Young Writer of the Year. *The Language Wars* (2011) completed what was in effect a trilogy of books about language. He is a prolific critic and has made several programmes for radio and television on subjects including Erasmus Darwin, the eighteenth-century English novel and the history of manners. He is a Fellow of the Royal Society of Literature.

'Hitchings himself could be said to provide positive proof of Dr Johnson's benign influence on the world. As this delightful book goes on, his own aphorisms grow more like Dr Johnson's, as though infected with that robust sympathy and intelligence. Looking through my notes for this review, I sometimes found it hard to recall which phrase was coined by Henry Hitchings, and which by Samuel Johnson.'

Craig Brown, *Mail on Sunday*

'Witty, engaging . . . Hitchings proves an amiably convincing advocate for his hero's enduring significance.'

Nick Rennison, *Sunday Times*

'Enjoyable . . . Hitchings is at his best when un-entwisting some of Johnson's most quoted and misquoted sayings.'

The Times

Also by Henry Hitchings

Dr Johnson's Dictionary

The Secret Life of Words

The Language Wars

Who's Afraid of Jane Austen?

Sorry! The English and their Manners

The WORLD in Thirty-Eight CHAPTERS or DR JOHNSON'S Guide to Life

HENRY HITCHINGS

PICADOR

First published 2018 by Macmillan

This paperback edition first published 2019 by Picador
an imprint of Pan Macmillan
20 New Wharf Road, London N1 9RR
Associated companies throughout the world
www.panmacmillan.com

ISBN 978-1-5098-4194-3

1 3 5 7 9 8 6 4 2

A CIP catalogue record for this book is available from the British Library.

Printed and bound by CPI Group (UK) Ltd, Croydon, CR0 4YY

For Marina

Contents

1. An inscription over the door, to show what kind of a Book this is — *1*

2. Of personal oddity, which is no obstacle to personal authority — *12*

3. The community of pains and pleasures – our subject's Origins and Upbringing, with some speculations on what we may learn from them — *24*

4. The description of a young man's disappointment, with some sidelights courtesy of a certain Switzer, Dr Jung — *33*

5. A philosophical meditation upon the nature and rewards of Accident, in which are used the strange words 'Galilean serendipity' — *42*

6. In which Samuel Johnson, being entrusted with a mission of Love, proceeds to execute it; with what success will hereinafter appear — *49*

7. The mournful truth of London life: or, an author embarks upon the sea of Literature (with but a smattering of wormy cliché) — *57*

8. In which we observe the peculiarities of Friendship, manifest in Samuel Johnson's association with the notorious Mr Richard Savage — *68*

9. A resting-place – where the reader may take refreshment, and where vexed matters are resolved — *74*

10. Of Genius, with sundry other scenes from the farce of life — *77*

11. In which the craft of literary biography is expounded   *87*

12. An excursion to the Theatre, with some brief diversions   *95*
     into other arts

13. In which we ponder the making of a Dictionary – with   *105*
     thoughts on the true meaning of lexicography and the
     particular flavours of its solitude

14. A chapter about Grief (for one word must serve where   *114*
     in truth no assemblage of words will be sufficient)

15. Containing some essential points of information on the   *127*
     life of reading, whereamong are the most fugacious
     mentions of Mrs Elizabeth Montagu and even Mr Stephen
     King

16. A chapter that reflects on the uses of Sickness, and of   *133*
     Patrons

17. An essay, or 'loose sally of the mind', upon the methods   *140*
     of a moralist, in which are considered prose style and
     its higher functions

18. Some further thoughts on the *Rambler* and the intricacies   *149*
     of ordinary life

19. A short musing, upon exemption from oblivion (or what   *154*
     is otherwise called Memory)

20. Containing much to exercise the reader's thoughts upon   *160*
     the questions of Fear and Sanity

21. A chapter one might, in a more facetious spirit, have   *171*
     chosen to label 'Shakespeare matters'

22. In which Samuel Johnson idles, to some avail, not least   *180*
     by enquiring into the soul of advertisement and our
     artificial passions

23. Of tea and Abyssinia – a chapter about Choices, in which   *188*
     we have chosen to include the word 'lumbersome' (a curio
     you may reasonably think a mistake for 'cumbersome')

24. In which the definition of *network* provides an   *199*
     opportunity to appraise certain marvels of the twenty-first
     century, not least the inventions of Mr Mark Zuckerberg

25. On the business of a Club – being not 'a heavy stick;   *205*
     a staff intended for offence' but rather 'an assembly of
     good fellows' (where the staff may cause offence, without
     intent)

26. A chapter upon Samuel Johnson's lawyerly inclinations, 215
    in which we may wonder at the conduct of Signor
    Giuseppe Baretti and the philosophy of Dr George Berkeley
    – of whom, we can be sure, only the latter was fit to be
    a bishop

27. In which at last we attend to the life and loves of Hester 221
    Thrale, a foisonous fund of Anecdote

28. Some ruminations upon scepticism, amid which 232
    appear the names of both Sir Thomas Browne and
    Scratching Fanny

29. A short chapter on politics and public life, wherein the 240
    radical John Wilkes does rear his head

30. Containing a sketch of Dr Johnson's visit to the 246
    Caledonian regions – and matters pertinent thereunto

31. On the fleeting nature of Pleasure and the state of Felicity 258

32. In which thought is applied to an awkward question: 267
    whether Dr Johnson subscribed to the doctrines of
    S****ism

33. Upon Charity – whether it be cold, and how it is 274
    performed

34. A chapter about Boredom, which may serve to remind 281
    us that there are no truly uninteresting things

35. Of Johnson among the Bluestockings – though it behoves 287
    us to remark that he did not refer to them thus, and that
    we might now be wise to forswear this somewhat disdainous
    appellation

36. One of our longer chapters, directed with no little 294
    incongruity to the matter of life's brevity

37. Some thoughts upon the business of Cultural Legislation, 307
    which is less atrocious than it sounds

38. In which this account of the great Johnson is concluded, 320
    with a Farewell to the reader

Acknowledgements 327
Bibliography 328
Notes 343

An inscription over the door, to show what kind of
a Book this is

A SCRAP OF LAND, a speck in the sea's breath. On an October evening, a Tuesday, two travellers arrive after dark. The sea has been rough, and their craft's four oarsmen can find no easy place to disembark; it seems they must carry the visitors to dry land, though one of them chooses to spring into the water and wade ashore. In the moonlight the two figures embrace. It is late to be inspecting monuments, so they retire for the night – sleeping fully clothed in a barn, nestled in the hay, using their bags as pillows.

The next day they explore the island. Its buildings have been battered by storms and stripped by locals needing materials for their homes; now they are ruins, caked in filth. The old nunnery is a garden of weeds, and the chapel adjoining it a cowshed. The two men walk along a broken causeway – once a street flanked by good houses – and arrive at the roofless abbey. Its altar is damaged; islanders have carried off chunks of the white marble, believing that they afford protection against fire and shipwreck. A few intricately carved stone crosses still stand.

Later, the visitors will write about what they saw. One will comment that the island used to be 'the metropolis of learning and piety' and wonder if it 'may be sometime again the instructress of the Western Regions'. The other will reflect that 'the solemn scenes of piety never lose their sanctity and influence': 'I hoped that, ever after having been in this holy place, I should maintain an exemplary conduct. One has a strange propensity to fix upon some point of time from whence a better course of life may begin.'

This is a sketch of Iona, where in AD 563 the energetic Irish exile St Columba founded a monastery. Today, the island's great sites have been restored and are often mobbed with day trippers – a mix of Christian pilgrims and happy-snapping tourists. Yet in 1773, when Samuel Johnson and James Boswell visited, few people went there. It was Johnson who reflected on the island's lost role as 'the metropolis of learning and piety', recalling how, as he experienced its decay but also its tranquillity, he was transported into the past – to a time when it was 'the luminary of the Caledonian regions, whence savage clans and roving barbarians derived the benefits of knowledge and the blessings of religion'. This was a place where earth and heaven seemed only a finger's width apart. Somehow it cheered the soul.

'Whatever withdraws us from the power of our senses,' Johnson wrote, and 'makes the past, the distant, or the future predominate over the present, advances us in the dignity of thinking beings.' This is a rallying cry, an appeal for historical understanding. He doesn't mean that we should refuse to live in the moment, ignoring the pith of the present to spend our lives dwelling on how idyllic the past was or how ambrosial the future might be. Instead he is arguing that we are dignified by our ability, through the operations of our minds, to transcend our circumstances, to reach beyond the merely local, to appreciate difference.

It is an insight typical of Samuel Johnson, a heroic thinker whose intelligence exerted itself in a startling number of directions. A poet and a novelist, a diarist and editor and translator, as well as the author of numerous prefaces and dedications, he produced the first really good dictionary of English, invented the genre of critical biography, and shaped the common understanding of what is meant by 'English literature'. He would not have recognized the term 'Renaissance man'; not until half a century after his death did English import the word *Renaissance*, and *Renaissance man* is a twentieth-century coinage. But that is what he was: an astonishing all-rounder. A great moralist and essayist, he also practised the virtues he preached.

Today Johnson is not an obvious role model, for we live in an age when anyone laying claim to that title is expected to be golden – attractive and infallible. He wasn't the sort of person that modern media companies lionize. His Instagram feed would be wack. Diet tips? Forget it. Although his Twitter might deliver a bit more sizzle, he'd be an infrequent tweeter, what with his lethargy and dejection. Yet he has a lot to say to us. For instance, about role models: 'Almost all absurdity of conduct arises from the imitation of those whom we cannot resemble.' This is a maxim for the era of social media, if ever there was one. Not least because, inside the designer heels or sleek sports shoes, the golden idol has feet of clay. Humanity is flawed, and if we allow ourselves to believe that any specimen of it is wholly unblemished, we see only a persona, not the person. Glossy role models conceal reality from us, rather than helping us navigate it.

Seeking a better example of how to live, we might not be quick to choose someone with several gruesome features. But faults are part of our magic. A person is stitched together out of both charms and imperfections, and we can only be inspired – really and deeply inspired – by someone whose virtues cohabit with weaknesses.

Samuel Johnson was precisely such a person. His achievements made him famous – a public figure who, in the words of his friend William Maxwell, took on the role of an 'oracle, whom everybody thought they had a right to visit and consult'. Vividly present in his own writings, he appeared even more colourfully in what others wrote about him: imposing and unkempt, quirky yet robust, courageous in his honesty, a supporter of the neglected and the needy, cutting through the thickets of trumpery and going down into all the dark places of the soul.

His days were full of crisis and suffering. He spent countless weeks and even years lost in what he called 'the maze of indolence', worried that he could not exclude the 'black dog' of depression (his words) from his home and his head. Dramatically, and alarmingly, he pictured himself 'suspended over the abyss of eternal perdition only by the thread of life'. Much of the time, he regarded himself as a failure. His many difficulties meant he had to be an expert at finding ways to handle misery and pain. Not all of these were good: in the belief that it would ease his breathing, he was often bled, and he made use of opium, valerian and the sea onion known as squill (a diuretic, otherwise employed as rat poison). But he put greater faith in what seemed to him the most effective natural painkillers: humour and friendship.

It was the humour that I found especially appealing when I got to know him, at nineteen, through Boswell's *Life of Johnson*. I had a vague awareness that he was famed for his wit, yet was surprised by what I found: not the dry superiority that frequently passes for *bel esprit*, but something more daring, a vibrant candour. Often, reading about Johnson, there was the simple pleasure of sampling his verve, as when he wrote to his great friend Hester Thrale, 'I received in the morning your magnificent fish, and in the afternoon your apology for not sending it.' Sometimes he might raise a smile that was close to being a wince by squashing some fond notion or ambition, for instance informing Boswell, 'As to your History of Corsica, you have no materials which others have not, or may not have. You have, somehow or other, warmed your imagination . . . Mind your own affairs, and leave the Corsicans to theirs.' But what I saw above all was his belief in the utility of humour – as a social lubricant, and also as a means of negotiating the world's incongruities and accessing the truth.

Johnson's capacity for laughter – for exciting it, and for sharing in it – was essential to his closest relationships. He loved being able to 'compare minds', and the warm glow of intimacy eased his psychological burdens. It pleased me then, as it has often pleased me since, to think of friendship as a connection that at once enriches and disencumbers us. I was impressed, too, by the words of one of those nearest to him, the painter Sir Joshua Reynolds: 'He may be said to have formed my mind, and to have brushed from it a great deal of rubbish.' The verb *brushed* is so unexpected and immediate, and the second half of Reynolds's sentence captures a significant function of friends: we rely on them to sweep away our drossy ideas and free us from fatuous preoccupations.

As I read further, venturing beyond Boswell, I admired Johnson's independence and incisiveness, his ability to finish a mighty judgement with a little twist of idiosyncrasy. I enjoyed the precision of his attacks on flattery, sophistry and the tendency of shallow people 'to ridicule and vilify what they cannot comprehend'. But I grew to understand that he has a greater gift to offer: in diagnosing the mind's bad habits, which he does by reference to his own, he invites us to confront the less noble parts of ourselves.

I had in fact come across him before – and been less appreciative. Aged sixteen, embarking on my A-levels, I'd been given the *Cambridge Guide to English Literature*; the front cover reproduced a head and shoulders painting of a grave-looking man, and on investigation I found that this was Samuel Johnson. But the first encounter had been two or three years earlier, when a tetchy version of him turned up in the sitcom *Blackadder*. I've several times revisited the episode, in which Dr Johnson, having completed his *Dictionary of the English Language*, solicits the patronage of the Prince Regent, a fop who pronounces himself 'as thick as a whale omelette'. This deliciously daft half hour of TV doesn't pretend to be historically accurate (Jane Austen is said to be a huge Yorkshireman with a beard), but in my experience it has played a large part in shaping popular ideas of who Johnson was, right down to his failure to include the word *sausage* in the *Dictionary* – although in reality it's there, 'a roll or ball made commonly of pork . . . minced very small'. *Blackadder* contributes to an image of the good doctor as a pedantic grump. Certainly it's common to picture him as cantankerous, a thunderingly patriotic champion of monarchy and hierarchy, and it is possible to find things he said that support such a reading. Some of his devotees, keen to correct this simplistic take, choose instead to present him as an out-and-out progressive or an agitator who spurned the authority of institutions. This, too, lacks nuance. Although it is true that some of his attitudes – to women's education, for instance, and to race – were enlightened by the standards of his day, it's fanciful to claim for him some sort of revolutionary now-ness.

This book is animated by different ideas: that the dead do not vanish completely, that we aren't obliged to embroider the past or sex it up to make it pertinent to our world, and that great writers and thinkers speak in eternity. In parts it is microscopically biographical, because to understand how to live we need to look at life as it is actually experienced, or as it has actually been experienced. In an essay for his periodical the *Rambler*, Johnson wrote in praise of biography: 'no species of writing seems more worthy of cultivation . . . since none can be more delightful or more useful, none can more certainly enchain the heart by irresistible interest, or more widely diffuse instruction to every diversity of condition'. Everyone 'in the mighty mass of the world' will find great numbers of people in a condition similar to theirs, for whom an account of their 'mistakes and miscarriages, escapes and expedients, would be of immediate and apparent use'.

In the pages that follow I offer a chronological account of Johnson's life – the playful chapter titles redolent, I hope, of those eighteenth-century novels that luxuriate in the details of an individual's day-to-day existence. But each chapter is also an exploration. What, to borrow his phrasing, are the immediate and apparent uses of Johnson? How does swimming among his thoughts and experiences enable a better, more reflective approach to living? How might the service he performed for Reynolds – that vital task of brushing rubbish from the mind – be something he can do for all of us? I present him as an example of how to act or think; occasionally his role is the opposite, as an illustration of how not to; and often I draw attention to something he wrote or said that perfectly condenses an important truth.

He is a quotable commentator on so many departments of life: 'All distant power is bad', 'Whoever thinks of going to bed before twelve o'clock is a scoundrel', 'We are more pained by ignorance, than delighted by instruction', 'This is one of the disadvantages of wine: it makes a man mistake words for thoughts.' Often his judgements make us pause. I can remember faltering the first time I came across his statement that 'No man is a hypocrite in his pleasures'. It took me a moment to catch what it meant, namely that our amusements show our true character. His most astute judgements reward a second or third reading. 'All censure of a man's self is oblique praise. It is in order to show how much he can spare.' 'The tenderest love requires to be rekindled by intervals of absence.' 'It is seldom that we are otherwise, than by affliction, awakened to a sense of our own imbecility.' 'It is the practice of good nature to overlook faults which have already, by the consequences, punished the delinquent.'

'How he does talk! Every sentence is an essay,' observed a Miss Beresford, an American living in Worcestershire, when she shared a coach with Johnson and Boswell one summer's day in 1784. The assessment is itself pleasantly quotable – and perceptive. The remarks that inform our sense of the quotable Dr Johnson are often fragments of longer sentences, or of more substantial utterances. He is not so much an aphorist as a perpetual essayist, even in speech. In his *Dictionary* he defined *aphorism* as 'an unconnected position' – a statement, that is, detached from context and even its source. It is thus rather like an oxbow lake, a free-standing pool (of thought) cut off from the flow of the river (of conversation or prose) where it originated. He has the aphorist's crispness, the verbal artistry required to reinvigorate familiar ideas or respond ingeniously to other people's coarser generalities. He has, too, the aphorist's prudent irony.

Not all the aphorisms attributed to Johnson were actually written or uttered by him. He never said that 'A fishing rod has a hook at one end and a fool at the other', or that 'I did not have time to write you a short letter, so I wrote you a long one instead'. It is not true that he was interrupted in bed with his wife by a maid who exclaimed 'I am surprised,

Dr Johnson'; nor did he reply, 'No, my dear, it is *we* who are surprised; *you* are astonished.' It's telling, though, that these lines are often taken to be his. Among the reasons for his lasting fame is a facility for witticism, so it is natural to attach his name to stray examples.

Yet even the authentic Johnsonisms that fill the pages of dictionaries of quotations are only part of his story. His observations are the product of strenuous thought, and rather than simply firing off bons mots he likes to untie the knot of an aphorism. While he can come up with glorious new sayings of his own, other people's exist to be unravelled. Are they true? Are they consistent? Are they helpful? His idea of instruction isn't the soothing banality of the modern self-help guru, who plays shamelessly on the reader's insecurities; his willingness to argue, explain and exemplify means that his wisdom is less reductive than aphoristic writing tends to be.

We could dwell on any of the quotations I have cited. But what's most striking is that, although they appear impersonal, Johnson is present in all of them; these are distillations of his experience, and his voice reverberates in each. When he speaks of want and of the intervals of absence that renew love, he is drawing on memories of his own suffering and missteps, and when he refers to the absurdity of imitating people we can never match, he is in fact thinking of a particular type of person, who has come by the idea that retreating to the countryside – or into solitude – is a guarantee of creative freedom, yet in practice has managed only 'to quit one scene of idleness for another, and, after having trifled in public, to sleep in secrecy'.

Because of his abilities as an aphorist, there is a tendency to think of him as a sententious man with a sharp pen and no less sharp a tongue. We may also imagine him as a master of the imperative mood, issuing diktats from a lofty perch. But though at times Johnson's talk is high-handed, that is seldom how he writes. In the *Rambler* he describes 'the task of an author', which is either 'to let new light in upon the mind' or 'to vary the dress and situation of common objects' and in doing so 'spread such flowers over the regions through which the intellect has already made its progress, as may tempt it to return, and take a second view of things'. The key words here are the last. The author who takes a second view is changing perspective, challenging their existing notions, renewing the act of looking. As he writes in another of his periodicals, the *Adventurer*, 'we see a little, and form an opinion; we see more, and change it'. This is something Johnson does on a pedestrian level – for instance conceding that pigs, which he'd once held in low regard, are 'unjustly calumniated' – and on a more elevated one – such as by revising his *Dictionary* to beef up its stock of morally instructive quotations. Taking a second view isn't just a task for authors; it is the essence of the examined life, in which we seek to understand events and ideas, or indeed people and emotions, from more than one vantage point. Here we begin to see a more supple and empathetic Johnson, among whose favourite words are *yet* and *but*.

Even once we get the measure of this two-handed Samuel Johnson, he continues to surprise, looking with approval or interest on something we might expect him to deplore or dismiss. He argues that playing card games 'consolidates society', and writes the preface for a book on the game of draughts (which he believes can sharpen one's foresight and vigilance), though he doesn't go in for either activity himself. He recognizes that women who become prostitutes do so out of necessity rather than weakness – not a remarkable insight now, but a bold one at the time. He claims that gambling is less likely than flashy business ideas to be a cause of harm, and can even make the case for smoking – 'a shocking thing' that involves 'blowing smoke out of our mouths into other people's mouths, eyes and noses', yet one that 'requires so little exertion, and yet preserves the mind from total vacuity'. This willingness to deviate from received wisdom also allows him to condemn popular pursuits, as when he reflects that 'It is very strange and very melancholy that the paucity of human pleasures should persuade us ever to call hunting one of them.'

One of the special qualities of Johnson's judgement is its power to jolt us, perhaps because it feels radically truthful or lays its emphasis somewhere unanticipated: 'all intellectual improvement arises from leisure', 'the insolence of wealth will creep out', 'vivacity is much an art, and depends greatly upon habit', 'histories of the downfall of kingdoms, and revolution of empires, are read with great tranquillity'. As we trace his personal journey, these moments when his ideas unsettle us are frequent – and invaluable.

2

Of personal oddity, which is no obstacle to
personal authority

JOHNSON'S EXISTENCE calls to mind an image coined by his
fellow poet Alexander Pope – 'this long disease, my life' –
and it began with ominous difficulty in September 1709. On
Wednesday the 18th, late in the afternoon, he was 'born
almost dead'. The phrase is his, used in one of his few fragments of autobiography. This inauspicious start was one he
shared with some of the eighteenth century's most august
figures – Voltaire, Rousseau, Goethe, Newton. To be born
almost dead and to know that this was so is to understand
the preciousness and precariousness of life, to think that one
has been given a second chance and that whatever follows
is a gift.

'Here is a brave boy,' said the man-midwife George
Hector, hoping to reassure the child's mother. Forty-year-old
Sarah Johnson was exhausted by her difficult labour, and her
newborn was placed with a wet-nurse, Joan Marklew. He
returned from her care after just ten weeks, 'a poor, diseased
infant, almost blind'; whether from her milk or exposure to
some other source of infection, he contracted scrofula, a disease of the lymph nodes that caused angry abscesses. He
would later be taken to London to be touched by Queen
Anne – the royal touch was supposed to cure the condition
– but the scars remained with him till he died. From infancy,
his hearing was imperfect and he had little sight in his left eye.

The mature Johnson struggled with asthma, gout and rheumatism; other afflictions included a painful swelling inside his scrotum. Worse, he suffered from a deep melancholy that seems to have caused two collapses (of a kind we might now call nervous breakdowns), and his efforts to overcome dark thoughts often failed. James Boswell, the most influential of his biographers, provides a vivid image of his mind, which 'resembled the vast amphitheatre, the Coliseum at Rome'. In its very centre 'stood his judgement, which, like a mighty gladiator, combated those apprehensions that, like the wild beasts of the arena, were all around in cells, ready to be let out upon him'. At length 'he drove them back into their dens', but they could at any moment return to assail him. This has long struck me as a peculiarly powerful vision of mental disturbance and the recurrent need to withstand its assaults. It suggests, too, that life itself is a trap and that the individual caught in the trap is an object of voyeuristic fascination, perpetually being given a thumbs up or thumbs down.

Though Johnson had it in him to be jovial and gregarious – and coined the word 'unclubbable' to describe his self-important, difficult friend Sir John Hawkins – he kicked against the conventions of polite society. He was 'beastly in dress', according to one squeamish observer; his protégée Frances Reynolds (sister of Sir Joshua) thought he looked like a beggar, and those meeting him for the first time commented on his loose clothes and his shrivelled wig, which sat askew. In other respects he lacked polish, and he was either puzzled or amused by refined manners. He treated books with cavalier disregard; his personal library was 'miserably ragged', and when the actor David Garrick lent him some fine volumes of Shakespeare, he defaced them and then rather implausibly claimed that such marks as he had made could be rubbed away using breadcrumbs.

There is evidence that he suffered from what we now call Tourette's syndrome (after Gilles de la Tourette, who described the disorder a hundred years after Johnson's death). Certainly he had symptoms of Tourette's. He didn't engage in the involuntary bursts of profanity that the name now brings to mind – in fact exhibited by only 10 per cent of sufferers – but there were other forms of disturbance and excitability, tics and jerks and grimaces and noises that sometimes embarrassed him and deepened his feelings of guilt and unworthiness.

In his later years, his odd mannerisms attracted the startled attention of people wedded to new ideas about the body as an instrument of politeness. Those ideas derived from many sources: the writings of the French surgeon Nicolas Andry, whose notions about correcting physical deformity began to impress an urbane English audience in the 1740s; the philosopher David Hartley, whose *Observations of Man* (1749) emphasized that the functions of the body and the mind were related; and works of less medical and philosophical substance, such as the letters of the Earl of Chesterfield (published in 1774), which aimed to inculcate politesse and preached total mastery over the movement of one's limbs and face. The result was a surge of interest in the mechanisms – both mental and physical – for regulating the body. Johnson, it's fair to say, failed by some distance to meet the standards required by the votaries of this physical self-discipline.

Boswell describes how Johnson would rock back and forth in his chair, clucking and whistling and breathing out explosively like a whale. Tom Davies, the Covent Garden bookseller who introduced the two of them, said that Johnson laughed like a rhinoceros. The novelist Fanny Burney noticed his habit of twirling his fingers, twisting his hands, see-sawing up and down, and chewing at the air – 'in short, his whole person is in *perpetual motion*'. He would touch every post he passed when out walking and squirm unnervingly before he swept through a doorway with a single giant stride. Another compulsion led him to collect scraps of orange peel, which he pocketed mysteriously. When the artist William Hogarth encountered him for the first time, he concluded that this odd figure, 'shaking his head and rolling himself about in a strange ridiculous manner', was 'an idiot', and when he heard him speak, the eloquence that poured from him was such that Hogarth imagined the idiot had for a moment been touched by divine inspiration.

Johnson was aware of his many oddities. He was aware, too, that they caused others to regard him as a misfit, even an undesirable, and that many people thought he was therefore unqualified to write for a broad audience. His relationship with his oddities was ambivalent. Although he was often sociable, he stood a little removed from the routine and the regular, and as a result he was well placed to survey the contours of everyday experience. But while a sense of his own peculiarity deepened his perceptiveness about norms and patterns of behaviour, he also knew that his quirks could be distracting. What was more, the efforts he made to control his unruly body could heighten the impression of strangeness. Sir John Hawkins's daughter, Laetitia-Matilda, described him walking with his left arm pinned across his chest, and recalled her brother Henry seeing him descend from a coach on Fleet Street and head off at high speed 'in the zig-zag direction of a flash of lightning'. According to Frances Reynolds, he would often 'with great earnestness place his feet in a particular position, sometimes making his heels to touch, sometimes his toes, as if he was endeavouring to form a triangle'.

Some of Johnson's peculiarities were endearing, or could be channelled to entertaining effect. Many observers left behind accounts of his relish for extreme physical feats. Attacked in the street by four robbers, he was able to hold them at bay until assistance came, and when a fellow the-atregoer in his home town of Lichfield stole his seat and refused to surrender it he tossed both the man and the seat into the theatre's pit. In the summer of 1762 he visited Devon, and in Plymouth met a young woman who claimed she could outrun anybody; he duly raced her across a spacious lawn and won, though at first he lagged behind because he had to kick off his slippers, which were much too small for him. Another time, having challenged the book-seller John Payne to a footrace, he picked him up halfway through the agreed distance and unceremoniously deposited him on a branch of a nearby tree, before hurtling off as if the race was not yet done. Even in the final year of his life, aged seventy-four, he was able, when he found a bone-weary prostitute lying in the street, to carry her on his back to his lodgings (where he nursed her back to health). On a lighter note, he amused his friend Bennet Langton by rolling all the way down the steep hill behind his Lincolnshire home, and had amused him more in the early days of their acquain-tance, answering the door at three in the morning with a poker in his hand, an unexpected willingness to join in Langton's carousing and the more than faintly alarming promise that 'I'll have a frisk with you.'

One of Johnson's most memorable performances occurred during his trip with Boswell to Scotland in 1773. Though not much given to mimicry, he astonished guests at a dinner in Inverness when the conversation turned to recent British discoveries in Australia: among these was Joseph Banks's sighting of a creature that, according to the recently published official account, moved 'by successive leaps or hops, of a great length, in an erect posture' (and proved 'most excellent meat').[1] At the mention of this marvel, Johnson rose from his chair and, gathering the tails of his massive brown coat into a pouch, put out his hands like feelers and bounded across the room. It was not enough to hear about the kangaroo; he needed to *be* the kangaroo.

This is the behaviour of an armchair traveller, projecting himself into foreign experiences, and of someone sympathetic and inquisitive, keen to imagine what it might feel like to inhabit others' worlds (including that of a large marsupial he'd never seen). His actions promised to induce mirth and amazement, but he also risked looking silly – and he was prepared to run that risk in order to make the moment dramatic and animate the otherwise rather vague image of the kangaroo.

It was not unusual for him to shock his companions. Even his friend Edmund Burke, whose career in parliament and as a political theorist had accustomed him to boorish talk, thought him 'a little rough in conversation'. Johnson's roughness could simply be a haste to assert himself, but was sometimes offensive. He often drew pleasure from being contradictory, and admitted that he 'talked for victory', enjoying the contest more than was seemly. As a critic of literature, his defence of high standards could seem belligerent; he would delight in finding fault with writers who were usually revered, claiming that the task was important because such writers might otherwise be held up as perfect examples. He would promote a point of view he knew to be spurious, because supporting it would allow him to display his wit and ingenuity. Recalling an evening when Johnson took pride in his own 'colloquial prowess', Boswell commented that 'you tossed and gored several persons'. Mostly he resembled not a mad ox, but a bear huffing and snorting: he was brusque more often than rude. Regret, even remorse, often followed these outbursts, and when he strained to seem remarkable – when others marvelled at him – the pleasures of audacity soon gave way to feelings of self-disgust. He was harder on himself than on anybody else.

Johnson's confrontational spirit reflected his suspiciousness about refinement. The routines of gentility, to which Lord Chesterfield in the 1750s applied the French term *etiquette*, were no more than a veneer. As far as Johnson was concerned, being a good friend or a good guest should have nothing to do with such cosmetic performances. Even in talking up politeness, he referred to it as 'fictitious benevolence'. The phrase sounds like a whisper, full of gentle persuasion, and usefully conveys a sense of polite conduct as a ceremonial act of self-control. But while he could see the value of behaving agreeably and smoothly, social life was pointless if it consisted only of courtesies that propagated further courtesies. Candour should be at the core of one's relationships, and he encouraged others to act on this principle.

One of those he urged on in this way was Fanny Burney. When she was daunted at the prospect of coming face to face with the Shakespeare scholar Elizabeth Montagu, their host Henry Thrale suggested she should warm up for their encounter by testing her conversational gifts on another of those present, the less formidable Dorothea Gregory. But Johnson told her that 'when I was beginning in the world, and was nothing and nobody, the joy of my life was to fire at all the established wits'. Instead of behaving tricksily, by putting off the inevitable contact and needlessly ruffling another guest, she should not hesitate to face the woman she wanted to meet. 'Always fly at the eagle,' he counselled. Procrastination, he knew, was not the opposite of crude impulsiveness but its cousin, a failure of self-control. It results from incorrectly framing our understanding of the situation we are in. His instruction to Burney made her think of both herself and Mrs Montagu as birds, similar even if not equal, whereas her first instinct was to visualize the encounter as more like one between, say, a mouse and a lion. Being socially courageous, or just socially fluent, requires this kind of shift in perspective: it involves not only thinking and talking more affirmatively about oneself, but also reimagining one's environment.

Thanks chiefly to Boswell, we know a lot about Johnson's own skirmishes and engagements, the tossing and the goring – and, thanks again to Boswell, we know their perpetrator as 'Dr Johnson'. The doctorate was honorary; in fact, two were bestowed on him, by Trinity College Dublin in 1765 and by Oxford ten years later. He did not like to use the title, preferring to be 'Mr Johnson', partly because there were a lot of phoney doctors and bogus doctorates around, and partly because he hoped, as a 'Mr', to sound more like a gentleman and less like a person with something to peddle. But friends and critics made the name stick, and Boswell, though adept at capturing his subject's complexity, doctored his image in other ways. Readers of his *Life of Johnson* get used to its subject's utterances including a formal 'Sir' – 'Why, Sir, most schemes of political improvement are very laughable things', 'Sir, it is affectation to pretend to feel the distress of others, as much as they do themselves.' Boswell portrays himself going in for a lot of this *Sir*-ing, too, as he asks a question or ventures an opinion, but when Johnson does it, while issuing an edict or correction, he sounds pompous and peremptory. A modern audience feels this keenly: when someone calls me 'Sir', I suspect that I am about to be told off ('Sir, get in line' at the airport) or patronized ('I'm afraid, sir, that this is not a public area'). The image of Johnson as a bossy doctor, dishing out potent prescriptions, isn't an easy one to shake.

It's an image that obscures his attractions. For in his works, and in many of his recorded sayings, he reveals a profound intelligence about human nature. He understands that we don't always know our own motives and grasps the importance of cultivating kindness. He has seen things that appear clear-cut once they've been mentioned but mostly elude us: how often we lose all the good of some great labour for want of doing just a little more to wrap it up; or how wary we should be of simply despising sentiments that are not our own, since one day, under different circumstances, we may share them. He writes persuasively about disappointment, desire, delusion and the 'secret discontent' that accompanies wickedness; about envy, rivalry, pride and 'the treachery of the human heart'. Skimming this list, we might suppose that close examination of such subjects is a recipe for despondency. But Johnson shows that by thinking carefully about these matters we can steer a better course through life. From the jaws of despair he could wrest hope, and so can we.

For all his mental turbulence, he was fundamentally sane, and his rudeness was often also rightness. Thus when dining with Catharine Macaulay, a staunch advocate of egalitarianism, he proposed that she practise what she preached by having her footman join them at table – and when she was reluctant, observed that 'your levellers wish to level *down* as far as themselves; but they cannot bear levelling *up* to themselves'. Visiting St Andrews, he showed less interest in the professors at the university than in a woman who lived with her cat in the ruins of the cathedral; the woman's assertion of her legal right to reside there appealed more to him than the pride of scholars whose institution looked as if it was in decline. On another occasion, when the politician Charles James Fox launched into a finicky discussion of Roman history, an unimpressed Johnson 'withdrew my attention, and thought about Tom Thumb'. Fox wanted to talk about Catiline, a debauched, magnetic and treacherous senator of loftily patrician background; Tom Thumb, on the other hand, was a man with humble origins, a tiny hero who got the better of much bigger men.

Johnson's populism was audible when he expressed sympathy for the victims of everyday injustices, or revulsion at the elite's tendency to find lucrative sinecures for its most useless members. Observing the way that the lower classes were demonized for being uncouth, he pointed out that 'those who complain, in peace, of the insolence of the populace, must remember that their insolence in peace is bravery in war'. He professed himself 'a great friend to public amusements', on the grounds that they kept people from more vicious activities, and objected to the vogue for petitions ('a new mode of distressing government, and a mighty easy one'), not because they unlocked democracy but because they created the illusion of democracy and were often signed out of vanity rather than commitment. Yet sometimes he could take up a position that seemed starkly un-egalitarian, and would then provide a strange but credible explanation. When George III's coronation procession was planned, he objected to the shortness of the proposed route: 'All pomp is instituted for the sake of the public. A show without spectators can no longer be a show. Magnificence in obscurity is equally vain with *a sundial in the grave*.'[2]

He lived at a time that was propitious for a person capable of such analysis and vigorously expressed opinions. The growth of newspapers and magazines provided him with a wealth of everyday detail on which to comment, as well as the channels through which to do so. For all its interest in refinement and etiquette, this was an age of appetite, feverish with cravings for gossip and for celebrities fit to be its subject. Johnson was perfect for its purposes. Cogent and contradictory, always ready with some gem of invective or critique, and endowed with an astounding range of knowledge, he seemed an ideal luminary for a society where bookish accomplishments were treasured and fame was achieved through the medium of print. That he was eccentric, a struggler made good, simply meant he was even better suited to be wrapped in its myth.

His was an age, too, of consumerism and expanding foreign trade, of innovation rather than blind faith in providence, and of belief in the idea that 'progress' meant moving both forwards and upwards. One in which it was respectable to indulge the ego, and in which being acquisitive ceased to be seen as brash or selfish and began instead to be thought of as an expression of prudent interest; in which the glee and sport of the privileged often rested on exploiting a servant class; and in which one could (at least from 1757 to 1795) buy a directory of the prostitutes who worked around Covent Garden, which served as a guide to prices and services, but could also be read one-handed. Yet this was a period in which the very people who saw themselves as exuberantly experimental in fact embodied a decorous traditionalism; society was dominated by an oligarchy of great proprietors, and there was no workable programme for changing that state of affairs. Characterizing an entire century in this way – or offering such a sketch of the 'high' eighteenth century (1730–1780) – is inevitably reductive. But maybe this world, with its dynamic commercialism, its reliance on credit and its inventive approaches to taxation and fiscal policy, its cult of the pursuit of leisure and its myriad new opportunities to indulge the imagination, sounds just a little bit familiar?

In our own age, attentive to the drama of the self in all its intricacy, we can appreciate Johnson's finely tuned scrutiny of his own thoughts and feelings. As we acknowledge the mind's battles rather than repudiating them, we can prize his intuition that inside our heads we carry not a neatly ordered box of offal, but a furrowed landscape dense with ridges and valleys. His struggle adds authority to his judgements, insights and ideas.

3

The community of pains and pleasures – our subject's
Origins and Upbringing, with some speculations
on what we may learn from them

LICHFIELD IN STAFFORDSHIRE, where Samuel Johnson was
born and grew up, was at the time the cultural hub of the
West Midlands. His parents' dignified new house stood in
the marketplace. His father Michael, who had spent more
than he could afford on its construction, ran a bookshop on
the ground floor. Johnson would later refer to his family's
poverty, which will surprise anyone who now visits the house
at the corner of Breadmarket and Sadler Streets. Its solid
facade and fifteen rooms suggest prosperity, but Michael
often found it hard to pay his taxes, and to keep afloat he
had to be versatile, selling patent medicines and stationery,
binding books and presiding over auctions, and even dishing
up practical or professional guidance to people who dropped
in at the shop and treated it like a citizens advice bureau.

When Johnson compiled his *Dictionary of the English Language* in early middle age, he would salute his birthplace.
In the entry for *lich*, meaning 'carcass', he explained that
Lichfield was 'the field of the dead . . . so named from
martyred Christians'. To this he added the Latin phrase
'*Salve, magna parens*' ('Hail, great parent'), a deliberate echo
of a line in Virgil's *Georgics*, from a section in which the
Roman poet praises his country – the mother of vigorous
men, as he puts it. Thanks to his origins, the poet feels able

to unseal the sacred fountains of poetic inspiration (or 'divulge the hallowed sources', according to the translation I have to hand). He can make his voice heard. He can 'plunge into material and measures prized in days of old'.[1] The reference is apt, since Virgil is saluting the influence of the place he is from and the traditions that shape it. The challenge – for the poet, and for Johnson – is to leave this special place, vanquish the wider world's hardships and then return, ever loyal, to add something to its greatness.

Johnson portrays his childhood as an ordeal, but with pride rather than self-pity. His stock of anecdotes about his early years is small, perhaps because a few well-rehearsed set pieces were enough to satisfy people's curiosity without obliging him to revisit anything too sensitive. Yet the stories are evocative. For instance, when he was just a few weeks old 'an inflammation was discovered on my buttock, which was . . . taken for a burn': soon 'it swelled, broke, and healed'. Later in infancy an 'issue' was cut in his left arm so that pus from his tubercular infection could drain away. He reports his mother saying that he took little notice of this painful procedure because he was otherwise engaged – 'having my little hand in a custard'. The issue was kept open until he was six, which must have drawn unwelcome attention from other children.

The first school he attended was a short distance from home, but his eyesight was so poor that he had to be shepherded back there after lessons. According to legend, he once decided to make his own way and, crossing the marketplace, crawled near the gutter. As he did so he became aware that his teacher Anne Oliver was following him; he sprang to his feet and, feeling she had insulted his independence, attacked her. Another story, which he would eventually disclaim, centred on his pronouncing, aged three or four, the first half of a short poem to commemorate a duckling he had trodden on and killed – apparently one of a fleet of eleven that he had been allowed to look after. These tales of the infant Johnson have endured because they show him pugnaciously refusing assistance and responding creatively to death. Both behaviours were themes of his whole life.

It is tempting not to quote the poem on the duckling, because it's feeble. But this is the first of the many epitaphs he wrote, and gives a flavour of his later direct and rather droll approach to the form's standard element of *what if?* 'Here lies poor Duck / That Samuel Johnson trod on! / If it had liv'd, 'twould have been good luck / Because it was an odd one.'[2] In maturity, when he wrote about the deaths of others, it was with the hope that some detail from their lives could be turned to use – 'to exhibit patterns of virtue'. But he usually included a hint of the incongruous and even the absurd, of life's fragility being both painful and farcical. Though terrified of death, he could cherish the insight that its very 'uncertainty' is 'the great support of the whole system of life'.

Early on, school was a relief from the tensions of home. When Sarah Ford wed Michael Johnson in the summer of 1706, they were thirty-seven and forty-nine respectively. Their famous son later reflected that they 'had not much happiness from each other'. Part of the problem was that his mother came from a landowning family and had little time for her husband's relatives – 'those indeed whom we knew of were much lower than hers'. 'This contempt,' he explains, 'began . . . very early: but, as my father was little at home, it had not much effect.' When his father was present, he disliked talking about business, and when his mother broached the subject 'her discourse was composed only of complaint, fear, and suspicion'. Another revealing detail: when Michael was short of funds, he expressed shock at the price of tea and discouraged Sarah from socializing with their neighbours, with the result that she festered at home, unfulfilled.

Samuel's relationship with his mother was complicated. (Whose is not? But still . . .) There was tenderness on both sides; she sometimes spoiled him, and he and his brother Nathaniel, born three years after him in the autumn of 1712, were rivals for her affection. Yet at other times, unsettled by his ill health or by having too little money, she treated him less warmly. She nagged him about his failure to learn 'behaviour' and bridled when he objected to the vagueness of this; he wanted precise instruction, not woolly platitudes. As he grew older, his disrespectfulness increased – when she called him a puppy he asked if she knew what people called a puppy's mother – and he seems to have gone to some lengths to avoid her. Part of the problem was that she saw in him some of the same traits that she found unattractive in her husband and his relations. He recorded her letting him know what an embarrassment it was when he visited his aunt and gobbled a large quantity of boiled leg of mutton; his mother had lived 'in a narrow sphere, and was then affected by little things', so 'told me seriously that it would hardly ever be forgotten'. Children get used to the words 'You haven't heard the last of this'. Typically, the punishment is the threat itself, but in Samuel's case the episode suggested a future in which his shame would extend in every imaginable direction.

Sarah was right to think that, at least in terms of temperament, her elder son had more in common with his rugged, brooding father. For Sam this was no great source of satisfaction, and in adulthood he would grumble that he had inherited from Michael a 'vile melancholy'. Today we are likely to associate melancholy with a blue pensiveness or bittersweet autumnal mood of introspection, but for Sam it was akin to madness. It heightened his awareness of the animal energies within him, of urges that needed to be restrained and voices he wanted to silence, and gave him a foretaste of death – not the moment of death itself, but the slow shutting down of the powers of reason. Like insanity, it could be considered an illness (a medical problem) or a character fault (a moral one), according to his mood. He was heir, then, to a corrosive wretchedness, a psyche with the blackest of undercurrents.

Michael Johnson had some standing in Lichfield, serving as sheriff in 1709 and becoming a magistrate three years later; in 1725 he would be the senior bailiff, chairing the local council. Yet his moodiness affected his work and he tended to overstretch himself. For instance, in the year following his marriage he chose not only to erect a new house, but also to add to his shop's stock 2,900 volumes – mostly folio – that had previously belonged to the Earl of Derby. At the same time, he began a sideline as a manufacturer of parchment. In his lighter moments, Michael liked to exhibit his son to friends and visitors, and Sam would rush off and climb a tree to avoid being his father's plaything. Later he would reflect that the offspring of a doting old man were likely to have 'much the same sort of life as a child's dog'.

One of the childhood episodes that Sam pictures most sharply is being sent, aged ten, to Birmingham. There he and Nathaniel stayed with their uncle John Harrison, whom Sam describes as 'drunk every night, but drunk with little drink, very peevish, very proud, very ostentatious, but luckily not rich'. On another occasion around the same time, his Birmingham cousin Sally Ford visited Lichfield; one day, as he sat in the kitchen writing, believing himself alone, he momentarily became aware of her presence and saw that she had begun to dance, but he was so absorbed in his work that he barely paid her any notice. His biographer John Wain suggests that this scene may have looked like a painting by Vermeer, one of those small images of an interior where nothing much is happening, its detail at once limpid and elusive. Sam's own take on the episode was that it illustrated vividly 'the power of continuity of attention, of application not suffered to wander or to pause' – but 'This close attention I have seldom in my whole life obtained.' Given what we know of his later literary output, it seems strange that he should refer to his errant attention. Therein lies a paradox: it requires an unusual degree of attentiveness to one's self to know how fallible one's powers of attention really are.

At the grammar school in Lichfield, which he entered aged seven, he was initially in the care of Humphrey Hawkins, a kindly teacher of about fifty who was 'very skilful in his little way'. After a couple of years he moved on to the upper school and received less congenial tuition: first from Edward Holbrooke, a recent Cambridge graduate who apparently used ill temper to mask deficiencies of knowledge, and then from the stern and scholarly John Hunter, who could be savage in his treatment of difficult pupils. Sam belonged in that category; a schoolmate described him as a 'long, lank, lounging boy', and he had an adolescent's urge to question authority – one third genuine curiosity about why things are the way they are, two thirds recalcitrant cockiness. Unsurprisingly, Hunter's methods didn't endear him to his pupils. He joked that he was cruel in order to save them from what would otherwise be their certain fate – the gallows. Sam would recall Hunter with horror, but conceded that he was 'a very good master' and 'whipped me very well. Without that . . . I should have done nothing.' Half a century later he would reflect on how much educational practices had changed, concluding that 'There is now less flogging in our great schools than formerly, but then less is learned there; so that what the boys get at one end, they lose at the other.'

Few readers today will share his apparent enthusiasm for corporal punishment, and in Sam's lifetime it became increasingly contentious. Beating was widely regarded as therapeutic and a means of visibly and palpably underscoring schoolmasters' authority; it was common to claim that it could harm no one besides the recipient (Sam told Boswell that 'The rod produces an effect which terminates in itself'). Yet arguments against the practice stressed how counterproductive it could be, achieving discipline in the short term but causing longer-term resentments. Its decline owed much to the philosopher John Locke's *Some Thoughts Concerning Education* (1693), which noted that such methods did nothing to reward good habits. For Locke, shame was more effective than pain in getting pupils to recognize their offences, and incentives were essential in order to reinforce positive conduct. In the second half of the eighteenth century, Jean-Jacques Rousseau would restate the case against corporal punishment. But Sam's schooldays made him think of public education as a system of correction; guidance and edification barely came into it. The problem, as he saw it, was that education worked best when self-administered. Children who were educated together, in public, learned more about obstinacy than mental elasticity, more about self-preservation than free expression, and more about crime than virtue – and sometimes it took a sadist with a rod to cut through the mephitic atmosphere of vice. By contrast, self-education was a happy mixture of freedom, volition and purposeful exertion, a kind of 'learning to learn' and a process rather than a product.

At sixteen, he escaped Hunter and enjoyed a taste of a more cosmopolitan life. He went to stay for more than six months with Cornelius Ford, his thirty-one-year-old cousin, who had recently become a clergyman and was living in the Worcestershire village of Pedmore. Ford had taught at Cambridge, was a wit and a drinker, and mixed in bookish London circles; now he was married to Judith Crowley, a woman twelve years his senior who had paid off debts he had incurred in Cambridge, and had renounced her Quaker upbringing to join him in the Church of England. Cornelius relished the presence of his well-read, unusual and oddly rustic relation, and encouraged him to make the most of the fine library he maintained at Pedmore. The time Sam spent with this sophisticated figure gave him a notion of what intelligent conversation could be, and it introduced him to the idea of London as a centre of literary excellence.

It was not the last time that Sam would revel in the witty company of a charming, dissolute man. In his edition of Shakespeare, forty years later, he writes shrewdly about Falstaff, in terms that illuminate his experience of dissolute charmers. Falstaff is a 'compound of sense and vice; of sense which may be admired but not esteemed, of vice which may be despised, but hardly detested'. For all his faults, he 'makes himself necessary . . . by the most pleasing of all qualities, perpetual gaiety, by an unfailing power of exciting laughter'. What moral can be drawn from Shakespeare's complex portrait of this boastful, cowardly, engaging glutton? Simply this: 'that no man is more dangerous than he that with a will to corrupt, hath the power to please'. Although this is not an exact image of Cornelius

Ford or of Sam's later debauched yet likeable companions, it speaks revealingly of his capacity to succumb to the seductions of a person he knew he ought to condemn. In a note on Falstaff's failure to form a bond with Prince Hal's brother, he identifies 'community of pleasures' as the root of friendship, and a few years later he would repeat the phrase, with a little more focus, when telling Boswell that 'Many friendships are formed by a community of sensual pleasures'.

As he says this, in his sixties, he is thinking over the friendships he has enjoyed, and he is looking back to his time with his cousin Ford. The sharing of pleasures builds relationships, and the sharing of illicit or decadent ones builds relationships that contain a hint of the flirtatious and the competitive. Friendships are undergirded by ideas of respect, and (on the whole less explicitly) by the potential for benefit, but they also involve an element of risk, the consciousness of laying oneself open. Sam's experience at Pedmore showed him that we form such bonds by chance, not choice, though we may pretend otherwise, and that part of their magic is that there is always a hint of something unequal in them. It is usual to claim that friendship must be evenly proportioned, and Sam is sometimes held up as an advocate of this state of affairs, since he wrote in the *Rambler* that 'Friendship is seldom lasting but between equals'. Yet he thought that its essential property was that it 'enlivened' us: through friendship 'our virtues may be guarded and encouraged, and our vices repressed . . . by timely detection and salutary remonstrances', and at any moment only one of a pair of friends can occupy the role of guardian and booster. In practice, it was what he called 'conformity of inclinations', rather than their parity, that buoyed such a relationship.

❧ 4 ❧

The description of a young man's disappointment, with some
sidelights courtesy of a certain Switzer, Dr Jung

RETURNING HOME, Sam again felt stifled. After a period
that had augmented his sense of life's possibilities, he came
across as rather precious, and the perennially severe Hunter
would not accept him back at school, regarding his long
absence as impertinent. His parents, buckling under the
pressure of money worries, now also fretted about what
this exclusion meant for their son's prospects. He had to
complete his schooling elsewhere – twenty miles away in
Stourbridge, lodging at the headmaster's house and teaching
some of the younger children. He made a nuisance of himself there, took too much pride in his command of Latin,
wrote a few elegant pastoral poems, and expressed contempt
for his father's business.

Once more back in Lichfield after a year away, he
worked resentfully in Michael's shop, complaining that
attending to customers was a poor substitute for the pleasures of reading the stock. Around the house, he and
Michael and Nathaniel must sometimes have squeezed past
one another awkwardly and seemed, in John Wain's nice
phrase, 'like mastiffs in a terrier's kennel'. His appetite
for mischief remained, yet it was redeemed by his friendship with Gilbert Walmesley, a scholarly bachelor who lived
in the bishop's palace and kept an impressive library; he
liked to stay in touch with literary fashion, had been a good

customer of Michael Johnson's, and around the time Sam began to receive his hospitality was reacting with horror to *Gulliver's Travels*.[1]

Ford and Walmesley were mentors of a kind Sam was never to have again. He would become a mentor to others, but struggled in early adulthood for want of someone to guide him in this way. He valued access to an older, cultivated, judicious man who could serve as an advisor, coach and model, an illustration of what was possible, a listening ear. At a time when his existence seemed unpromising, these mentors were lifelines. They gave him purchase on ideas and inspirations that weren't available from among his own family or from his teachers. For instance, Walmesley was a lawyer and led him to contemplate a legal career. He also introduced Sam to a forceful style of intellectual debate, often charged with an eagerly businesslike politics very different from the bumbling Toryism he had tended to encounter in Lichfield.

Sam's prospects brightened when his mother received a legacy of £40 from her cousin, Elizabeth Harriotts. The money could have helped shore up Michael's ailing business, but was earmarked for Sarah Johnson's personal use, and she decided that it should be spent on enabling her son to go to university. Further help came from a well-off former schoolmate, Andrew Corbet, who was at Pembroke College, Oxford, and liked the idea of having Sam join him there – as a mixture of companion, auxiliary and teacher. The destination seemed apt; Sam's godfather Samuel Swynfen had studied at Pembroke, as had one of his mother's cousins.

On the final day of October 1728, Sam entered Pembroke College, hopeful of adding to his already considerable learning and testing his intellect in conversation with the university's scholars and his fellow students. But his time there was a disappointment. Although one of his tutors, William Adams, would recall his being a 'gay and frolicsome' student who was 'caressed and loved by all about him', Sam corrected this, insisting that 'I was rude and violent. It was bitterness which they mistook for frolic.' The teaching did not impress him, and he got more pleasure from sliding on the ice in the meadow that belonged to Christ Church, the college opposite, or from loafing by Pembroke's entrance and amusing other students. He read a lot of Greek, grappled with the study of metaphysics, and flustered acquaintances with his mixture of erudition, irritability and nervous energy. It says something about the temper of his time at Oxford that he eventually wore out his shoes by clumping around the city streets, and that he indignantly threw away a replacement pair that a fellow student left outside his door.

In the winter of 1729 he quit the university. His father was sick, and money was tight. It's possible, too, that he had become uncomfortably aware that, if he stayed, in order to graduate he would have to take an oath of allegiance to the monarch, which would have troubled his conscience. What's certain is that he went back to Lichfield and slipped into a period of apathy. He was, in a sense true to the word's etymology, disappointed: deprived of an opportunity, a position, an appointment (with destiny), the feeling of being *à point*. Writing about authors very different from Sam, the critic Laura Quinney has referred to disappointment as 'the state of the self estranged from the hopes of selfhood' and as 'a twilight of paralysis'. Those definitions are useful here. Sam was frozen by humiliation. He had lost his grip on a public identity as an Oxford student; he had believed this was his to keep hold of, and his relationship to the world – to time – had been broken. It was not simply that he was now in a cul-de-sac; he could see exactly how this looked to other people.[2] He would occasionally walk to Birmingham – a round trip of more than thirty miles – but without much purpose besides the exertion. Staring at the town clock without being able to tell what time it was, writing love poetry to several young women who he knew would not return his interest, he seemed on the verge of a breakdown, beyond the help of mentors or medics.

Cornelius Ford died in the summer of 1731, at the Hummums in London's Covent Garden; a century later, when Pip stays there in *Great Expectations*, it is a seedy hotel, but in Cornelius's day it was a place for Turkish bathing and furtive intimacies. His death was a shock, as he was in his thirties and had always seemed so full of vitality. Then, in December, Michael Johnson died too. Near the end, when a weakened Michael urged his elder son to go the fifteen miles to Uttoxeter to man the bookstall he ran there on market days, Sam declined. He believed himself above such petty business. This hauteur would afterwards make him feel shame, and half a century later he would do penance for it, standing in the rain in Uttoxeter's marketplace, 'exposed to the sneers of the standers-by'. But at the time his refusal to go there was a symptom of his determination to compensate for his father's failings. He associated all his own problems – temperamental, financial, religious, domestic, professional – with Michael.

Sam's was not a world in which people went in for word association tests, but 'father' and 'bookstall' would have elicited awkwardly delayed reactions from him, stirring up other disagreeable sensations. One of the key figures in the development of the word association test was Carl Gustav Jung, and in the Jungian model the father is a bridge to society at large, representing and enabling a young adult's transition into a world beyond the home. For Sam, this and all other such bridges seemed, in the space of a couple of years, to have collapsed. When Michael asked him to run the bookstall at Uttoxeter, it was an occasion not to embrace adult responsibility, but to discern parental deficiency. With one of his mentors gone forever and his educational prospects in tatters, his father's failure to be *instrumental*, to convey him safely into adulthood, seemed catastrophic, and the idea that he could make a tangible impression on the world receded from view.

Jung is in another respect a fitting point of reference here, for Sam's renunciation of that world – his isolation and turn inwards – was like the 'creative illness' that Jung would suffer immediately prior to the First World War. That the men and the contexts are different hardly needs saying, but Jung's episode is instructive. He would write, afterwards, that 'In order to grasp the fantasies which were stirring in me "underground", I knew that I had to let myself plummet down into them.'[3] Attending to the visions and voices that had taken residence inside him, he feared falling completely under their spell. But it struck him that, if he was going to progress beyond a merely theoretical sense of fantasies and their tyranny, he needed to face them. His attack of mental disturbance looked, according to one's perspective, like madness, an extended spell of narcissism, or an experiment in self-analysis. In the short to medium term it was crippling, but in the longer term it inspired a profound understanding of the need to confront the unconscious.

Sam's experience anticipated Jung's: from a bout of mental sickness, he learned the importance of exploring his inner life and documenting what he found there. It was a harrowing yet formative period and therefore, unsurprisingly, one he later had little wish to discuss. Jung furnishes another term that's useful here; he took from ancient Greek philosophy the term *enantiodromia*, meaning the tendency for things to turn into their opposite. He illustrated this with the story of a man who laughed all the way up a steep mountain and then cried on the way back down; as he climbed, he looked forward to his smooth descent, but on the way down he thought about how hard it had been to get to the top. Enantiodromia is embodied in tendencies we've all noticed: when people on the political left turn into arch-conservatives, atheists experience Damascene conversion, hedonists become anchorites, and punctilious scholars metamorphose into batshit visionaries. For Jung, when 'an extreme, one-sided tendency dominates conscious life . . . an equally powerful counterposition is built up, which first inhibits the conscious performance and subsequently breaks through the conscious control'. In his view, the psyche is a self-regulating system, in which the discord between opposite attitudes will eventually resolve itself. In Sam's case, the opposites were threefold: a strong sense of his own worth, and a hideous self-loathing; an unusually rich appreciation of the mind's astonishing power, and a crushing feeling of mental impotence; a pride in his origins, and a contempt for the psychological and financial woes inflicted on him by his family. See-sawing between these positions was exhausting, and one of the ordeals of his adult life was converting this fluctuation into a virtue – his capacity for balanced, even-handed argument.

When Sam began to emerge from his depression, he wasn't suddenly able to forge ahead. The lack of a degree frustrated efforts to earn money; it wasn't something he could wear as a badge of honour, in the style of many a modern university dropout who's grown sick of institutional constraint. When he applied for teaching jobs, as seemed natural for a young man of his gifts, it was a grave handicap. He became aware of the importance of badges, of the need to have the right credentials rather than just ability. Later, objections to appointing him had as much to do with his odd appearance and mannerisms. To be blunt, he was ugly, and ugly people struggle to find patrons; when he turned seriously to writing, it was in the knowledge that it was a field in which his odd looks wouldn't ruin his chances. In today's literary culture, where so much importance is attached to authors' marketability (a pretty transparent euphemism), he would be considered a poor prospect.

Eventually, in March 1732, he secured a position at a school in Market Bosworth, a Leicestershire market town. He was an usher, a role like today's classroom assistant. The school's main patron was Sir Wolstan Dixie, a legendarily violent and stupid man who was about as far as possible from being an ideal employer. Sam lasted there a few months, and that autumn, having failed to get a job as an usher at the grammar school in the Derbyshire town of Ashbourne, he went again to Birmingham. He expected to stay a few weeks with his closest schoolfriend Edmund Hector (a doctor, and nephew of the man-midwife who had assisted at Sam's birth), but he ended up spending a large part of the next four years there – mostly in a state of torpor, out of which he slowly managed to claw his way.

It was here that he wrote his first journalism, for the recently launched *Birmingham Journal*. The newspaper was the brainchild of Thomas Warren, a bookseller with whom Hector lodged. Well-known locally, Warren took an interest in his lodger's friend and introduced him to a new social circle. He also encouraged him in the idea of translating an account of the travels of a Jesuit missionary, Jerónimo Lobo, in Abyssinia (today Ethiopia). The original was in Portuguese, which Sam didn't know, and he worked from a previous translation, in French. Although the subject doesn't now sound enticing, travel writing, especially when it had a religious flavour, was in demand. Abyssinia was a spiritual battleground, where the Habesha people withstood Roman Catholic attempts to overhaul their long-established form of Christianity. Besides, it would have struck English readers as romantic and remote. Buyers, of whom there weren't in the end very many, must therefore have been disappointed to find the English translator explaining that Lobo's account contained no juicy material about exotic geniuses or inarticulate barbarians. Instead, explained Sam, it revealed 'that wherever human nature is to be found, there is a mixture of vice and virtue, a contest of passion and reason'. In other words, there were such things as universal psychological truths – a theme to which he would return.

Even if *A Voyage to Abyssinia* didn't generate much buzz, it was a publication, and Sam received five guineas for his work. His name did not appear on it and in fact would feature on the title page of no complete work of his before the poem *The Vanity of Human Wishes* in 1749 (though in 1738 it popped up when he published a proposal for a translation of an Italian work of history). But at the beginning of 1735, or possibly even in December of the previous year, he had the satisfaction of seeing the bound volume – proof of his worth, and an artefact capable of outlasting him. On the title page of a copy he later gave to Edmund Hector he wrote, 'Sl. Johnson, Translator, 24 yrs.'[4]

Sam had some reservations about Lobo specifically and the overbearing Portuguese missionaries more generally, and his translation contains mistakes that suggest he wasn't fully engaged with the task. He renders *dix* as 'six', *sixième siècle* as 'sixteenth century' and *vers le couchant* as 'eastward' rather than 'westward'. These look like simple blunders, but can be seen as marks of his less than total respect for his source. Not doing the job as well as possible may have been a form of protest, as if the young author was quietly, even unconsciously, letting it be known that he was cut out for bigger things.[5] In other cases, he seems deliberately to have tweaked Joachim Le Grand's French translation in order to represent the colonists unfavourably and emphasize the noble resistance of the Habesha.[6]

This, too, would turn out to be a position he repeatedly adopted, and one of his most astringent statements on the subject comes more than twenty years later in 'An Introduction to the Political State of Great Britain', where he writes that 'surely they who intrude, uncalled, upon the country of a distant people, ought to consider the natives as worthy of common kindness, and content themselves to rob without insulting them'. Behind these withering words lies a humanity appalled by imperial thuggery, and the memory of his translation of Lobo hovers in the background as he concludes, here with obvious reference to the putative greatness of Britain, that 'no people can be great who have ceased to be virtuous'.

✂ 5 ✂

A philosophical meditation upon the nature and rewards
of Accident, in which are used the strange words
'Galilean serendipity'

I HAVE STARTED referring to Sam, rather than to Johnson
or Dr Johnson or even Samuel. It's not a very Johnsonian
manoeuvre or one that's in step with scholarly punctilio, but
I think it is a small risk worth taking. To call him Johnson
over and over is to keep him at arm's length. A single easy
syllable, rather than a lugubrious pair, makes him more
present. As Sam, his story is immediate and his wisdom current; only when stepping back to view him in a broader
historical context will I refer to him as Johnson.

Sam grew up above, and often in, his father's bookshop.
He was evidently able to browse among its extensive stock,
reading extracts of whatever took his fancy. The catalogue
for a sale Michael held at Worcester in 1718 lists what must
have been a typically rich assortment of titles. In it he
addressed prospective customers, and this introduction
includes the now rather tart-seeming detail that 'to please
the ladies, I have added store of fine pictures and paper-
hangings'. He explains that the sale will begin with 'small
and common books', after which comes more serious fare:
works of divinity ('the best of that kind'), as well as law,
mathematics and history.

One of Sam's recent biographers, Peter Martin, calls
Michael Johnson's shop 'a huge biblio-cabinet of curiosities,

a bookish bower of bliss tempting him into divergent and crisscrossing intellectual, cultural, . . . scientific and geographic paths'.[1] Access to such abundance was unusual, and Sam made the most of it. But his reading was often spontaneous; living in a bookshop created opportunities for happy accidents. He told Boswell the story of how, as a boy, he went looking for some apples that his brother Nathaniel had hidden on a high shelf in the shop. It may be that he'd imagined this stash, for he located no apples, but in his search he came across a sizeable volume by Petrarch. He had previously read some praise of this Italian scholar, and he now sat down with the book and read it for a long time. 'The story is too good to be true,' says another Johnson expert, Robert DeMaria, who sees it as a convenient allegory about a youngster who 'reached for immediate and simple gratification but grasped instead the old, intensive European Latin culture, in which he then laboured throughout his life'.[2] Yet I'm not sure that it is too good to be true. Isn't this exactly what happens in bookshops and libraries? We go looking for one thing and happily find another. If the bookshop were our home, wouldn't this sort of discovery occur frequently?

Large projects often have their origins in a stroke of luck or a chance encounter: ability stumbles on opportunity, and events that might well have happened separately instead concur. As a Christian, Sam could argue that 'nothing in reality is governed by chance', for the universe is 'under the perpetual superintendence of him who created it'. Yet he was struck by what he couldn't help feeling was the randomness of his personal history. He claimed that we arrive at our occupations by accident, and while his choice of a career as a writer feels apt and natural, we can see the events that set him on that course. In an essay that pictures Sam's greatness being achieved 'by committee', as friends and associates prompt his conversation and adventures, Hugo Reichard describes how 'it is mainly inner resistances that hold the man back, chiefly outside forces that start him, route him, and keep him going'. 'What he badly needs, others come prepared to give', and many of his key moments are 'decided by others, by persons in his shadow'.[3] This underestimates his resourcefulness, but it captures the mood of a life in which many grand enterprises had casual or unplanned beginnings.

Opportunities rarely come from where we expect. My path has been shaped – to a greater degree than I may choose to recognize – by chance. We tend to underplay the role of chance because it threatens to make us look and feel like pawns; it diminishes our claim to genius. People who achieve great success will argue that every step of their ascent was planned. But this is the amnesia of victory. I'd argue that an unwillingness to acknowledge the importance of chance is a mark of a pedestrian mind, and accommodating it is a talent, not a weakness.

In an intriguing essay on the relationship between chance and creativity, Lewis Hyde writes of how 'a chance event is a little bit of the world as it is – a world always larger and more complicated than our cosmologies'. He describes 'smart luck', which is 'a kind of responsive intelligence invoked by whatever happens', a form of wit that 'responds and shapes, the mind-on-the-road, agile, shifty in a shifting world'. Conventionally, we think of luck and intelligence as opposites (or near enough), but Hyde proposes that luck is a form of intelligence. He quotes Paul Valéry's strangely satisfying claim that 'the bottom of the mind is paved with crossroads'.[4] It's an image of juxtaposition as something at once magical and logical – and one that implies our failure to recognize that boundaries are zones of transition rather than limits.

Inspiration is a receptiveness to accident and its effects. We see this principle in its crudest form, perhaps also its most absurd, in the ink spill on a writer's desk which causes a gloriously suggestive Rorschach blot to form on the page. Not something that happens as often as it used to; the modern equivalent of the fortuitously ornamented page may be a website we blunder upon, which initiates some new and fruitful course of action or the possibility of a collaboration we'd not previously considered.

Mostly we have been taught to be sniffy about accidental discoveries, and this is part of a larger cultural agenda of belittling luck. We have learned to think that people who frequently refer to luck are superstitious, unreliable and stupid, and that they are irresponsible, excusing their failures with the weak explanation that some things are simply beyond their control. At the same time, we persuade ourselves that our understanding of how things happen – the how, the why and the when – is impeccably scientific. But the world is more volatile than we are generally willing or able to accept, and our path through it less systematic than our pride will allow us to admit. As Nassim Nicholas Taleb argues in *Antifragile*, a provocative book about the rewards of disorder, 'our minds are in the business of turning history into something smooth and linear, which makes us underestimate randomness'.[5]

Sam's life is an instructive story of using uncertainty rather than hiding from it. This, after all, is someone whose education proceeded 'by fits and starts, by violent irruptions' (the phrase is Boswell's) and whose career developed haphazardly. In his life of the poet Abraham Cowley, he argues that 'Genius is a mind of large general powers, accidentally determined to some particular direction', and the words 'accidentally determined' are key. Cowley found a copy of Edmund Spenser's epic poem *The Faerie Queene* lying in the window of his mother's room, and from that moment had his 'particular direction'.

Today, when we speak of happy and accidental discoveries, the word that comes to mind is *serendipity*. It was coined by Horace Walpole in 1754, as Sam was at work on the *Dictionary*, but its popularity didn't take off till the second half of the twentieth century, and the *Oxford English Dictionary*'s first citation for *serendipitous* is as recent as 1958. Both noun and adjective are adored by self-professed word lovers, who like to point out that the island of Sri Lanka was once known as Serendip and that Walpole was inspired by a story, 'The Three Princes of Serendip', in which the main characters 'were always making discoveries, by accidents and sagacity, of things they were not in quest of'. But, as so often, delight in a nugget of etymology is an end in itself; it doesn't inspire further reflection on the nature of this accidental sagacity or sagacious embrace of accidents.

The historian Robert Friedel describes three kinds of serendipity. First there is Columbian serendipity: 'When one is looking for one thing, but finds another thing of value, and recognizes that value', as when Christopher Columbus, seeking a new trade route to Asia, landed in America. Then there is the Archimedean version: 'finding sought-for results, although by routes not logically deduced but luckily observed', as when Archimedes, wondering how he might measure the volume of an irregular solid, settled into a bath and noticed his body displacing a quantity of water equal to his own volume. Finally, we have Galilean serendipity: 'the discovery of things unsought for', a 'facility for using new instruments or capabilities to generate surprises', as when

Galileo pointed his newly constructed telescope skywards and saw celestial phenomena no one had previously been able to perceive.[6]

We tend to think of Columbus, Archimedes and Galileo as glorious pioneers. Yet their experience discloses a simple truth: you can't plan to make discoveries, but can only plan the type of activity that could lead to discoveries. To this we might usefully add Einstein's insight that 'No worthy problem is ever solved within the plane of its original conception.'[7] Inspiration happens when the ego acknowledges, at least for a moment, the existence of something bigger. 'Whatever be our abilities or application,' writes Sam in *Rambler* 154, 'we must submit to learn from others what perhaps would have lain hid for ever from human penetration, had not some remote inquiry brought it to view; as treasures are thrown up by the ploughman and the digger in the rude exercise of their common occupations.'

His definitive statement on the subject comes in *Rambler* 184. 'It is not commonly observed,' he writes, 'how much, even of actions considered as particularly subject to choice, is to be attributed to accident.' He goes on: 'Let him that peruses this paper review the series of his life, and inquire how he was placed in his present condition. He will find, that of the good or ill which he has experienced, a great part came unexpected, without any visible gradations of approach; that every event has been influenced by causes acting without his intervention; and that whenever he pretended to the prerogative of foresight, he was mortified with new conviction of the shortness of his views.' The productiveness of accident is not a reason, or an excuse, to shirk being purposeful. But to pursue ambition and feed a sense of adventure is to lay ourselves open to mishap. 'We set out on a tempestuous sea in quest of some port, where we expect to find rest, but where we are not sure of admission', and 'we are not only in danger of sinking in the way, but of being misled by meteors mistaken for stars, of being driven from our course by the changes of the wind, and of losing it by unskilful steerage'. Yet sometimes it happens 'that crosswinds blow us to a safer coast, that meteors draw us aside from whirlpools, and that negligence or error contributes to our escape from mischiefs to which a direct course would have exposed us'.

৯৶ 6 ৶ৎ

In which Samuel Johnson, being entrusted with a mission
of Love, proceeds to execute it; With what success
will hereinafter appear

WE LEFT SAM at a critical moment – the publication of his
first book. If this seemed to mark the start of a new chapter
in his existence, an even more significant change occurred
in 1735 when, after a brief but eager period of courtship, he
married. Elizabeth Jervis Porter, affectionately known as
Tetty, was a widow whom he probably met through Edmund
Hector, and at forty-five she was twenty years his senior. Her
husband Harry, a mercer in Birmingham, died in the
autumn of 1734, and she and Sam were wed the following
July, not in Birmingham or Lichfield but on neutral ground
in Derby.

In marrying someone so much older than him, he must
surely have recalled the circumstances of his cousin Cornelius Ford, who had shown that, whatever other people might
think, an age gap of this kind need not be a problem. It was
the first time that his affections for a woman had been
returned, and that sensation – of love, of reciprocity, of
someone being willing to make sacrifices for him – was
enough to fortify him against criticism. There was plenty of
that. To many in Tetty's social circle, the appeal of this
poor, strange and dishevelled young man was impossible to
fathom. Of her three children, only her nineteen-year-old
daughter Lucy was willing to accept him, and even she was

unnerved by his appearance. The standard image of Dr Johnson is of a man built like a Toby jug – well-fed, even fat. Such is the portraitist's privilege (or obligation). But although in later years his body became large and unwieldy, until middle age he was formidably built rather than overweight. When Lucy Porter met him, he struck her as 'lean and lank', his imposing bone structure alarmingly visible even through his clothes. Her brothers found his arrival in their mother's life both physically and morally repugnant. Tetty's elder son, eighteen-year-old Jervis Henry, refused to have anything more to do with her, and the younger, Joseph, took many years to get over his disgust.

Tetty brought £600 to the marriage, and as a result Sam was able to set up a school. This was at Edial, a hamlet a few miles from Lichfield, and an advertisement in the *Gentleman's Magazine* sought to attract interest from all around the country, boasting that 'At Edial, near Lichfield in Staffordshire, Young Gentlemen are Boarded and Taught the Latin and Greek Languages, by SAMUEL JOHNSON'. Readers of this London publication, launched in 1731 by a fellow Midlander called Edward Cave, could have had no idea of who Samuel Johnson was, and the advertisement failed to inspire great confidence. But the school seemed at first both a brave experiment and a reproof of all who had cast doubt on Sam's suitability as a teacher.

Later, when he was famous, people struggled to see other motives for the union with Tetty and concluded that it was odd or opportunistic (or both). She was not an obvious match for a man of his powers. Imprisoned by the affectations of faded beauty, she had weaknesses for gaudy make-up, trashy romances and opium. One of Sam's Victorian biographers, Leslie Stephen, puts the matter with wry succinctness: 'The attractions of the lady were not very manifest to others than her husband.'[1] But to her husband they were clear. He apparently trusted her judgement, and she declared him 'the most sensible man I ever met' (*sensible* at the time meant 'judicious' or 'capable of tender feeling'). It also seems likely that she was receptive to the affections his mother had seldom encouraged or welcomed, and that she embodied an idea of nurturing womanhood he had heard about but not experienced. She grounded and pacified him. Yet the possibility that she saved him from himself – that their private life together had a substance outsiders couldn't divine – seems scarcely to have occurred to any of his biographers until the twentieth century.

While the couple didn't need the rest of the world to approve of their union, they were wounded by its mockery. The school at Edial opened in the autumn of 1735 and attracted a handful of pupils; it is possible that there were as many as eight, but we know the identity of only three. Among them was David Garrick. In later life, established in fashionable London society, Garrick would turn party tricks for his admirers. One of these involved impersonating Tetty ('a little painted poppet, full of affection') and exaggeratedly recalling certain amorous scenes between man and wife that he had witnessed through a keyhole. Hard luck for Sam that, of the tiny number who could have witnessed the newlyweds' fumblings, one turned out to be the age's leading actor.

By his own account, Sam married for love. But love, he argued, was not a guarantee of marital happiness. Boswell records his saying that 'marriages would in general be as happy, and often more so, if they were all made by the Lord Chancellor, upon a due consideration of characters and circumstances, without the parties having any choice in the matter'. It is tempting to dismiss this as flippant or say that

Sam was reflecting his own experience of an unsatisfactory union. Yet he touches on an interesting issue. While marrying for love is today exalted in most cultures, and we perhaps tend to sneer at those where arranged marriage is common, there is a history of love marriages being regarded as foolish. According to this school of thought, passion makes us blind. Arranged marriages, widely considered coercive and authoritarian, often work. They have pragmatism at their core and are supported by both families involved. Comparatively untroubled by the problems that cause love matches to fail – a lack of realism, tension between the couples' relatives – they can be secure rather than flighty, and love, at first absent, may gradually emerge.

Am I advocating arranged marriage? No. But there is evidence all around us that people aren't very good at judging whether they should bind themselves in perpetuity to a particular individual, and while 'due consideration of characters and circumstances' is something most of us are likely to carry out before marrying, an impartial expert may perceive points of incompatibility that someone lovestruck will overlook. Sam's line about the Lord Chancellor engineering marriages shouldn't be read as a serious suggestion, but it is the comment of someone who has observed the arbitrariness of people's decisions about marriage – the imprudence with which they enter into it, or indeed the callousness with which they are shepherded in its direction. We hear a similar note of realism in Sam's short romance *Rasselas*; the title character is an Abyssinian prince, and his sister Princess Nekayah says that 'Marriage has many pains, but celibacy has no pleasures.' She is immediately accused of 'exaggeratory declamation', yet imagine being charged with that – it's like being told you're right.

In Sam's lifetime, there was a marriage crisis. Anxiety

about the relationship between love, sex, property and matrimony took many forms: the denunciation of fortune hunting, a fretfulness about the large number of bachelors, an insistence that regulating marriage was a means of preserving the boundaries of social class. The vigorous debates surrounding the Marriage Act of 1753, which sought to prevent clandestine marriages, focused political attention on this anxiety. Before the Act, the laws governing this institution were a curious hotchpotch. The Act's sponsors were unhappy about the number of marriages contracted without parental consent. Many of these were worryingly 'unequal', and the result was social chaos; the attorney general Sir Dudley Ryder wondered 'How often have we known a rich heiress carried off by a man of low birth, or perhaps by an infamous sharper?' When the Act was debated in parliament, one of the most compelling speakers was the Earl of Hillsborough, who argued that 'mutual love' was 'a very proper ingredient' of marriage, but that it should be 'a sedate and fixed love, and not a sudden flash of passion which dazzles the understanding but is in a moment extinguished'. Critics of the Marriage Act saw it as an assault on the freedom of the individual – an attempt to curb love and control the circulation of wealth – and it is hard to avoid the conclusion that the motives for the new legislation were at root economic.[2]

In the build-up to the Act, Sam was mulling over his own marriage. No one has ever pretended that it was exemplary. But, like his parents' uneasy bond, it prompted a lot of thought about how marriage could and should work. When he writes in *Rambler* 18 that marriage is 'the strictest type of perpetual friendship', he's proposing something that would have struck most of his contemporaries as radical: not a hierarchical relationship, but a balanced union, a place of confidence and integrity. In *Rambler* 167 he pictures a couple who in their 'connubial hopes' are 'less deceived' than is common. On the face of it they have a 'general resemblance'. Yet 'a nearer inspection discovers . . . a dissimilitude of our habitudes and sentiments', of a kind that 'affords that *concordia discors*, that suitable disagreement which is always necessary to intellectual harmony'.

The theory of the *concordia discors* can be traced back to the Greek thinkers Pythagoras and Empedocles, but the expression itself was first used by Horace. The world, so the theory goes, is in perpetual flux between harmony and strife. When it comes to relationships, the ideal state is one of dynamic tension. In *Rambler* 167 Sam goes on to say that each half of a couple has thoughts 'tinged by infusions unknown to the other', yet they can be 'easily united into one stream, and purify themselves by the gentle effervescence of contrary qualities'. While this could be more appealingly phrased, his thinking is suggestive. Although relationships need solid foundations, they are kept alive by our from time to time experiencing the frisson of difference: the person you know so well surprises you with an opinion or attitude that is at odds with your own, and you feel the fizz of chemistry, the pleasure of being tested, the same pulse of excitement that surged when you first met.

Sam's understanding of what mattered in marriage was tested in 1773, when his friend Henry Thrale got involved in trying to block the marriage of his niece, Frances Plumbe. The fifteen-year-old Frances wished to be wed to her sweetheart, Jack Rice; her father, Samuel, known in the family as Old Sammy, opposed the match and threatened to have Frances locked up. Our Sam surprised the Thrales by taking Frances's side. Alert and hostile to the ways in which marriages could be contrived for dynastic convenience, in order to keep assets in the family, he argued that a child's duty of obedience to its parent was not absolute: 'There wanders about the world a wild notion which extends over marriage more than over any other transaction. If Miss Plumbe followed a trade, would it be said that she was bound in conscience to give or refuse credit at her Father's choice? And is not marriage a thing in which she is more interested and has therefore more right of choice?' It was a while before Old Sammy Plumbe came round, but Frances and Jack Rice married, in Holland, and together they would have thirteen children before her premature death at thirty-two.[3]

This episode again shows Sam's soberly businesslike attitude to how one chooses a spouse. The individual is entitled to select a course of action – and to get it wrong. In *Rasselas*, the prince discusses 'the common process of marriage', which is 'a choice made in the immaturity of youth, in the ardour of desire, without judgement, without foresight, without inquiry after [the couple's] conformity of opinions, similarity of manners, rectitude of judgement, or purity of sentiment'. He claims that all the evils of a bad marriage could be averted 'by that deliberation and delay which prudence prescribes to irrevocable choice'. But Nekayah puts him straight: delaying marriage means that a couple 'suspend their fate upon each other at a time when opinions are fixed and habits are established'. Although a youthful or hasty marriage may be made in a mood of 'desultory levity', the alternative is a union between people too set in their ways (and guilty of a 'pride ashamed to yield, or obstinacy delighting to contend'). It's not possible, she says, to resolve the question of a marriage's suitability simply by applying reason and logic; intense feelings can pass, but well-advised arguments in favour of a marriage or against it are equally fugitive.

Nekayah may not strictly speak for Sam, but in its fundamentals her position is his: the most frisky or facile case for matrimony can sometimes stand up, and the most considered can founder. In his sermon on marriage (written for his friend John Taylor to deliver), he comments that it is 'an institution designed . . . for the promotion of happiness' but 'sometimes condenses the gloom, which it was intended to dispel'. This is because many married couples neglect their duties, for instance failing to maintain the 'continual acts of tenderness' that keep the flame of love burning. There are lots of reasons why this happens, scarcely foreseeable at the point when one marries. Among them is this: the demands of life can erode our capacity for tenderness. In *Rambler* 45, Sam observes that people who complain of the unhappiness of their marriages will often say that they were wed in a moment of folly, yet 'the days which they so much wish to call back, are the days not only of celibacy but of youth, the days of novelty and improvement, of ardour and of hope, of health and vigour of body, of gaiety and lightness of heart'. Such people's expressions of regret for what they have lost are the tokens not of superior judgement, but of jaundiced maturity, since 'whether married or unmarried, we shall find the vesture of terrestrial existence more heavy and cumbrous the longer it is worn'.

~ 7 ~

The mournful truth of London life: or, an author embarks
upon the sea of Literature (with but a smattering of
wormy cliché)

THE FIRST TWO YEARS of Sam's married life were dominated by his efforts to launch and then maintain his new
school at Edial. When it failed, he decided to try his fortunes
in London. On the morning of 2 March 1737 he left
Lichfield, travelling with David Garrick. He was Garrick's
mentor and friend, and their journey – sharing a horse,
which they took it in turns to ride – now sounds like a story
contrived by a nutty scriptwriter, rather than something that
actually happened. To picture them in transit is to picture,
let's say, Marlon Brando crossing America on a motorbike,
with Ernest Hemingway in his sidecar. Except it's bigger
than that.

Garrick's name is indelible in the history of British
theatre. His approach to portraying a character was sympathetically imaginative, rather than declamatory like that of
his predecessors. Besides redefining what it meant to act a
part, he promoted the idea that a cast should work as an
ensemble instead of largely ignoring one another onstage.
He revolutionized the theatre's understanding of how to
achieve its effects, particularly through lighting and scenery,
and overhauled the mechanisms of management and publicity.[1] Yet when he quit Lichfield, a few days after his
twentieth birthday, he had no definite plans. In hindsight,

his ascent looks astonishingly swift – a decade after arriving in the capital he would be earning more than £1,000 a year. But before he blazed across the stage, there was a fallow period. His father believed that his loquacious energy suited him to a legal career – and was hardly the first person, or the last, to misconstrue acting skills as a gift for advocacy. That career did not materialize, and in fact his early years in London were spent working in the wine trade with his elder brother Peter, selling bottles of port at eighteen shillings a dozen.[2] It was only in 1741 that he made his professional stage debut, stepping in to replace an unwell performer as the harlequin in a pantomime. That year he had several roles as part of a small company in Ipswich, and in October he made an astonishing breakthrough, as the king in Shakespeare's *Richard III*.

But in March 1737 Garrick was a volatile young man whose eagerness to amuse others had not yet found a proper outlet, and his mentor was scarcely any more sure of the road ahead. As Adam Gopnik has observed, Sam had the misfortune to arrive in London 'in a time not unlike this one, with the old-media dispensation in crisis and the new media barely paying'. Aristocratic patronage, which had tended to deform writers' endeavours, was dwindling, but authorship was not yet securely established as a career.[3] At the time, Alexander Pope was perhaps the only living English author who had grown rich from writing. Many others were 'writers by profession'. The term, later interchangeable with 'authors by profession', seems to have been coined by the critic James Ralph in 1758, and he used it disapprovingly of the quill drivers he had come across since arriving in London from Philadelphia more than thirty years before. After trying his hand at poetry, political pamphleteering and writing for the theatre, Ralph was conscious of how precarious professional authorship tended to be. Sam, who would follow in Ralph's footsteps as a parliamentary reporter, was entering a realm in which writers were expected to work quickly, be versatile and embrace political causes with gusto – all for very modest rewards.

By unhappy coincidence, on the day of departure his brother Nathaniel died, aged twenty-four. Three days later he was buried at St Michael's Church in Lichfield. We can't be sure how or when news of this reached Sam, but it is safe to assume that he left without knowing of his brother's death. Ignorance was in this case a blessing. Had he been aware of Nathaniel's fate, he would have delayed his journey. Instead, for a moment, he had the pleasure of not knowing: he was relinquishing a scene with which he was tediously familiar to venture to a place he had visited once as a child. He could imagine himself stepping into freedom: a life with more elbow-room and fewer threads binding him to the Johnson family and its gloomy legacy. But the journey itself was the moment of psychological liberation.

Before we continue to London, let us pause to think of Nathaniel Johnson. He is a murky figure, and it is a grim irony that his passing is one of the few moments that bring him into view. It seems that he drank too much and shared the melancholy temperament of his brother and father. He may well have had little genuine interest in the family's bookselling business, but there is evidence that he practised that trade in the West Midlands and in Somerset. The one document that survives to shed some light on his life is a letter to his mother, written the year before his death. In it he speaks of a plan to emigrate to America. Hoping to go to Georgia, which was then being settled under the guidance of James Oglethorpe, he admits that he has little idea of what to expect there – but is sure that his new life can be no worse than the one he will leave behind. In the letter he refers to 'these crimes . . . which have given both you and me so much trouble' and to his brother who 'would scarce ever use me with common civility'.[4] We can only speculate about the nature of the crimes – forgery is one suggestion – and what passed between him and Sam. As to the manner of his death, nothing is known. Suicide seems plausible, save for the detail of his being buried in consecrated ground; perhaps he had an accident or was felled by sudden illness. It is clear, though, that in adulthood the older brother, who as a child had been encouraged to think of Nathaniel as 'little Natty', barely acknowledged that he had existed. When Sam mentioned that memories of Nathaniel had surfaced, he was tantalizingly unspecific about them. On the day of their mother's burial in January 1759, he wrote in his diary, 'The dream of my brother I shall remember.' More than twenty years later he wrote to Mary Prowse, who had once employed a cousin of his and lived near Frome in Somerset, asking if she could find any information about a bookseller who had resided there 'more than forty years ago' – 'He was my near relation.'

Because we know so little about Nathaniel, it's easy to overlook him completely. But it is clear that their cheerless fraternity was something Sam felt glad to leave behind. London promised different flavours. His awareness of the possibilities of a literary life there, begun during his teenage stay with Cornelius Ford, had been strengthened by his reading of the *Gentleman's Magazine*. Edward Cave's periodical was the first to call itself a magazine – the word had previously denoted a storehouse or centre of commerce – and aspired to be a sober, useful publication. Its audience consisted not so much of gentlemen as of the middling sort: professionals and tradesmen and their families.[5] Many of the people who wrote for it weren't Londoners, and Cave welcomed new voices. About half of each number consisted of contributions from readers, and in 1734 he ran the first of several generously funded poetry competitions – nothing out of the ordinary now, but an innovative scheme at the time, and one that suggested to Sam that an outsider with no secure standing and no rich backers could find ways to make a living in the capital.[6]

Although he had several literary projects in mind and dreamed of being recognized as a serious scholar, Sam's most pressing task in the spring of 1737 was to complete his stately tragedy *Irene*. He believed that it would make him a fortune if only he could get it finished and put on, yet it wasn't a good time to be trying to do this. New plays were not often staged, and in June his prospects worsened when parliament passed the Licensing Act, which restricted both the subject matter of theatre – so as to quash political satire – and where it could be presented (a form of censorship that would last until the Theatres Act of 1968). In 1739, he would write a heavily ironic pamphlet, *A Complete Vindication of the Licensers of the Stage*, arguing that, given the political will to keep the public in a state of ignorance by suppressing plays, it might also be sensible to stop teaching people to read. The pamphlet contains one especially chilling sentence: 'What is power but the liberty of acting without being accountable?'

By the time of the *Complete Vindication*, insults and frustrations had blighted his sense of London as a place of opportunity. Soon after his arrival, he met a bookseller known to Garrick, John Wilcox, who asked how he expected to make his living. When Sam replied, 'By my literary labours', Wilcox laughed and suggested that, given his burly appearance, he might be better off looking for work as a porter. Wilcox wasn't being needlessly mean; he was making the point – an enduringly true one – that anyone proposing to live off their literary labours had better come up with a Plan B (or a Plan A, around which the writerly ambitions can fit). But the judgement was still galling. No one delights in being told what they look like they should do. 'You should be a model', which is about as good as this gets, is usually an offer of a leg-over rather than a leg-up. My own experience on this front, which runs to 'You'd make a good bouncer' (a wild misreading) and 'You'd be perfect for one of those ads about hair transplants', is merely dismal.

In retrospect, Wilcox seems an outlier among Sam's acquaintances in the book trade, a source of discouragement rather than a generous sponsor of literature. Yet he was willing, despite his reservations, to lend Sam and Garrick £5. This was hardly a trivial sum at a time when £30 a year was reckoned enough for a young man to live frugally but not contemptibly. Furthermore, words that sound like discouragement can sometimes serve a different purpose: by challenging a person's ambitions we oblige them to stiffen their resolve. Wilcox's putdown was bracing, a useful illustration of the capriciousness and competitive spirit so prevalent in the literary marketplace. It also demonstrated how important perceptions could be in that sphere: authors' looks were thought a foretaste of their style.

The London in which Sam found himself was dangerous. At night, robbers skulked in the unlit streets. Armed muggers and pickpockets crawled over the open spaces of Spitalfields and Covent Garden. At any time of day one might be mown down by an out-of-control cart or startled by a stray animal. The city was a confusing patchwork of districts, divided by the Thames, with only one bridge connecting its northern and southern halves. The river itself was spectacular and often busy with ships – as later depicted by Canaletto, who moved to London in 1746 – but the bank-side neighbourhoods were squalid. Much of what we now think of as central London had yet to become urban: St Pancras and Paddington were villages, and anyone who walked along Oxford Street could glimpse open fields to the north, while west of Hyde Park lay a broad swathe of green.

As Sam wandered London's streets and ventured beyond its limits, from Chelsea to Bow and from Southwark to Hampstead, he got the measure of the city, which seemed overwhelmingly crowded. It had a population of about 700,000, whereas Birmingham was home to roughly 20,000 people, Oxford to 8,000, and Lichfield to 3,000. Violent and noisy, it was in the grips of a mania for gin, despite legislation the previous year to curb its consumption. The Gin Act had provoked riots, and so had competition in the building trade between British and Irish labour. The threat of mass protest was constant. The streets were dirty, too – Benjamin Franklin reported in 1742 that the gutters running up their centre were often glutted with offal. Grime from the street was popular with market gardeners, who bought cartloads of it and rejoiced in the richness of its 'glutinous mixture of animal manure, dead cats and dogs, ashes, straw, and human excrement'. No eighteenth-century citizen could avoid occasional over-intimacy with dung, but London's abundance of horse-drawn traffic – and the enduring habit of driving cattle through the streets – meant that the city's thoroughfares were alarmingly feculent.[7]

If we look at William Hogarth's famous prints of London life, which date from Sam's first decades in the city, we see its cobbles, signs and lamps, its paupers and fanatics, char-latans and tipplers, the mad and the sick, the textures of material profusion, the chaos of the crowd. But not all London is in Hogarth, and for a more Johnsonian flavour of the city we can turn to the *Gentleman's Magazine*. Its issue for March 1737 contains an account of 300 footmen rioting after being denied access to their usual places at the Drury Lane playhouse; the report mentions that they fought their way to the stage door, forced it open, and wounded twenty-five people. The following month it notes that the cost of rice has gone up dramatically as a result of a trade embargo, and a terse report of the sessions at the Old Bailey on Saturday 23rd records eight people being sentenced to death and thirty-three condemned to be transported to the colonies. A glance at April's bills of mortality shows that more than half the month's deaths were children under the age of five. In May there is a reference to Dick Turpin, 'the noted Butcher Highwayman', who 'almost every day this month, committed some robbery or other'; another small item concerns a mad ox that swam across the Thames, injured a couple of bystanders when it reached the shore, and was shot to prevent further nuisance. In June, 'the officers of excise gave information against 300 persons for selling punch'.

Sam would have read all this with less and less amazement. Depressed by the filth and hubbub around the Strand, where he first lodged, he moved for a few months to Greenwich, which was comparatively sedate.[8] Perhaps he remembered Daniel Defoe's claim that it had the best air and views in England, as well as the best conversation. But the point of moving to London had not been to find a salubrious spot to roost. When one chooses to live in a city, it's in order to experience its swarming density, to collaborate and be exposed to unfamiliar stimuli, to step outside oneself, to share in its madness and productive antagonisms. The retreat to Greenwich had to be temporary.

By the end of the year he appeared committed for good

to life in the capital. There would later be one last attempt to secure a teaching job in the Midlands, but that autumn Tetty felt able to join him in London. They lodged close to Oxford Street, first near Hanover Square and then in the house of a Mrs Crow on Castle Street, two minutes from Cavendish Square. This, you might think, was a fashionable address, but the square was embarrassingly unfinished, twenty years after building work had begun. In 1734 James Ralph, in a critique of London architecture, had cited its 'neglected condition' as a perfect example of how 'the modern plague of building' could produce dismal results, with many projects abandoned.[9] An all too familiar case, this, of a scheme of improvement that ends up being an eyesore, and Sam was quick to take an interest in the relationship between the city's fabric and the conditions of its people. Ultimately this would lead him to reflect on how London's infrastructure could be upgraded, and it would crystallize more than twenty years later in his support for the architect John Gwynn's proposal that the design of inner London be subject to central planning, not the piecemeal efforts of speculators. In the short term, he was simply unimpressed with the mess and muddle of his surroundings, and he was adamant that once *Irene* was a hit they could move somewhere better.

But he had to find ways to scrape a living. With the draft of *Irene* stashed in a drawer, he tried a more fluently populist style of writing, and it was not long before he gained notice – with a wittily disillusioned poem about his new home. *London*, published on 12 May 1738, pictures a city full of fiery fops, raging rabbles, prowling lawyers and thieves waiting to ambush unwary pedestrians. These images tumble from the mouth of Thales, a self-pitying poet who is leaving the town for a new home in the country; he addresses a younger man, who is planning to stay. He complains that in London the houses keep collapsing, hangings are so frequent that there isn't enough hemp to produce the necessary rope, and everything is for sale – even smiles. If you are really unlucky, a drunk will stab you for a joke.

This was a sensationalist image of the city, but not one that entirely misrepresented it. Plenty of Londoners could relate to Thales, and plenty who saw him as a caricature of an embittered satirist were nevertheless amused by his strident commentary on the city's corruption. The first printing sold out in a week, the second inside a month, and literary London was curious to know the identity of the poem's unnamed author. Its best-known couplet is 'This mournful truth is everywhere confess'd, / SLOW RISES WORTH, BY POVERTY DEPRESS'D'. The next line, 'But here more slow, where all are slaves to gold', makes it clear that the problem, though universal, is felt very keenly in the city. Yet the decision to set just one of the poem's 263 lines in capitals makes it stand apart from its context and look like a motto. Or perhaps it's an idea for an epitaph: Sam imagines that, if he were to die right now at the age of twenty-eight, this would be a suitable statement to chisel on his gravestone. It is not so much a 'mournful truth . . . everywhere confess'd' as *his* mournful truth, and feels like a lament for the time he has lost, in London certainly but also before arriving there.

That his condition was truly one of 'poverty' is open to question. Yet by convention poets were regarded as beggarly – a generation later, one of the members of Sam's circle, Oliver Goldsmith, could write that 'The poet's poverty is a standing topic of contempt' – and for the next few years, whenever Sam earned money by his pen, lax management and generosity to others meant that too much of it slipped through his fingers.[10] In *London* his references to poverty form part of a complaint about the gulf between ordinary citizens and their unprincipled overlords. He writes with feeling about society's grossest insults being directed exclusively at the poor. 'All crimes are safe, but hated poverty,' he claims, and 'This, only this, the rigid law pursues'. By contrast, the rich persist in fraud, knowing they'll get away with it. Sam attacks the corruption of a parliament full of hypocrites who are easily bought, and attacks the prime minister, Sir Robert Walpole, who can resist no opportunity to increase his personal fortunes. In the end, *London* is less about the physical detail of the city than about the moods it provokes: outrage, disgust, and an exhilaration that his attempts at satirical aloofness can't quite disguise.

By the time he wrote *London*, Sam was often consorting with other writers, inhabitants of Grub Street, a place associated with plague, penury and, on account of its proximity of the lunatic asylum at Bedlam, mental infirmity. In his *Dictionary* he would identify the physical space it occupied: 'originally the name of a street in Moorfields in London, much inhabited by writers of small histories, dictionaries, and temporary poems'. But Grub Street was also a state of mind: to be there was to be a literary hopeful, trying to scrape a living. The name makes one think of worms and maggots; since the seventeenth century, *grub* has been a word for a person with unlovely manners or limited abilities, and Nathan Bailey's *Universal Etymological Dictionary* of 1731 defines the plural *grubs* as 'a kind of white, unctuous, little pimples or tumours'. Inevitably we picture not just hacks manufacturing third-rate literature – people who can't hold their ink – but also filth and parasitism. Here, in the valley of the shadow of books, one might learn a lot about human motives.[11]

⊷ 8 ⊷

In which we observe the peculiarities of Friendship, manifest
in Samuel Johnson's association with the notorious
Mr Richard Savage

AMONG SAM'S Grub Street associates was Richard Savage,
a poet whose best-known works were *The Bastard* and *The
Wanderer* – titles that sum up the main themes of his existence. Much about Savage's life remains unclear, but among
the details that are certain two stand out: in 1727 he killed a
man in a fight at a Charing Cross coffee house, and in 1743
he died penniless in a Bristol jail. Altogether more mysterious were his origins. He alleged that he was the illegitimate
son of another Richard Savage, the fourth Earl Rivers, and
his mistress Anne, Countess of Macclesfield. His adult life
was devoted to trying to prove his nobility. Pursuing Lady
Macclesfield with violent persistence, he lurched from one
drunken accident to the next. Obsessive, vain and malicious,
but also a wit and an outrageous mimic, he had twin talents
for making friends and for turning friends into enemies, and
seemed doomed to repeat a pattern of intimacy, extrava-
gance, insult and disaster.

Sam fell in with him in 1738, at a time when Savage often
spent his nights roaming the London streets. By Sam's
account, he would sleep 'in cellars among the riot and filth
of the meanest and most profligate of the rabble' or out-
doors on the warm ash from a workshop. Down in the dirt
with the derelicts and vermin, he seems the archetypal liter-

ary vagabond/bum, a precursor of the Beat poets, hungry and delinquent but convinced that he holds the keys to the palace of wisdom. It is tempting to identify him with the character of Thales in *London*, although it's not clear that Sam had met Savage at the point when he wrote the poem. Rather, the great testament to the two men's relationship is Sam's *Life of Savage*, published in February 1744. This is a story of Grub Street and also very much a Grub Street product, yet even as it depicts its subject at his lowest points it transcends the squalor of that world, dignified by the precision of its insights.[1]

What Sam doesn't mention, though, is that he joined Savage on his weary night-walks, and that in the dark they talked at length. Their conversation was of a sort I associate with pubs: they spoke of dethroning authority and creating new forms of government, and as they set the world to rights – for that is what we'd now call it – they clung to the principle that, no matter what, 'they would stand by their country'. Those words stink of booze. But the truth is that Sam and Savage often couldn't afford to drink much, and they were full to the brim with fervour, not ale or brandy. Sam's new friend was an egalitarian and a critic of imperialism. In politics, as in all other things, Savage was erratic, but he could be counted on to rail against the cruelty of colonial exploitation. Sam was repeatedly struck by 'the extent of his knowledge, compared with the small time which he spent in visible endeavours to acquire it'. The two men shared an appreciation of poetry and the belief that society had not properly acknowledged their talents. They may also have bonded over their feelings of resentment towards their mothers; each thought that he had not been accepted by the person whose acceptance would have meant most to him. Savage was the closest Sam came to having a mentor in

London; while for the most part his example was cautionary, he was a rich source of information about how the literary world worked. Richard Holmes, who has written sympathetically about their relationship, likens Sam at this time to a young Faust, guided by Savage's Mephistopheles, and pictures them 'walking in enemy territory' – the west of London, associated with power and privilege, into which the two of them crept 'like spies in the night, their very presence a provocation'.[2]

For a couple of years they enjoyed a degree of closeness that would later puzzle and appal the guardians of Sam's reputation. Boswell hints that Savage caused Sam to do some sleazy things that he would later find distressing to recall. When Sam told Boswell that 'There is a certain degree of temptation which will overcome any virtue', he wasn't thinking of his time with Savage, but he spoke with a knowingness born of experiencing temptation rather than just speculating about it. We can imagine Savage's bad habits being at least briefly contagious. Yet if Sam regretted some of his actions during those vagrant years, he was nonetheless grateful for Savage's friendship and the truths about human nature that it taught him. The *Life of Savage* concludes with an account of its subject's personality: he 'appeared to think himself born to be supported by others' and was 'the slave of every passion'; 'easily disgusted', he retained hatreds 'tenaciously', and 'very small offences were sufficient to provoke him'. Mingled with these criticisms, though, are tributes to his 'eminently exact' judgement, 'open and respectful' style of conversation, powers of focus ('his attention never deserted him') and readiness 'to reject that praise to which he had no claim'. These are recorded partly in order to exonerate a figure who certainly needs exonerating, and partly in order to account for how Sam could be close to such a person. He needed to explain this to others, and also to himself.

Sam suggests that Savage's vindictiveness meant that his friendship was of limited value, but the *Life of Savage* is a celebration of the paradoxes of friendship. To be a friend is to have a relationship that is at the same time binding and informal, robust and fragile, voluntary and exigent, luxuriant and sacrificial. Friendship involves discovery but also stability; it is closer than the relationships we inherit yet more combustible, and manages to feel both precious and ubiquitous. At any moment it seems fully formed, yet at every moment it is under development. And though we for the most part know just who our friends are, the precise features and definition of friendship are blurry, suggesting something that is simultaneously happily snug and completely without boundaries.

Time spent with Savage was an education in such contradictions – or rather, in the difference between what seems incongruous and what feels right. In 1743, the year before the *Life of Savage* and the year of its subject's death, Sam published 'An Ode on Friendship', a poem that praises its 'guiltless joys'. He explains that love is the 'parent of rage and hot desires' and that it finds its way into both 'the human and the savage breast', which it 'inflames alike with equal fires'. By contrast, the role of friendship is as a guide that helps us negotiate the 'darksome' journey of life; its pleasures are 'all transporting, all divine'. It is tempting to see this as a comment on his unlikely bond with Savage. A similar reference to that bond seems to be embedded in the *Dictionary*, for, as Richard Holmes has pointed out, the few words that it illustrates with quotations from Savage are *elevate*, *expanse*, *fondly*, *lone*, *squander*, *sterilise* and *suicide*, and these 'to an analyst . . . might suggest something about the nature of that most puzzling relationship'.[3] Associating with this prodigal figure deepened Sam's sense of the perils, both practical and psychological, of life as an author, and made him apprehend more keenly the need for some means of relieving life's darkness.

There is no greater cliché of social life than 'Opposites attract'. Yet even if we resist the glibness of that two-word formula, we know the allure and interest of friendship (and other kinds of relationship) with people whose qualities and inclinations differ from our own. Who hasn't enjoyed being taken somewhere entirely unfamiliar by an acquaintance whose tastes and attitudes seem exotic? Who hasn't observed the frisson of gracious disagreement? More than that, though, friendship is an escape from oneself that is also a journey deeper into oneself. It begins, as C. S. Lewis observed, when we say to another person 'What! You too?' (the words are in many cases thought rather than spoken), and at its rarest moments it creates a sense that part of our soul resides in another person's body. Yet it's the sharing across a divide, not the closing of the divide, that makes the magic; the pleasure of friendship is not finding someone who does everything just as we do it, but finding intense similarities with someone who, in also differing from us, can enlarge who we are.

In Savage we find a classic story of pretence solidifying into conviction – of a person who makes a claim about himself with such persistence that he erases the truth from his mind. But Sam sees instead a story that calls for compassion; the impulse to judge is always matched by sympathy, and he reflects that no one could sensibly say, 'Had I been in Savage's condition, I should have lived or written better than Savage.' At one point he offers the dry comment that Savage, 'having no profession, became by necessity an author'. This is both a good joke and an unpleasant truth. It's a vignette of himself and of the literary sphere they both inhabited. But it's more than that. For although the impulse to write is fired by passions for reading, sharing, inveighing and inventing, writers are very often people constitutionally and temperamentally unsuited to other forms of work. In Savage's struggles he saw the likeness of his own, and saw too a man within whom vice and virtue were perpetually at war – not a unique ordeal, but a paradigm of the human condition.

Savage's most significant poem was *The Wanderer*, which in its strange and meandering way praises a life of quiet contemplation. Its title would influence Sam's decision to call his first great series of moral essays the *Rambler*. The name wasn't in line with their sobriety, but it suited their improvised nature – as well as affording him a handy degree of flexibility about subject matter. For while the *Rambler* essays aren't loosely discursive, they are the product of a life spent roving and loitering, and of Sam's needing every few days to translate his excursions (around the city or literature) into a piece he could publish. Like the wanderer, the rambler gives the impression of being homeless; both are open and vulnerable figures, haunted by uncertainty about whether they can sustain their journey, yet ready to know the vastness of the world. Long after Savage's death, Sam continued to think of life as an unorthodox pilgrimage, and kept in mind some spirited words from his friend's best poem: 'Great my attempt, though hazardous my flight.'

❧ 9 ❧

A resting-place – where the reader may take refreshment,
and where vexed matters are resolved

THE PICTURE THAT emerges here of Sam's early experience
of London is at odds with the most famous of his sayings
– 'When a man is tired of London, he is tired of life.' There
is evidence that Sam, who spoke these words with more than
a trace of his native Staffordshire accent, was sometimes
tired of London; his first few years in the city made him
homesick for the West Midlands, and in old age he liked to
withdraw periodically to quieter places. But he uttered this
judgement in 1777, when Boswell wondered if living full-
time in the city might dampen appreciation of its 'exquisite
zest', and by then he had been in London forty years;
piqued by Boswell's doubts, he was saluting the place that
had been the backdrop for all his success. In any case, what
he meant by these words was a little different from what we
now understand. In 1777, London was Europe's largest city,
having within living memory surpassed Constantinople,
and, given Britons' lack of awareness then of the world
beyond Europe, it was assumed to be the largest city in the
world. As such, it was a symbol of the possibilities of urban
life. Whoever asserted its inexhaustibility was applauding its
role as a temple of commerce, invention and art.

When today's crapulent hacks recycle Sam's remark, it
lacks this particular resonance, and I'm tempted to argue
that it is untrue: when one is tired of London, one is simply

tired of London, and most people who have lived or worked there will know that feeling, even if they have also savoured the city's charms. But the line has become so well-known that it obliterates pretty much everything else Sam said – or, more importantly, wrote – on the subject. 'More importantly', that is, because we can be confident that what he wrote was what he thought at that moment, whereas his sayings are inevitably a little warped by the people who recorded them. It's not that we should reject the quotations attributed to him; many are too richly attested for that to be necessary, as well as too good to be given up. Yet what he wrote should take precedence. There we can find plenty more evidence of his delight in London's social and cultural inexhaustibility, but there are hints in his letters that an occasional retreat from the city was essential to his continuing appreciation of it.

Another possible objection to Sam's celebrated aphorism is that it appears to confine itself to male experience. But while it's true that at the time Sam was writing (and speaking), *man* could certainly mean 'the male human being', often it was used simply to denote 'a person', without any implications of gender. Even if it was no longer natural to write of Adam and Eve, as the preacher John King had in the sixteenth century, that 'The Lord had but one pair of men in paradise', an author generalizing about humankind would refer to the behaviours and attitudes of *men*. It was the norm to use *he* where an author might now prefer *he or she*, *s/he* or a less cumbersome singular *they* – the last of which is of course guaranteed to incense those guardians of the galaxy who otherwise go by the name of grammar pedants. (While this is not the place to present a sustained case for singular *they*, I make no apology for having used it in these pages.) More to the point, although Sam's aphorisms often look gender-specific, they rarely need to be interpreted that way: 'If a man is in doubt whether it would be better for him to expose himself to martyrdom or not, he should not do it', 'Men are seldom satisfied with praise introduced or followed by any mention of defect', 'There lurks, perhaps, in every human heart a desire of distinction, which inclines every man to hope, and then to believe, that nature has given him something peculiar to himself.'

This is also the place to observe that, if some of Sam's most celebrated remarks are far from being his best, some of his best are commonly misunderstood. A perennial favourite is 'Patriotism is the last refuge of a scoundrel', which is trotted out by cynics eager to make the case that any flicker of patriotic sentiment is contemptible. Sam had something more specific in mind: the feigned love of country so often used to cloak the self-interest of tycoons and cheapjack politicians. It's not that all attachment to one's homeland is corrupt and boneheaded; rather, the most noxious individuals will claim, in moments of extremity, that the destructive things they're doing must be performed for their country's good, and that those who want to stand in their way are traitors. Exploited thus, the notion of patriotism has nothing to do with affection or a commitment to certain principles one thinks are embedded in one's community. Instead, it's a psychopath's excuse for violence – and here it seems apt to add the judgement of Isaac Asimov's character Salvor Hardin, a diplomat and master of the morally charged epigram, that 'Violence is the last refuge of the incompetent.'

🦥 10 🦥

Of Genius, with sundry other scenes from the farce of life

BY THE 1740s, the territory known to modern literary tourists as 'Dr Johnson's London' had been staked out. Over the course of the forty-seven years Sam spent in the city, he would reside at more than twenty addresses. But 'his' London was, as the historian Jerry White explains, 'a tightly circumscribed district about three-quarters of a mile long – from Durham Yard, Strand, to Shoe Lane, Fleet Street – and only half a mile wide'. When he worshipped it was at St Clement Danes, a High Church establishment on the Strand, and the parish was mixed, a mosaic of fine streets and poor ones that included not one but two Pissing Alleys.[1] This was the part of town where printing and publishing happened. It was a scene of pleasure, too: here were inns and shops and shows, as well as many potentially fatal attractions.

Three decades later, Sam would survey this domain and say that 'Fleet Street has a very animated appearance, but I think the full tide of human existence is at Charing Cross'. These were the words of a man who felt a sense of ownership and believed he had an overview of London's commerce and vitality. Yet during his early years in the city he was part of its surge and flow, a mere Grub Street peon. Feeling financially and morally responsible for Tetty, whose health was in decline, he took on a string of thankless projects. It was these that cemented the unillusioned attitude that would later find expression in statements such as 'A man may write at any time, if he will set himself doggedly to it'. By this reckoning, a real writer wasn't one who coyly waited for inspiration and ideal conditions: 'Composition is for the most part an effort of slow diligence and steady perseverance, to which the mind is dragged by necessity or resolution.'

Even when one of Sam's Grub Street gigs held promise, in the very moment of savouring that promise he saw, as writers do, how small his chances were. In the *Rambler*, he would define the 'writer's malady' as the dream of success. 'Perhaps no class of the human species requires more to be cautioned against . . . anticipation of happiness, than those that aspire to the name of authors.' A few years later he began his preface to Richard Rolt's *Dictionary of Trade and Commerce* by returning to this theme: 'No expectation is more fallacious than that which authors form of the reception which their labours will find among mankind.' Sam had not met Rolt or even read his work, but, inadvertently anticipating the poor reception of this volume, noted that scarcely anyone publishes a book 'without believing that he has caught the moment when . . . the world is disposed . . . to learn the art which he undertakes to teach'. From the very start of his own literary career he understood the delusions of authorship: the conviction that one's current idea is brilliant and opportune, destined to express the spirit of the moment or of the moment that's just about to be, and the necessarily sanguine belief, when that idea shows signs of being no more than a slushy brainfart, that the real magic lies in the next one, already taking shape.

In his thirties, one of the most exacting tasks he took on was writing up parliamentary debates for the *Gentleman's Magazine*. This occupied him from July 1741 to March 1744, and was a job that called for some ingenuity. Since the

House of Commons had resolved in 1738 that it was a 'breach of privilege' to report these debates, parliamentary coverage had to be dressed as something else – in the case of the *Gentleman's Magazine* as 'Debates in the Senates of Magna Lilliputia'. Sam, who seems to have entered the House of Commons only once, would write his account of a debate long after the event, with the help of notes provided by Edward Cave, who had some clout with the House's doorkeepers. He was also able to refer to the *London Magazine*, which was quicker to report the speeches, and where he added drama to his account it was in order to make the *Gentleman's Magazine* seem superior to its brisker rival. At best a reconstruction, his reporting was often more like an inspired fiction. Yet most readers, while aware of the limits on parliamentary reporting, accepted that these reports were as close to the truth as they would get. This preyed on Sam's mind. Many years later, when a literary acquaintance, Philip Francis, pronounced a speech by William Pitt one of the masterpieces of modern oratory, Sam astonished his companions by explaining that the printed version, rather than being a faithful transcript of Pitt's eloquence, was something he had cobbled together in a garret in Covent Garden. Near the end of his life he expressed regret over passing off these fictions as realities, which to Boswell was prime evidence of 'the tenderness of his conscience'.

A more bookish task that occupied him during this period was cataloguing the library of the Earl of Oxford, who had died in 1741. Acquired by the bookseller Thomas Osborne for £13,000, this was at the time Britain's best collection in private hands – around 50,000 books and 350,000 pamphlets, together with 7,639 volumes of manuscripts, and 14,236 rolls, charters and deeds. Sam worked alongside William Oldys, who had been the Earl's literary secretary but now had to earn his keep as a literary hack. 'In this painful drudgery both editors were day-labourers for immediate subsistence,' writes Oldys's Victorian biographer James Yeowell.[2] It says something about the nature of this drudgery that Osborne objected to Sam's pausing to read a little of one of the books he was meant to be cataloguing, and that Sam responded by thumping him with a particularly large volume and then stood on his neck. Here, in a nutshell, is one of his life's recurring problems: his appetite for literature could hamper his work on projects where time was of the essence and other people's livelihood was at stake. And here, too, is the stout-hearted Samuel Johnson of legend, subduing a bully, though it is worth adding that the details of what happened are disputed, with Sam conceding only that 'he was impertinent to me, and I beat him'.

His life in Grub Street made him aware of how the literary world functioned. It exposed him to good writers who existed in a state of perpetual penury, their gifts unrecognized, and to writers whose success and reputation were vastly in excess of their talent. He saw at close quarters the mud-slinging and sharp practices of a culture in which plagiarists mixed on equal terms with poets and pornographers. In the *Idler*, another of his series of essays, he would reflect on the surfeit of violent propaganda and the ease with which it could be commissioned from desperate hacks: 'I know not whether more is to be dreaded from streets filled with soldiers accustomed to plunder, or from garrets filled with scribblers accustomed to lie.' This was a milieu in which belligerence, jealousy and double-dealing were the norm. When he wrote that 'the reciprocal civility of authors is one of the most risible scenes in the farce of life' he was thinking of an incident in the literary career of Sir Thomas

Browne, a seventeenth-century Londoner who removed himself to the comparative obscurity of Norwich. Browne's first book, the anonymously published *Religio Medici*, gained publicity as a result of an inept commentary produced in the space of twenty-four hours by Sir Kenelm Digby, a writer at the time well-known, and the two men then exchanged polite letters in which Digby was at pains to emphasize his correspondent's brilliance and his own comparatively modest gifts. For Sam, this ritual courtesy was an example of the embarrassing ease with which authors stoop to mutual puffery. Of course, there are countless instances of authors doing the very opposite and trashing each other. Yet literary squabbles are to be expected; it is the secret ecosystem of flattery and covert patronage that needs exposing.

He noted with distaste how many of his contemporaries were content to bestow the word *genius* on people of modest ability. Where once it had signified a guardian spirit, presiding over a person, a place or an age, it had become a badge of individual excellence – of being, as Sam puts it in the *Dictionary*, 'endowed with superior faculties'. Writing in the *Spectator* in 1711, Joseph Addison had complained that writers were forever being called geniuses; even some puny scribbler of unoriginal poems could receive the accolade. In Addison's view, there were two types of ground (i.e. mind) in which genius could grow: one was 'like a rich soil in a happy climate, that produces a whole wilderness of noble plants rising in a thousand beautiful landscapes without any certain order or regularity', the other 'the same rich soil under the same happy climate, that has been laid out in walks and parterres, and cut into shape and beauty by the skill of the gardener'. In other words, there were extravagant geniuses and there were restrained ones. Shakespeare was in the first class, along with Homer; Plato and Sir Francis Bacon were in the second. When Addison wrote this, the vulgarization of *genius* was in its infancy. By mid-century, it was an established problem. In *Tom Jones* (1749), Henry Fielding had fun at the expense of the fashion for finding genius inside thick skulls: 'several gentlemen in these times, by the wonderful force of genius only, without the least assistance of learning, perhaps without being well able to read, have made a considerable figure in the republic of letters'. The result, joked Fielding, was that critics had begun to claim that any kind of learning is useless to a writer and acts like 'fetters on the natural spriteliness and activity of the imagination'.

It was understandable, then, that Sam should argue in the early 1750s that 'the present generation' suffered gravely from feeling it could 'rely wholly upon unassisted genius and natural sagacity' – on 'sudden irradiations of intelligence' and 'immediate intuition'. Within a few years there was a new spokesman for that generation, the poet Edward Young, who claimed in his *Conjectures on Original Composition* (1759) that the difference between genius and competence was like that between a magician and an architect. For Young, uncovering one's genius was a matter of examining oneself profoundly rather than of applying oneself to study; it was a native endowment rather than an acquired art. He also argued that genius was far from rare, and that there had been many geniuses whose gifts had gone undiscovered because they'd not been afforded the benefits of literacy.

By the end of the century the distinction between *genius* and *talent* had widened. This was thanks in large measure to the influence of the philosopher Immanuel Kant, who argued that genius was an attribute of artists, not scientists; whereas a scientist carried out careful investigation, an artist could fire off new ideas with fierce spontaneity. In the early years of the nineteenth century the Romantic poets, especially Samuel Taylor Coleridge, advanced the cult of artistic genius – a belief that the individual's unique personality is the source of art, and that art is the sublime expression of the individual's feelings.

Sam's understanding of genius was very different – grounded rather than airy. His attitude to Shakespeare illustrates this. Whereas the Romantics' insistence on the category 'genius' was in large measure a means of coming to terms with the playwright's originality and extraordinary capacities, for Sam he was an 'exact surveyor' of the world, whose insights arise from 'contemplating things as they really exist'. As it happens, *Exact Surveyor* was the title of a book published in 1654, in which a certain John Eyre described the use of theodolites and protractors, as well as how to 'prove the truth of your work by a decimal table'. I have no evidence that Sam knew this, but Eyre's is the sort of book he found interesting, and its image of what it meant to be an 'exact surveyor' is a nice sidelight, a droll hint at how far his conception of genius was from Edward Young's. Fanny Burney reported hearing him say that 'Genius is nothing more than knowing the use of tools', and elsewhere, as we have seen, he wrote that 'Genius is a mind of large general powers, accidentally determined to some particular direction.'

Today this isn't the usual perception of genius. We think, as the Romantics did, of geniuses as a breed apart, possessed from birth of special qualities: they may fritter away their gifts, and such gifts may thrive only in certain sorts of environment, but genius is a natural endowment, not an acquired trait. The genius, as commonly conceived, is wild and godlike. Alongside this, Sam's position seems lacklustre. *Tools? Large general powers? Some particular direction?*

But wait: the most important part of his hostility to the cult of genius is moral. The geniuses glorified by his contemporaries were allowed, even encouraged, to get away with not knowing the use of tools, not having large general powers, and not channelling their abilities in a particular direction. Worse, they were allowed to get away with behaving like jackasses. Sam's apparently drab notion of genius is not an attempt to belittle inventiveness, but is instead a criticism of a culture that insists on anointing people as magicians and by doing so gives them licence to be pricks. He is attuned to a problem that's with us today: a willingness to indulge the vileness of people who are believed to be gifted, and a willingness to indulge the mediocrity of people whose vileness is understood as a symptom of their nascent, latent or dormant gifts.

It's too easy to dismiss Sam's notion of genius as merely grey. In fact, he wants to establish two things: the first is that geniuses are still human, and the second is that genius is basically exploratory. He understands genius as 'the power of combination', and describes a genius for poetry as 'that energy which collects, combines, amplifies, and animates'. In this he's much closer to the philosopher Alexander Gerard, who set out his claims about imagination and aesthetics in essays published in 1759 and 1774. Gerard thought of genius as having a mechanism; it involves the filtration and association of ideas. While the sudden blaze of imagination may seem marvellously inexplicable to the person who experiences it, it's a feat of computation rather than a moment of magic.

There's another good reason to cherish Sam's antipathy to the cult of the wild and effortless genius. It is a corrective to our present obsession with creativity (or 'creativity'), which, rather than stimulating genuine inventiveness, prizes supposititious guff at the expense of rigorous execution. People who boast about their creativity – and who revel in job titles such as Creative Director – tend not to be fresh thinkers. They act as though it's a special faculty that they possess and the rest of us don't. At the same time, conversely, there's a widespread fixation with insisting that each of us is already a creative hotshot: if I can't tie my shoelaces and express myself intelligibly, the most likely explanation is that I'm about to invent video tattoos or air-conditioned underpants. But anyone who brags about their creativity ('I'm a thought sherpa', 'Meet the Ideas Ninja!') is no better than a snake oil merchant. Individuals who are especially creative don't tend to make a noise about it; they just get on with producing things that are the best possible advertisement for their talents.

The achievements that the self-applauding 'creative' attempts to wrap in mystique are actually the fruit of everyday intelligence and abilities. To call these 'everyday' isn't to trivialize what they can accomplish. Rather, it recognizes that we all have it in us to be creative. We combine familiar ideas in unfamiliar ways, shift the frontiers of the conceptual space we're used to inhabiting, or transform what happens inside that space. In doing so, we bring into being things that are new and valuable. What's more, preparation and incubation – much of them barely conscious, and possibly social rather than solitary – will precede the moment of creative illumination, and that moment is followed by a phase of evaluation or elaboration. Creative people tend to be rule-breakers, but they must also, rather more prosaically, have access to the domain they want to influence, possess a huge amount of information about it, understand its rules and norms, and be motivated to see an idea through to fruition and transmit it to others. The keynote of creativity is not a bullish desire to be conspicuous, but curiosity.

The question of motivation is present in Sam's aphorism that 'No man but a blockhead ever wrote, except for money.' This is both seductive and simplistic. It is true that the desire or need to make money has driven many people to write, and there are a lot of writers who profess noble motives but are impelled by financial necessity or a craving for wealth. Yet this is a saying that trivializes writers and their art. It was Boswell who extracted it from Sam, and in recording it he added that 'Numerous instances to refute this will occur to all who are versed in the history of literature.' The fact that Boswell is right doesn't make his behaviour endearing: he gets Sam to say something that he can then correct or undercut, in order to make himself appear more worldly than his subject.

As for the applicability of Sam's claim: his own career abounds with examples of projects he took on without any hope of financial reward. But while the quotation is usually treated as a quip about the self-delusion of writers who claim to have no interest in money, it can be interpreted rather differently, as a call to arms. Only a blockheaded writer would neglect money matters. Writers should drive a harder bargain and shouldn't give their work away. In an age when writing is referred to as 'content', to be aggregated on websites that enrich people who've never written anything more substantial than their signature, that's a principle worth setting in stone. What's more, Sam's words tease us in the direction of another insight: that just as even the most romantic and idealistic writers desire commercial success more than they'd care to admit, so those writers most intent on commercial success are more fastidious about their craft than one might imagine.

✺ 11 ✺

In which the craft of literary biography is expounded

NOTWITHSTANDING his dislike of the overused term 'genius', Sam several times attached it to the subject of the *Life of Savage*. It is thanks to this book that Savage's name endures, and with his account of his recently deceased friend Sam rebooted assumptions about who matters and why. The story of a failure and an outcast, it suggests that a marginal figure can be interesting, worth treating with compassion and psychological acuity. It is also, as Richard Holmes observes, a kind of 'displaced autobiography'. Savage is Sam's 'demonic *alter ego*', embodying what he might under other circumstances have become.[1] In this respect, too, the *Life of Savage* is influential, for we now accept, as Sam's contemporaries did not, that biography will always contain an element of displaced autobiography – part calculated, part unintentional. Paying deep attention to another person's life demands that one pay equally deep attention to one's own.

In Sam's conception, a biography is an act of rescue. By imagining people's lives and minds, it reclaims them for history. 'The biographical part of literature,' he told Boswell, 'is what I love most'; he thought of it as essentially humane, a sympathetic activity rather than a dusty, antiquarian one. Excavating facts is part of the biographer's mission, but registering character – especially by reproducing conversation – is more important. The biographer's subject is not just some symptom of the past; the texture of his or her existence must be palpable.

This is a principle that has filtered down to Sam's own biographers. Each of the many 'lives of Johnson' claims for itself some special licence to reanimate him and invoke his spirit. The first person to produce a substantial account was his executor Sir John Hawkins, who has tended to be considered an uncharitable biographer. Anyone who reads him soon notices his habit of introducing sly little digs – at the expense of Sam's 'inattention to historical facts' or the fondness for rhyme that was 'one of the blemishes in his judgement'. He could claim a deep knowledge of his subject, having met Sam as far back as 1738. He was particularly close to him in his final months, and he writes with insight about his spiritual life. But Hawkins was no stylist. Struck by the stilted prose of his *Life of Samuel Johnson*, an early reviewer joked that there were plans for the book to be translated into English, and others complained that it was digressive, grudging and inaccurate.

Hawkins's efforts were soon surpassed, for in 1791 there appeared Boswell's *Life of Johnson*, the full title of which ran to more than sixty words.[2] The *Life* is both intimate and immense – about 550,000 words. More thoroughly researched than Hawkins's biography, it contains a vast quantity of Sam's sayings and observations. As a record of his conversation it is astonishingly rich. Boswell tells us that he has provided a faithful transcript of 'his occasional talk at such times as I had the good fortune to be in his company'. Yet we should be wary of taking this at face value. Boswell's gifts included a good memory, but not total recall. The two men did not meet until May 1763, by which time Sam was fifty-three and established as a literary celebrity, though not prosperous. Boswell was twenty-two, ambitious and naive. He had first travelled from his native Scotland to London in 1760, when he'd been struck by the city's abundance of 'the great, the gay, and the ingenious', and in November 1762 he had returned, hoping to deepen his acquaintance with all three types. He immediately saw documenting Sam's life as an opportunity to make his own name as a writer, and guessed that the childless Sam might enjoy his puppyish company.

Boswell worked hard to distil the essence of his subject. He wanted to portray Sam as a (mostly) heroic figure and to correct the less flattering impression created by Hawkins, though he inevitably wasn't above nabbing some of his predecessor's material. Sam's first fifty-three years occupy less than 20 per cent of the *Life*, and in the twenty-one years that Boswell documents more fully he includes plenty about himself. We might infer that he was Sam's constant companion – but he was not. In the two decades they knew each other, there were about 420 days when they were together; 117 of those were in a single year, 1773, and there were in total eight years in which they didn't see each other at all.[3] That's not slender acquaintance, yet it means that they saw each other on average once every three weeks. Would you, in old age, be happy to say that someone you have met 420 times after the age of fifty-three knows every recess of your mind? I'm not sure I would. Most biographers, it's true, exercise a far greater degree of presumptuousness, but Boswell has the knack of making it seem as if he is at Sam's shoulder, looking on and listening in. It's a shock, then, to realize that sometimes he reports as an eyewitness events from which he was certainly absent. He uses what he knows of the mature Sam as he seeks to understand his earlier years. It's an inevitable approach, and one that allows him to claim that Sam was from his early years 'a king of men'.

The *Life* makes Boswell look tender-hearted and curious-minded, but also gossipy and inquisitive to the point of being tactless. He records Sam's irritation at 'hearing a gentleman ask . . . a variety of questions concerning him': 'Sir, you have but two topics, yourself and me. I am sick of both.' It was Boswell's practice to reel off query after query, and the 'gentleman' was probably not some third party, but the biographer himself. On another occasion, Sam snapped that 'I will not be baited with *what*, and *why* . . . why is a cow's tail long? why is a fox's tail bushy?' Yet while there was more than this to their relationship, it is clear that each man was useful to the other: if writing about Sam gave Boswell a rich subject, and one that might find a large audience, it was also true that Sam wanted to be written about. He knew that his posthumous reputation would be defined by the information his biographer so busily gathered, and he knew that he could shape that information. Every aspiring Johnson needs a Boswell, though the real Boswell was less reliably adhesive than the proverbial one.

In the nineteenth century, thanks largely to the dashing disparagement of the historian Thomas Babington Macaulay, it became common to think of Boswell as a conceited parasite – 'one of the smallest men that ever lived', a creature of feeble intellect, bloated with booze and self-importance, who produced a great book by accident. The satirical poet John Wolcot, writing under the pseudonym Peter Pindar, called him a 'shark for anecdote and fame', 'the pilot of our literary whale' and 'a tomtit twittering on an eagle's back'. Sam himself spoke of his 'noisy benevolence', and the first of the two words stuck in others' minds.

Since then, Boswell's reputation has been rescued. Crucial to this was the recovery of his private papers – from Malahide Castle near Dublin, where they'd been stored in a cupboard, in a box that had once contained croquet balls. In these, Boswell revealed himself to be a tormented and sometimes thrilling chronicler of eighteenth-century life. To Macaulay his manner might have seemed impertinent, shallow and vain, but today he feels grippingly candid about his weaknesses and desires. In the *Life of Johnson* there's an arresting moment, in the autumn of 1777, when Boswell complains of 'a wretched changefulness, so that I could not preserve, for any long continuance, the same views of anything'. Relief came from Sam, whose 'steady vigorous mind held firm before me those objects which my own feeble and tremulous imagination frequently presented', and we're impressed by the biographer's acknowledgement of his own fallibility and his friend's mixture of dynamism and dependability.

The appeal of Boswell's book derives in large part from its set pieces. For instance, there is a dinner party at which Sam tries to praise a woman by saying she had 'a bottom of good sense'; at first he can't figure out why most of his companions are tittering, but then he twigs, collects himself and has another go at expressing his opinion – 'I say the *woman* was *fundamentally* sensible'. Or there's the occasion, in February 1767, when he goes to the Queen's House (where Buckingham Palace now stands) to make use of the fine collection of books known as the King's Library. One of its young members of staff, Frederick Augusta Barnard, introduces him to the king. They exchange polite talk, not unlike the sort that reputedly passes today between the monarch and people who work in the arts. Is Johnson writing anything? What are people up to at Oxford? Which are the largest libraries? Asked his opinion of John Hill, an ambitious botanist regarded as something of a quack, Sam starts to say that he is unreliable, but cuts himself short, aware that he is depreciating this man in the king's esteem. And when the king pays him a compliment, Sam chooses not to reply, for as he later explained, 'It was not for me to bandy civilities with my Sovereign.' All of this is droll, and it seems more so in retrospect because the king in question, whom Sam calls 'the finest gentleman I have ever seen', was George III, then in his twenties and far from exhibiting symptoms of mental illness – but in today's popular imagination Mad George, all erratic notions and purple-tinged pee.

The *Life*'s charm also comes from its parade of telling little particulars. Here is Johnson, watering and pruning a vine in order to fill a few idle moments, and here he is, buying a heavy oak stick in case he has a ruck with a writer he has nettled. Here he sees a man gesticulating to ram home a point in argument and snaps at him, 'Don't attitudinize', and here he reports drinking three bottles of port and being none the worse for wear, adding the details of where he did so in case anyone wants to check up on him. Here he is, very frankly putting George III straight on a point to do with microscopes, and here he is in less exalted company, explaining that the reason why some of the London poor go about gathering bones is that the best ones can be sold as mock ivory for knife handles, with the rest being boiled to produce grease for lubricating wheels. Here he is, in an unpowdered wig that is much too small for his great head, and here he is, paying twice the usual fare to a waterman on the Thames, impressed by the young man's curiosity about the Argonauts.

Snippets of this kind punctuate mightier moments, in which he reflects on the nature of memory, the importance of kindness or what one should read. But while the hero of the *Life* often appears to be a literary and social colossus, there are times when Boswell seems eager to emphasize his provincialism and quaintness, describing his ancestry as 'low' and then thinking better of this and calling it 'obscure'. This urge to put him in his place is most apparent where sex is concerned. A carnally voracious man who suffered at least nineteen attacks of venereal disease, Boswell prided himself on his success with women (whom he managed to find both alluring and uninteresting) and shuddered at the idea that any woman could think Sam was physically attractive. When Sam's friend Elizabeth Desmoulins, daughter of his godfather Samuel Swynfen, revealed that he had sometimes fondled her and admitted she could not have resisted him if he had chosen to 'proceed to extremities', Boswell was aghast. He pressed her to confirm that she hadn't 'felt any inclination for him', and, relieved when she confirmed that she had not, blurted that 'I cannot imagine it of any woman. There is something in his figure so terribly disgusting.' He labelled his notes of this conversation with the Latin word *tacenda*, 'things that should be kept silent'.

Although one reason to be discreet was, of course, that Sam's behaviour to Mrs Desmoulins was at odds with his image as a man of scrupulous moral character, it is clear that Boswell preferred to play down any suggestion of his master's sexual appetites. For instance, Sam told Garrick that he felt he must give up going backstage at the theatre because 'the silk stockings and white bosoms of your actresses do make my genitals to quiver'. When Boswell reproduced this admission, he changed the final words to 'excite my amorous propensities'. Perhaps he was trying to strike a suitably Johnsonian note of dignity. Yet the polysyllables of 'amorous propensities' smother the awkward and important fact that Sam felt sexually frustrated. On another occasion, Boswell made a note of a story in which Sam, asked to name the greatest of pleasures, replied, 'Why, fucking.' This, too, didn't make it into the *Life*. Boswell may have thought it uncharacteristic, but usually he enjoyed representing the more surprising aspects of Sam's behaviour.

Because Sam's life has been generously documented and closely analysed, by Boswell and the many biographers who have followed, he is that strange beast, an author who is well-known more than 200 years after his death, even though his works are not widely read. True, his prose still has many admirers, yet for every person who has read *Rasselas* there must be a hundred who know that he liked drinking tea and was fond of cats. As a result, he resembles a character in a work of fiction, an institution, a mythic treasury of anecdote and aphorism. What's more, in the many biographies and jaunty character sketches his brilliance as a speaker is on show; not all the things he says in them are his considered views, but the best of them have been allowed to eclipse his virtues as a writer.

✒ 12 ✒

An excursion to the Theatre, with some brief diversions
into other arts

SAM'S BIOGRAPHERS represent him as no connoisseur of
the arts. At his most philistine he could say that music was
loved by all 'except myself', and that it was an 'idle and
frivolous pursuit' fit to occupy 'no man of talent'. Sir John
Hawkins, who besides being Sam's biographer was a historian of music, commented that he was impervious to the
delights of a good tune – and recorded his saying that a
skilled musician had no more merit than a canary. 'Of the
beauties of painting,' noted Hawkins, 'he had not the least
conception'; when he looked at a statue he perceived only
'an unshapen mass', and he claimed that he would rather
see a portrait of a dog that he knew than look upon the
whole world's stock of fancy allegorical pictures.

Yet he struck such attitudes to be provocative. He was
sometimes affected by music and paintings – Handel, an old
ballad, historical canvases such as Benjamin West's. He was
interested, too, in the principles of aesthetics, as well as in
practical applications of artistic skill, and enjoyed confound-
ing critics who felt they knew the limits of his interests, as
when in 1759 he waded into the public debate over the best
design for a new bridge across the Thames at Blackfriars.[1]
He was often among artistic people, and when the Royal
Academy was founded in 1768, with Sir Joshua Reynolds
as its president, he took a keen interest in its activities.

Reynolds, the most successful portraitist of the day, was one of his closest friends and painted him at least five times. Sam also sat for Johann Zoffany, John Opie and the sculptor Joseph Nollekens. Although sitting for a portrait doesn't make one an art expert and involves a degree of vanity, it is hardly the mark of someone who thinks that paintings are contemptible. Equally, he wrote thoughtful dedications for two works by Fanny Burney's father, Charles: his *General History of Music* (1776) and *Commemoration of Handel* (1785). There he described music as 'one of the first attainments of rational nature' and 'the art which unites corporal with intellectual pleasure'.

It is clear, though, that his poor eyesight and hearing impaired his appreciation of art and music, and those same deficiencies limited his pleasure in going to the theatre. He was scathing about the people who made a living on the stage, and in the *Life of Savage* claimed that most actors were 'insolent, petulant, selfish, and brutal'. That animosity later softened, but he continued to think that the theatre and its practitioners were shallow and obsessed with fashion. It therefore seems strange that, notwithstanding his own modest appetite for attending plays, he imagined he could delight others by writing one. Or perhaps that's not so strange: how many people today find the theatre unbearable and conclude that the solution is to pen a drama of their own?

Sam began his one play, *Irene*, before he arrived in London, and throughout his early years there he clung to the idea that it would transform his fortunes. To modern eyes and ears its first underwhelming feature may well be the title. When I first became aware of the play I supposed that its main character's name was pronounced *eye-reen* (at the time there was such an Irene, a permanently pissed-off matriarch, in the BBC's *EastEnders*), and it took a while for me to gather that it was actually *eye-ree-nee*. Sam's Irene is based on a Greek woman of great beauty who appears in a book he admired, Richard Knolles's *General History of the Turks* (1603). Captured by the Turkish emperor Mahomet, she is told that her life will be preserved if she converts from Christianity to Islam. The play depicts a religious and cultural confrontation, between the 'wolves of Turkey' and the 'ill-fated' children of Greece. A modern audience may shrink from its abrasive image of Islam, or be intrigued that the subject was on his mind – Mahomet speaks of the need to 'pursue the task of war, / Till every nation reverence the Koran'. But for Sam's contemporaries the main issue was the failure to do justice to a potentially exciting subject, for as *Irene* ponders the question of what it means for a person to abandon her religion, it resembles a moral essay rather than a drama. I've seen claims that *Irene* was far ahead of its time – in its appeal to reason and its preference for the episodic rather than the seamless, a forerunner of the revolutionary techniques of Bertolt Brecht. But Sam, in trying to write a play that was concerned more with thoughts than with feelings, ended up creating something inert.

The opportunity to put it on came about through Garrick. Sam's former pupil was now a star. In 1747, he had become the manager of the Theatre Royal Drury Lane, and he launched his tenure there in September by reciting verses specially commissioned from Sam. He promised a new regime that would feature fresh infusions of 'useful mirth' and 'salutary woe' – the replacement of amusing trash with works of real artistic merit. Sam knew Garrick well enough to be aware that he might have more selfish priorities, but could point to his own play as a specimen of 'salutary woe'. At the start of 1749 Garrick finally gave him the chance to resurrect *Irene*, though not without some bruising arguments about how it could be made more pointed and performable.

The cast for the premiere was reassuringly strong. It included Garrick himself, along with the tall and handsome Irish actor Spranger Barry as Mahomet, while the popular Hannah Pritchard, who had recently played opposite Garrick in *Macbeth*, took the title role. But there were glitches. On opening night, 6 February, theatregoers applauded a speech that dwelled on the word *tomorrow*, apparently because it called to mind Macbeth's famous lines 'Tomorrow, and tomorrow, and tomorrow / Creeps in this petty pace from day to day'. This wasn't what Sam had been hoping for. Worse, they jeered the death of the title character – something which Sam would have preferred to be suggested, not shown, but which Garrick had insisted should happen onstage. As Hannah Pritchard struggled to utter her final lines while being strangled, there were cries of 'Murder! Murder!' Eventually she retreated, to die (of embarrassment) out of sight. For the rest of the run the audience was not subjected to this indecorous spectacle, but there were other sources of chagrin. Sam was not impressed with Mrs Pritchard's performance and would in due course condemn her mechanical approach, claiming that 'she no more thought of the play out of which her part was taken, than a shoemaker thinks of the skin out of which . . . he is making a pair of shoes'. As for her colleague Susannah Cibber, he'd have preferred to 'sit up to the chin in water for an hour than be obliged to listen to the whining'. Spranger Barry fared no better, in Sam's estimate 'fit for nothing but to stand at an auction room door with his pole'.

Those reproofs came later. When *Irene* opened, Sam was excited and not yet in a mood to blame the actors for failing to do justice to his mighty lines. He attended the performance in uncharacteristically fine clothes – a scarlet waistcoat, trimmed with gold lace, and a hat adorned in similarly extravagant style. He thought this was his moment and was eager to milk the attention. He quickly put the hat to one side, conscious of how ridiculous it looked on him, but we're struck all the same by his flamboyant image of how a successful playwright ought to present himself and by his readiness to embrace this showy garb.

The production ran for nine nights – certainly not a flop by the standards of the time. Sam attended every performance, made just under £200 from his share of the profits, and received a further £100 from the publisher Robert Dodsley for the playscript. This was far from disastrous. But Sam experienced what many other fledgling playwrights have found: no amount of praise could make him forget the criticisms, which felt like punches in the gut. Boswell would record his commenting on the brief and meagre influence of critics: 'A fly, Sir, may sting a stately horse and make him wince; but one is but an insect, and the other is a horse still.' In his *Dictionary* entry for *brusher*, Sam includes a pointed quotation from Sir Francis Bacon: 'Sir Henry Wotton used to say, that critics were like *brushers* of noblemen's clothes.' The truth, though, is that critics are often more than flies and the objects of their criticism rather less than stately horses. Besides, the sting of a hostile review does more than make one wince. Writers who don't read reviews of their work tend to claim that they don't trust or value them, but it's more likely that they are uncomfortable with the degree to which reviews – even, or perhaps especially, stupid ones – can be upsetting, a cause of self-doubt and despair.

Boswell reports that when Sam was asked 'how he felt upon the ill success of his tragedy', he replied, 'Like the Monument.' The dutiful biographer interpreted this as meaning 'that he continued firm and unmoved as that column' – namely the flute of Portland stone that still stands today on the site of the first church destroyed by the Great Fire of London. But he may have missed some of the significance of Sam's words. Perhaps, like the Monument, he was *unable* to feel anything; the play's reception numbed him. Or perhaps he thought that the failure was inscribed indelibly upon his reputation; he would have known that the Monument was originally commissioned 'to preserve the memory of this dreadful visitation', and might have believed that the unhappy story of *Irene*'s first production would also be preserved, a founding feature of his personal myth.

The trouble was that Sam had an untheatrical imagination. He did not grasp what gave a play and a production their vitality. In *Irene*, many of the scenes consist of head-to-head confrontation rather than three- or four-way talk, with the result that speechifying outmuscles more nuanced, layered kinds of interaction. If we return to the verses written for Garrick in 1747, we find him presenting it as a matter of fact that 'The Stage but echoes back the public voice'. Yet while Garrick at Drury Lane responded pragmatically to the audience's apparent enthusiasms and dislikes, Sam had little concept of who that audience was or what it wanted. Their desire for fervent exchanges between vividly realized characters was alien to him. Garrick would reflect that Shakespeare, in writing tragedy, 'dipped his pen in his own heart', but when his former schoolmaster essayed it, 'passion sleeps'. An anonymous critique that appeared soon after *Irene*'s Drury Lane run called its poetry 'languid and unaffecting' and complained of characterization being 'mangled in a miserable manner'.[2]

Reading the play now, it's hard to imagine a remotely bearable revival, and Sam's later commentary on theatre hints at the reasons for its woodenness. In the 1750s he wrote theatre reviews for the *Gentleman's Magazine*, and like many critics before and since he had ideas about the theatre that were at odds with those of the day's leading practitioners, who must have groaned to find him holding forth about their efforts. 'A play read, affects the mind like a play acted,' he claimed. It's a striking statement, for the text of a play needs animating by a team, and although the imagination can simulate this, the solitary reading of a playtext will never match the four-dimensional work of bringing it to life in collaboration with a cast and crew.

The limits of his thinking about drama are apparent in his edition of Shakespeare. Love, he claims, is not an important subject on the stage. He thinks that Shakespeare was 'much more careful to please than to instruct' – and considers this a fault, evidence of his lacking moral purpose. No less telling is his belief that 'In his tragic scenes there is always something wanting, but his comedy often surpasses expectation or desire'. In his opinion, the tragic scene most charged with tenderness comes not in *Hamlet* or *King Lear*, but in *Henry VIII*, when Queen Katherine hears of the death of Cardinal Wolsey. It's a good scene in a play that was then much more popular than it is now, and perhaps Sam was taken with the description of Wolsey by the Queen's usher, Griffith: 'This cardinal, / Though from an humble stock, undoubtedly / Was fashion'd to much honour from his cradle. / He was a scholar, and a ripe and good one; / Exceeding wise, fair-spoken and persuading.' Perhaps, too, he was touched by the moment when Katherine, foreseeing her own death and 'that celestial harmony I go to', has a vision of white-robed spirits who invite her to a banquet. But there's a lot of *perhaps* here, and Sam's choice is a contrary one. He delights in the scene's unfolding 'without gods, or furies, or poisons, or precipices'. The mockery of other people's preferences – not least for key moments in *Hamlet* and *King Lear* – isn't hard to spot, and it doesn't make his opinion any easier to share. In any case, Shakespeare collaborated on *Henry VIII*, and the lines Sam admired may have been the work of John Fletcher. Selecting this as Shakespeare's most affecting scene is a bit like saying your favourite kind of wine is a kir.

But Sam was right about some of theatre's problems. In the Drury Lane prologue written for Garrick, he noted that the management needed to 'watch the wild vicissitudes of taste'. Anyone who has spent much time in the theatre will know what Sam is talking about when he writes that they must attend to every 'meteor of caprice' and 'chase the new-blown bubbles of the day'. A lot of theatre, it's true, is so utterly obsessed with being on-trend that it's deadly, so pious about the importance of speaking to the present moment that it's doomed to be both ephemeral and insufficient. Yet such suspicion of the arena in which he was working could go too far. In the prologue he wrote for *Irene*, he called the theatre's patrons 'sons of avarice' and insinuated that a lot of them were snoozy fops whose critical faculties didn't extend beyond being able to applaud or hurl catcalls. Although there will always be a contingent of theatregoers who enjoy being wound up, this was a risky gambit, and the substance of his play didn't do much to justify such disdain. Instead, its reception revealed to him an uncongenial truth about being a playwright – the audience can't be counted on to laugh when you want them to, or share your sense of pathos, and the actors can't be counted on to place emphasis where you'd like it. To be a playwright one has to accept the precariousness of live performance and its reception, and ideally one should enjoy it. But plenty of people who fancy themselves playwrights struggle to let go of their work in this way. Trusting others, including the audience, is the fundamental gesture of theatre, an optimistic art form.

Still, for all its dramatic limitations, *Irene* provides interesting evidence of Sam's sexual politics. The first time the audience sees Irene she is asking her friend Aspasia to teach her how to repel Mahomet's advances. Aspasia encourages her to stay true to her Christian faith, but points out that withstanding Mahomet will be difficult, for Irene has been instructed from infancy to act submissively. Their later conversation has a similar degree of substance, and when Aspasia returns to this theme, she reflects on the ways in which patriarchy silences women. Mahomet objectifies Irene – in his eyes she is fit to 'adorn a throne', and he says that he won't rest 'till I clasp the lovely maid, / And ease my loaded soul upon her bosom'. His coercive attitude leaves a rancid taste.

Irene is also full of robust Johnsonian language. We can briefly admire references to the 'dubious twilight of conviction', the 'dull serenity' of monarchs, the 'labyrinths of treason', 'glittering fallacy' and 'agonizing pomp', the unsettling effects of 'hooting infamy', and the moment when passions mingle and 'Fate lies crowded in a narrow space'. But the play's verse seems stilted compared to his most significant poem of the period: shortly before the premiere of *Irene*, Sam published *The Vanity of Human Wishes*. A devastating portrait of a brutally competitive society, it's often described as a poet's poem, admired by other writers for its dignified precision. Frequently misread, on the strength of the title, as a statement about the emptiness and pointlessness of life itself, it in fact depicts the emptiness of an existence controlled by desires (for status, wealth, beauty, longevity). Like the earlier *London* it is an imitation of the

Roman satirist Juvenal, whom Sam commended for his 'declamatory grandeur', and its attack on self-seeking materialism is a mighty catalogue of human failings, reverberating with a philosophically charged rhetoric that Garrick deemed 'as hard as Greek'. Perhaps unsurprisingly, it wasn't very popular, certainly not compared with *London*, but it is his signature poem – grave, melancholy, philosophical and formal, bookish but worldly.

The Vanity of Human Wishes also underscores Sam's role as a guide. It identifies some of the ways in which ambition causes people to become disorientated. For instance, he imagines a scholar who must 'pause a while from letters to be wise' – rather than being smothered by academic study and failing to take note of the rest of humanity. But the 'fever of renown' makes it difficult to do this; institutional life creates a very narrow sense of what it means to be successful, and scholars all too easily become blinkered. The problem, in essence, is one of framing: the scholar's judgement is limited to the options that seem available, instead of embracing the full range of what's actually possible. This is salience trumping intelligence, and it's normal; although at the very start of the poem Sam proposes taking an 'extensive view' of the world, in what follows he conveys the difficulties of doing this. Overwhelmed with images and impressions, we struggle to achieve a wider perspective. Yet while he acknowledges that he shares such weaknesses, he seems to perceive them with an unusual degree of clarity – a necessary endowment, for by the time of *The Vanity of Human Wishes* and *Irene*'s premiere he was at work on a project that would test him profoundly.

❧ 13 ❧

In which we ponder the making of a Dictionary – with
thoughts on the true meaning of lexicography and
the particular flavours of its solitude

ON 18 JUNE 1746, Sam had breakfasted at the Golden
Anchor, an inn near Holborn Bar. There he had signed a
contract with a group of publishers, led by Robert Dodsley,
who believed that a new dictionary of English was desirable
and could make them money. Dodsley had known Sam
since his early days in London and thought him well suited
to the task. On first hearing of the idea, Sam had been
unsure if it was something he should pursue, but when at
length he agreed to do so, he knew he was embarking on his
most substantial venture. He imagined it would take three
years.

The fee, to be paid in instalments, was 1,500 guineas
(£1,575), the equivalent of perhaps £150,000 today. This at
a time when a guinea might buy a smart new hat and a
housemaid earned perhaps £10 a year. For *London*, Sam had
been paid ten guineas, and for *The Vanity of Human Wishes*
he received fifteen. True, these were poems, each fewer than
400 lines long, but now he was entering an entirely different
league. For comparison: Henry Fielding received £700 for
his novel *Tom Jones* (1749) and Adam Smith would get £500
for the first edition of *The Wealth of Nations* (1776), though
he would ultimately make about three times that amount
from it, while Edward Gibbon earned more than £6,000

from his *History of the Decline and Fall of the Roman Empire* (1776–88).

The money promised to transform his life. Though never one of those people for whom money was the foundation of self-worth, he was mindful of its allure. The subject often occupied him in the *Rambler*. 'Money has much less power than is ascribed to it by those that want it,' he wrote; 'few men are made better by affluence', and 'the rich and the powerful live in a perpetual masquerade'. But 'no desire can be formed which riches do not assist to gratify', and wealth is 'useful . . . when it departs from us'. Insights into the disappointments of prosperity ('no sooner do we sit down to enjoy our acquisitions, than we find them insufficient to fill up the vacuities of life') were matched by insights into its potential to open doors ('The most striking effect of riches is the splendour of dress, which every man has observed to enforce respect and facilitate reception'). He would tell Boswell that 'you will have much more influence by giving or lending money where it is wanted, than by hospitality'. Affluence has the effect of 'overpowering the distinctions of rank and birth', and whoever has it 'imagines himself always fortified against invasions on his authority'.

Feeling more confident about his finances, he took lodgings at 17 Gough Square, a minute's walk north of Fleet Street. This red-brick house, which dates from the end of the seventeenth century, still stands, and strikes the modern eye as tall and sturdy. For Sam, it had obvious attractions. Close to his familiar haunts, it was conveniently near the premises of William Strahan, the *Dictionary*'s designated printer, and the single room on the top floor, which enjoyed good light, was large enough to serve as an office. Installed there, he could survey his task and the world at large with satisfaction; set up in the sort of property a respectable tradesman would have occupied, he seemed at last to have arrived as a professional writer.

Soon he began his research, reading widely and marking the books with a black lead pencil. For practical reasons he chose to confine himself to written sources, and he looked for illustrations of good usage; the list of headwords, rather than being something he drew up in advance, would grow out of these, and he arranged for them to be copied into notebooks. A skeleton text began to take shape. But obstacles lay ahead. The nature of language itself was a problem and, as he would eventually note in his preface to the finished volumes, 'no dictionary of a living tongue ever can be perfect, since, while it is hastening to publication, some words are budding, and some falling away'.

There is a false image of Dr Johnson the cast-iron prescriptivist, regulating language with unwavering certainty. The truth is a little different. In 1747, when he brought out his *Plan of an English Dictionary*, he spoke of his ambition to 'secure our language' and stop it being overrun with barbarous usage. He intended to arrest the language's supposed decay, and pictured the period between the accession of Queen Elizabeth and the Restoration – that is, between 1558 and 1660 – as a linguistic and literary golden age, the purity of which was worth recovering. Yet even at this stage he was aware of the limits of his authority. Dodsley suggested he address the *Plan* to that influential taste-maker, the Earl of Chesterfield. Sam did so, and claimed that in considering the pure and proper use of words he would be 'exercising a kind of vicarious jurisdiction . . . as the delegate of your lordship'. He was embarrassed by this posture of obsequiousness, but it was expedient: in the eyes of the public whose interest the booksellers hoped to attract, Samuel Johnson was nobody, but Lord Chesterfield was universally known, a diplomat and political operator with an appetite for supporting the arts.

As Sam gathered the materials for the work itself, his understanding of the lexicographer's role sharpened. When he began, he believed that a word could have no more than seven senses, but in time his reading demonstrated that this was wrong. Encountering words in the wild, he saw just how varied their lives could be. In the finished volumes, he distinguished 134 senses of the verb *to take*, twenty senses of *up*, and fourteen of *time*. Now he was awed by 'the boundless chaos of living speech'; rather than occupying a vantage point outside the forests of language, he sat in their midst. He did not like everything he found there, and stuck usage labels on about 10 per cent of the words he documented, but only a handful of these, between 1 and 2 per cent, expressed an opinion – such as that a word or sense was 'low', 'cant', 'ludicrous', even 'vicious'. His mission was to register language rather than debug it, and the heart of the *Dictionary* was his decision to provide quotations from other authors to illustrate words *as they are actually used*.

This shift is culturally significant. In recognizing that no dictionary can 'embalm' language, in coming to appreciate English's 'exuberance of signification', and in noting that some words are 'hourly shifting their relations', he rethought the nature of his project, and this influenced both the practice of lexicography and the wider public understanding of language. Previously, making a dictionary had been seen as a means of reform: the language could be sent to school, and indeed in 1712 Jonathan Swift had published a pamphlet proposing exactly this. By contrast, Sam was responsive to the variety he found during his research – the jaggedness and profusion of usage, which he did his best to register. None of this is to say that he gave up having views about how English ought to be written, but exposure to the realities of its uses meant that he had to relinquish some of the ideals he'd entertained when he set out.

Clearly, then, his task was bigger than he had at first supposed, and he soon began to find ways of distracting himself from it. We all know how this goes, the irritatingly reasonable conversation one has with oneself: 'I need to get the right tools. Mastering this one apparently unrelated subject will help me make sense of the larger task I'm facing. This isn't an auspicious moment to start. I need to do this when I'm better rested and more relaxed. I need to wait till I'm in the same frame of mind that I was in the last time I made some progress. My levels of nervous energy are too high. I think I may have offended X by not being in touch with her for ages, so I must do something about that immediately. Speaking to Y will help clear this mental blockage. If I just get this other thing out of the way, I'll feel liberated and ready. The muse isn't with me. I think I might be getting sick.' Sam's own internal jabber will have been more freighted with melancholy and moral scruple, but the effect will have been the same. Deferring work is usually more tiring than doing it, and the fuzzy patterns of enervation make it possible to convince oneself that the deferral *is* the work.

It was while working on the *Dictionary* that he established himself as an essayist, with the *Rambler*. He wrote the pieces that appeared there to make some extra money and relieve the slog of lexicography. The immediacy of writing twice a week an essay of about 1,400 words, for prompt publication, could not have been more different from what he called 'beating the track of the alphabet'. It is well-known that he defined *lexicographer* as 'A writer of dictionaries; a harmless drudge'. His reasons for doing so tend to command less attention. The definition is treated as a droll gesture, a buried joke. But Sam didn't really think he was a drudge (in his own explanation 'One employed in mean labour; a slave; one doomed to servile occupation'). The *Dictionary*'s preface leaves one in no doubt of how important he considered his work, and in the course of his labours he pictured himself in many other and very different terms – as a sailor on the sea of words, an explorer, a collector, even an invader and conqueror, ransacking the recesses of learning. As for 'harmless', it's fair to say that people who protest their own harmlessness are aware of their potential to cause harm; they are conscious that their actions have implications. Sam's wry portrait of the drudging lexicographer is typical of the self-deprecation with which all serious people state their professions. Whereas someone doing a job of little consequence will often take enormous pride in their status ('I am the assistant deputy director of customer experience'), and proprietors of one-person companies without apparent irony refer to themselves as CEOs, heavy hitters are less brassy. To understate what you do is to leave breathing space for excellence.

Still, when he referred to his work as mere drudgery, he was expressing a sense of worthlessness. Even though people he knew were never far away, and often under the same roof, he regarded the *Dictionary* as a lonely undertaking. Its preface would characterize the mood of this period as the 'gloom of solitude', and the text bears witness to his morbid feelings of isolation. Deep into the intricacies of the project, he wrote a piece for the *Adventurer* in which he rejected the idea that solitude is 'the parent of philosophy'; while it might provide the opportunity to increase one's learning, the purpose of doing so was to share it with others. Allergic to 'specious representations of solitary happiness', he suspected that beyond the short term a reclusive life was conducive not to wisdom, but to lassitude. Impressed by Robert Burton's simple direction in *The Anatomy of Melancholy*, 'Be not solitary; be not idle', he nonetheless modified it as follows: 'If you are idle, be not solitary; if you are solitary, be not idle.' The principle was one he found it hard to put into practice, as solitude and idleness were such natural companions.

In *The Lonely City*, an investigation of what it means to be alone, Olivia Laing writes that 'You can be lonely anywhere, but there is a particular flavour to the loneliness that comes from living in a city.' Though one may sense 'the massed presence of other human beings', it is no guarantee of not feeling isolated. Pondering the temper of this 'absence or paucity of connection', she reaches for a definition: '*Unhappy*, as the dictionary has it, *as a result of being without the companionship of others.*'[1] The dictionary she has in mind isn't Sam's, but in the pages of his work we find pointed references to what she calls 'paucity of connection'. In his entry for *companion* he quotes the poet Matthew Prior: 'With anxious doubts, with raging passions torn, / No sweet *companion* near with whom to mourn.' His entry for *visiter* [*sic*] quotes a letter from Jonathan Swift to John Gay, in which Swift complains, 'I have a large house, yet I should hardly prevail to find one *visiter*, if I were not able to hire him with a bottle of wine.' Under *stagnant*, he cites lines from his own play *Irene* that imagine being 'buried in perpetual sloth, / That gloomy slumber of the *stagnant* soul'. Among the quotations for *lone* is one from Savage's *Wanderer*: 'Here the *lone* hour a blank of life displays.' For *solitariness*, he quotes from Sir Philip Sidney's *Arcadia*: 'You subject yourself to *solitariness*, the sly enemy that doth most separate a man from well doing.' There is much more in this vein, and while it is easy to exaggerate the significance of any particular excerpt, the many quotations on this theme have a strong cumulative force.

In an age that regarded the individual's industry as the basis of national improvement, idleness seemed shameful. It's natural to suppose that Sam felt guilty because he thought he was lazy. But there is an alternative reading: he was lazy because he was wracked with guilt. He had failed to keep resolutions, had allowed his faith and friendships to lapse, had wallowed in fantasy. Troubled by his offences and notions of the suffering they had produced, he imagined he would never complete the *Dictionary*. In a book-length 'pathographic essay' on Sam, Ernst Verbeek explains that 'Postponement, difficulty in finishing things . . . and working in bouts, are characteristics of the sympathetic person'. Verbeek believes that 'Johnson's intelligence was an extension of his heart', and sees in him a special ability 'to displace himself affectively into another person, or into a situation'.[2] His innate complexity of feeling caused his energies to veer off in many directions, and in *Rambler* 134 (dating from June 1751) he wrote about this, describing the emotional climate of slow, fitful work, which consisted of 'false terrors', 'the seducements of imagination', a tendency to dwell on 'remote consequences' or to 'multiply complications', and a readiness to be consumed with 'reconciling ourselves to our own cowardice by excuses which . . . we know to be absurd'.

Many years later, reflecting on Alexander Pope's slow and anxious progress in translating Homer's *Iliad*, Sam would comment that 'Indolence, interruption, business, and pleasure, all take their terms of retardation; and every long work is lengthened by a thousand causes that can, and ten thousand that cannot, be recounted.' All large projects involve unforeseen delays. I'm reminded here of Hofstadter's

Law, framed by the cognitive scientist Douglas R. Hofstadter: 'It always takes longer than you expect, even when you take into account Hofstadter's Law.' This conjures up an image like the strange loops one sees in the graphic art of M. C. Escher: the eye follows a staircase down and down and down and down, only to find itself back at the starting point. But if Sam was experiencing a paradox of perspective, or no more than the illusion of progress, there were other factors retarding him that could easily be identified, and chief among them was grief.

❧ 14 ❧

A chapter about Grief (for one word must serve where in
truth no assemblage of words will be sufficient)

UNLIKE SAM, Tetty had never really settled in London and
had spent much of their married life in flight from its dirt.
The house at Gough Square had promised to be a proper
home, but sharing it with all the work on the *Dictionary* was
intolerable. Once it had become apparent that she did not
wish to stay there, Sam had rented a small property in
Hampstead, which was then regarded not as part of London
but as a genteel retreat from it. Breathing the better air of
this hilltop spa community, Tetty was attended by nurses
and expensive doctors. Sam visited her often, and it was at
Hampstead, one morning in the autumn of 1748, that he
wrote the first seventy lines of *The Vanity of Human Wishes*.
During a bout of sickness, she returned to live with Sam in
Gough Square. But then she was advised that it would be
better for her to sleep in a more peaceful environment; she
removed again to Hampstead, and when she complained
about her lodgings, noting that the plaster beside the staircase was in many places damaged, the landlord ominously
replied that this was 'nothing but . . . the knocks against it
of the coffins of the poor souls that have died'.

Her own death came not long after this, in March 1752.
She was sixty-three. Sam was devastated, floored by his
grief, for it was impossible not to feel that he could have
done more for her, especially while blundering through the

early stages of the *Dictionary*. Prayers he composed in the weeks that followed speak of his 'troubled soul' and 'tumultuous imaginations', and he wrote of his hopes that her spirit would watch over him – 'that I may enjoy the good effects of her attention'. He clung to the belief that mourning might awaken his conscience, and hoped not to 'languish in fruitless and unavailing sorrow', lest 'idleness lay me open to vain imaginations'. In early May, he wrote of preparing for 'my return to life tomorrow', but it seems that he could not return so soon, and six months later he was pleading for help in overcoming idleness: he must 'shun sloth and negligence', cease to 'lavish away' his life 'on useless trifles', and learn not to waste time 'in vain searches after things . . . hidden from me'.

He wrote these words for himself, but his friends could see the intensity of his suffering, and it puzzled all who had regarded the marriage as an embarrassment. The couple's spiritual kinship had been closer than others had realized. But to those who'd doubted Tetty's worth, it suggested not so much hidden depths of feeling as Sam's hidden shallows, an unexpected weakness. It is worth emphasizing that his grief, rather than being taken as evidence that there was more to Tetty than met the eye, was seen as a guilty, mawkish reaction to the end of a low and unworthy union. We can never fully understand what happens inside the privacy of other people's relationships, but most of Sam's friends, admirers and biographers have assumed that whatever happened in this one was indelicate or shameful – and best ignored.

Sir John Hawkins felt that there was something bogus in Sam's emotional response to the loss. The melancholy that took hold of him was, concedes Hawkins, 'of the blackest and deepest kind', but reading, he thinks, played a large part in this. Sam had been exposed to sombre theories about what happened to the souls of the departed, and he had also absorbed other people's ideas about what grief was meant to look and feel like. Hawkins claims that 'if his fondness for his wife was not dissembled, it was a lesson he had learned by rote, and . . . he knew not where to stop till he became ridiculous'. He adds, breathtakingly, that for his own part he never met or even saw Tetty.

It hasn't helped the marriage's reputation that Sam did not attend Tetty's funeral. This took place at Bromley in Kent, a place with which she'd had no connections; it was chosen because Sam's friend John Hawkesworth, a writer he'd got to know through Edward Cave, lived there and was able to make the necessary arrangements. Reflecting on the matter, Sam must have found this expediency pitiful. Surely he ought to have done more to ensure a respectful and appropriate burial? But at the time the practicalities were beyond him, and later he was nagged by the memory of this omission. He did not visit Tetty's grave till Easter Day the following year, and it would be more than thirty years before he had a memorial stone laid there.

This can be interpreted two ways: as a sign that Sam didn't care, or as evidence that he was prostrate with grief. The latter is far more likely. But real grief, as opposed to the tropical and spectacular variety performed by impostors who treat outdoor sadness as a competitive sport, can make us look like we care far less than we do. There is a gulf between the experience of distress and other people's expectations about how we show and manage it, between the disorientating effects of loss and the conventional rituals of grieving.

What happens when we are bereaved? First there is a period of numbness. Then we crave the touch of the person we have lost, and the word 'lost' is apropos, as we believe that we can find them. We are angry. We are on edge. We keep seeing reminders of the past – of when we weren't alone, of when we were complete. We feel the illusory presence of the departed. We feel we have been deserted. We may also believe we have lost some status; the world defines us differently, and the difference is unfavourable. We feel empty, and there is silence.

In Max Porter's sad and gorgeous *Grief is the Thing with Feathers* (2015), a crow appears to a bereaved husband and takes on multiple roles: among them friend, spectre, crutch, symptom, analyst and babysitter. The husband plays roles, too: blinded by 'other people's performances of woe', he becomes a 'list-making trader in clichés of gratitude', a 'machine-like architect of routines' for his now-motherless children, and a scholar of orbiting grievers' moods and gestures. Loss makes him an anthropologist, a documentarist, an artist, and when he draws his dead wife's picture, her ribs appear 'splayed stretched like a xylophone with the dead birds playing tunes on her bones'. Grief is a project, says the bereaved husband in Porter's book, and it is one for the long term. We think we have put it behind us – have not so much banished it as forgotten its face – and then it returns, black-feathered, and perches in our room, staring down at us with gimlety precision. Of course, Sam didn't associate grief with this malign, anarchic comic-book bird, which Porter has adopted from the poet Ted Hughes's volume *Crow* (1970). But he too experienced it as a dark, insidious presence, blocking out the light, and among the images coined by Porter none seems more apt here than that of the grieving husband's house being 'a physical encyclopedia of no-longer hers'.[1]

Sam was stalked by reminders of Tetty. He kept her

wedding ring in a small round wooden box, along with a piece of paper on which he wrote the dates of their marriage and her death, and it seems he sometimes consulted the box, almost as if to reactivate memories. The box can be interpreted as a means of compartmentalizing his sorrow, as a symbolic miniature coffin, or as a *memento mori*, an object of remorseful meditation. How often did he see it? How often did he seek it out? We don't know. But I can picture his simultaneously wanting to look at it, maybe to hold it and ritually examine its contents, and wanting not to do this – his heart fit to burst, his soul riven with contradiction. One of the anomalies of grief is that our desolation at not being able to bring a loved one back from the dead is intruded on by the unworthy feeling that we don't want to.

Nearly thirty years later he would write to a recently bereaved friend, Thomas Lawrence, 'He that outlives a wife whom he has long loved, sees himself disjoined from the only mind that had the same hopes and fears.' As a result, 'The continuity of being is lacerated' and 'life stands suspended and motionless till it is driven by external causes into a new channel'. He wraps up the letter's weightiest paragraph with seven solemn words: 'But the time of suspense is dreadful.' This conjures an image of Sam, not as he is in 1780 but as he was in 1752 – alone at home and numb, as if Tetty's death is his own.

Grief made him feel older than his forty-two years, and it revealed to him a part of himself he preferred not to see. Tetty's death was a reminder of the fragility of existence – especially his own. When we grieve we are meant to witness the honour of the person we have lost, and to cherish our memories of them, but it's normal at this time to think about ourselves, to feel guilty for thinking so much about ourselves, and then to plunge deeper into those very thoughts – to see the possibilities that our loss opens up, to notice the ways in which others' views of us change as a result of our loss, even to exult in the status with which bereavement endows us (for now we are sad and serious and substantial). The most pious griever will still think 'What now?' While for some that's an entirely unhappy thought, it's frequently tinged with an awareness of what we can at last become.

Sam found that thoughts of other women crowded in on him, and for a while in 1753 he considered remarrying. A decade later he would pronounce that a second marriage was 'the triumph of hope over experience', but in the aftermath of Tetty's death it promised to be something else: a coping mechanism, or an act of atonement. Among several candidates, the most likely was Hill Boothby, a learned woman he had met fourteen years earlier on a trip to Derbyshire. But while he was contemplating a deeper kind of relationship with a woman he referred to as 'my sweet angel', she was busy looking after the household and six children of a recently deceased friend. Sam's thoughts of a second wife faltered, and the exhausted Hill Boothby's health deteriorated – she died in January 1756, aged forty-seven. In the weeks before her death he wrote to her repeatedly. In one letter he says that 'It is again midnight, and I am again alone. With what meditation shall I amuse this waste hour of darkness and vacuity?' (For as long as he spent on the letter, the action of composing it relieved the loneliness.) In another he proposes 'a very probable remedy for indigestion and lubricity of the bowels'; it involved orange peel, which perhaps explains his odd habit of pocketing such scraps of it as he could. His final letter to her is short and intense: 'I beg of you to endeavour to live . . . I am in great trouble, if you can write three words to me, be pleased to do it. I am afraid to say much, and cannot say nothing when my dearest is in danger.' Imagine receiving this under any circumstances, let alone when dying. Here we see how intimate he believed their connection to be, and we sense his fear that once again he will be abandoned.

Two years after Tetty's passing, in a letter to the literary scholar Thomas Warton, author of a poem on 'The Pleasures of Melancholy', he would reflect that her death had made him 'a kind of solitary wanderer in the wild of life, without any certain direction'; he had become a 'gloomy gazer on a world to which I have little relation'. That dissociation will make sense to anyone who has experienced bereavement: to grieve is to be adrift, to feel like an outsider, to have to learn afresh one's relationship to the most customary features of daily life. In truth, Sam always thought of himself as an outsider – rambler, adventurer, idler. But in picturing himself as a 'solitary wanderer in the wild of life', he captures something important: in time of grief and mourning we feel the world's wildness more keenly, and grasp how many conventions and comforts there are that ordinarily distract us from seeing ourselves as the empty eye of life's tornado.

Yet in the aftermath of Tetty's death Sam had plenty to occupy him. Lodgers roosted at 17 Gough Square; they paid nothing to be there, and the pleasures of their company, never exactly obvious, were frequently offset by the cost to his domestic tranquillity. Among the others who came by, adding to the discord, were the clerks who helped with work on the *Dictionary*. Now usually referred to as his amanuenses, these Grub Street habitués were capable rather than dependable; one of them, V. J. Peyton, seems to have been a particular cause of nuisance, and Sam's friend Giuseppe Baretti, a linguist who knew a thing or two about low living, commented, 'I never saw so nauseous a fellow.' Nauseous or not, Sam's helpers needed paying and must also have needed to be kept amused.

For most of the rest of his life, Sam would accommodate others whose condition he thought meaner than his own. Three of these stand out. The first is Anna Williams, who was three years his senior. She joined him after the death of her father Zachariah, a friend of Sam's who had devoted a large chunk of his life to finding and promoting a method of measuring longitude at sea. Anna, who went blind in her early thirties, preferred to channel her energies into poetry and would shepherd Sam through some of his darker nights, sitting up to drink tea with him. Then there is Robert Levet, an unlicensed and unmannerly doctor who would briefly leave Sam to take up with a prostitute who operated out of a nearby coal shed. Whereas the attractions of Williams were just about fathomable – she was peevish but undeniably clever – Levet was a puzzle. As with Tetty, Sam's friends couldn't divine this deficient character's appeal. When Levet eventually died, in 1782, Sam would mark their thirty-six years of friendship with a moving poem that testified to both his lack of refinement and his usefulness: he had been 'obscurely wise, and coarsely kind', a friend to those in distress, busily ministering to others without much thought of personal gain. Though Sam was thinking mainly of Levet's work among the poor, the poem also pictures his role closer to home. It begins: 'Condemn'd to hope's delusive mine, / As on we toil from day to day, / By sudden blasts, or slow decline, / Our social comforts drop away.' The last of those four lines contains a heavily compressed statement about what Sam valued in Levet. As he had written in the

Rambler, unhappiness is 'interwoven with our being' and 'The cure for the greatest part of human miseries is not radical, but palliative'. Thankfully, there are people who, rather than feeling the need to try and solve our problems, can soothe us by their very presence. Levet was such a person, his power of giving comfort not easily explicable but quietly reliable.

A few weeks after Tetty died, the household acquired another remarkable member. This was ten-year-old Francis Barber, who arrived from Jamaica via a Yorkshire boarding school. Barber had spent his early years as a slave on a 2,600-acre sugar plantation that belonged to Colonel Richard Bathurst, the father of one of Sam's friends (also called Richard Bathurst). The exact nature of his new role in London is unclear. To the various people who wrote about Sam's life he was his 'faithful negro servant', a sort of usher, helpful and handsome but never much more than a footnote in their accounts.

Francis Barber's biographer Michael Bundock believes that they were brought closer by others' tendency to look on them as outlandish oddities. David Olusoga writes in *Black and British: A Forgotten History* of Sam's being 'an extremely liberal and accommodating employer', and explains that while 'black Georgians were everywhere, scattered across London', they were still sufficiently rare to be 'an exotic novelty, worthy of mention'. 'For those clear-eyed enough to make the connection they were a reminder,' says Olusoga, of 'that vast empire of sugar, slavery and misery three thousand miles away across the Atlantic', but other, less far-sighted observers entertained visions of 'their nation brought to chaos by a large and rapidly expanding black community, whose unrestrained sexuality was contaminating the blood of the English'.[2]

Sam, who was accustomed to being treated as strange and barbarous, would have understood better than most what it felt like to be abused on account of one's appearance. For some of his contemporaries, having a black servant was a fashion statement, but he had little use for a servant, especially one who was still a child. The truth may be that his friend Bathurst thought Francis would be a welcome distraction. If so, the plan worked. Their relationship was not always easy, especially when Francis volunteered for the navy. Sam's feelings about that decision are apparent in his remark that 'No man will be a sailor who has contrivance enough to get himself into jail; for being in a ship is being in a jail, with the chance of being drowned.' But despite their differences, the bond endured, and more than thirty years later Francis was one of two people present at Sam's deathbed (the other being Elizabeth Desmoulins's son John), as well as being the chief beneficiary of his will.

Because Francis Barber has tended to appear almost parenthetically in lives of Dr Johnson, we can make the mistake of thinking the connection a slight one, but from the moment of his arrival he brought out Sam's latent paternalism. In letters, he refers to Francis as 'my boy' – an affectionate form of words, though of course it can also be read as possessive. At first, the presence of a child in his household created opportunities – even a need – for a playfulness and gamesome physicality that would otherwise have been absent. Then, as the bond deepened, he seems to have regarded Francis as a surrogate son. The relationship was a channel for emotional needs that his marriage had not fulfilled. Twenty-two years later, when Francis was married and had a son of his own, he and his wife Elizabeth chose to name him Samuel; the child died, but when they had another son they called him Samuel too. He had learned from his master that the emotional apparatus that enables us to vent our grief is also what makes it possible for us to transcend it.

'Sorrow is a kind of rust of the soul,' Sam had written in the *Rambler* in August 1750, borrowing an image from a letter by the Roman philosopher Seneca, who believed that '*Aerugo animi rubigo ingenii*' (roughly, 'The rust of the soul is the erosion of genius'). Like Seneca, Sam thought that the antidote for sorrow was employing the mind to other ends: when we engage with a new idea, it scours the rust away, and by exerting our minds we ensure that grief doesn't eat through us. A few weeks later, he found himself returning to the subject as he consoled James Elphinston, who was producing an edition of the *Rambler* for a Scottish audience and had recently lost his mother. 'The business of life summons us away from useless grief,' he wrote to Elphinston, 'and calls us to the exercise of those virtues of which we are lamenting our deprivation.' This is far from being his only reference to the 'business of life', and the word *business* had more complex associations for him than it usually does for us now. Before his time, it had been a synonym for *anxiety* or *care*, but in the *Dictionary*, where he identifies nine distinct senses, he emphasizes not so much the uneasiness of business as the necessity of paying it attention. It is 'serious engagement', 'something to be examined or considered', 'something required to be done'. In *Idler* 72, written in the autumn of 1759, a couple of weeks before his fiftieth birthday, he offers the simple judgement that 'The business of life is to go forwards.' He makes this statement while discussing the tendency to dwell on unpleasant aspects of the past, and, although he is thinking here about the defects and discomforts of memory, those eight words summarize his view of how to respond to loss.

He was unimpressed by the tropes of consolation, which all too often amounted to nothing more than a frayed and faded rhetoric. Instead, as the editor of the standard edition of his letters explains, he applies a very different kind of formula: 'first, a declaration of fellow feeling, based on shared or anticipated experience; second, a steady look at the hard facts of human mortality; third, an invocation . . . of shared beliefs; and finally, an injunction to activity'.[3] When Hester Thrale was grieving for her recently deceased and much-loved uncle in the winter of 1773, Sam wrote with advice: she should not dwell on what she might have been able to do to prevent his death, for 'You perhaps could not have done what you imagine, or might have done it without effect.' He concluded, 'Remit yourself solemnly into the hands of God, and then turn your mind upon the business and amusement which lie before you.' It is easier to give this sort of advice to others than to put it into practice oneself, but Sam's counsel was born of experience. He had put the matter more strongly in a letter to her earlier that year, when her mother was sick and looked likely to die. Pointing out that her need to mourn her mother should not outstrip her other obligations – chiefly to her children – he argued that 'Grief is a species of idleness'. Attending to the present 'preserves us . . . from being lacerated and devoured by sorrow for the past'.

'Do not suffer life to stagnate,' says Imlac, a philosophically minded poet Sam portrays in *Rasselas*. He is addressing people who believe that they may never again see a kidnapped friend, and tells them not to let the stream of time 'grow muddy for want of motion'. Instead, he urges, 'commit yourself again to the current of the world'. The mind needs stimulation. 'Life,' Sam told Hester Thrale, 'must be always in progression; we must always purpose to do more or better than in time past', and in the *Rambler* he declares that 'To act is far easier than to suffer', a sentiment one can imagine many other writers casting as the less encouraging 'To suffer is far harder than to act.' In the chasm of bereavement, we find a spur: as we think about death, we have the choice to think about how we live.

Containing some essential points of information on the life
of reading, whereamong are the most fugacious mentions of
Mrs Elizabeth Montagu and even Mr Stephen King

THOUGH WRITTEN AGAINST a backdrop of sorrow, the
Dictionary is a triumph – one not of innovation, but of execution. True, there are mistakes: a *dabchick* is not 'a chicken
newly hatched', a *pastern* not 'the knee of an horse'. Some
definitions are unhelpfully imprecise: *archery* is 'the use of a
bow', and *to worm* is 'to deprive a dog of something, nobody
knows what, under his tongue, which is said to prevent him,
nobody knows why, from running mad'. Sam omits words
he had certainly come across in his reading, or even used
himself: *euphemism*, *irritable*, *literary*, *shibboleth*, *underdone*. His
spelling is occasionally inconsistent, and some of his ety-
mologies are poor. As he would write to his friend Francesco
Sastres, twenty-nine years after publication and a few
months before his own death, 'Dictionaries are like watches,
the worst is better than none, and the best cannot be
expected to go quite true.' Yet the entries are crisp and
clear, and his definitions are confident. The ones that are
well-known – such as '*excise*, A hateful tax levied upon
commodities' – are unrepresentative in being so opinionated, but many have a lovely succinctness: a *thumb* is 'the
short strong finger answering to the other four', an *embryo* is
'the offspring yet unfinished in the womb', and a *rant* consists of 'high sounding language unsupported by dignity of

thought'. Others raise a smile with their sheer briskness: a *lizard* is 'an animal resembling a serpent, with legs added to it', *opera* 'an exotic and irrational entertainment', *tree* 'a large vegetable rising, with one woody stem, to a considerable height', and an *orgasm* simply 'sudden vehemence'.

This is not to say that there are no innovations at all. Sam changed attitudes to the very idea of a dictionary: he made people think of it as a significant cultural object, and inspired others to compile new works of reference. He was the first lexicographer to make a creditable attempt to work on historical principles by exhibiting the development of words. His use of illustrative quotations to support his definitions was an inspired move. One of its effects was to make the *Dictionary* an encyclopedia of treasurable literary and historical nuggets, embodying a belief he set forth in its preface: 'The chief glory of every people arises from its authors.' Besides being educational, it is a work of literature, and by 'showing how one author copied the thoughts and diction of another', he created 'a genealogy of sentiments', which amounted to 'a kind of intellectual history'.

The *Dictionary* was a triumph of reading, and it was reading of a persistent, dogged kind. 'A man will turn over half a library to make one book,' he told Boswell more than twenty years later, and this project bore out those words. The image is appropriately physical and unromantic; it makes me think of Sam rummaging his bookshelves or staggering across his garret room laden with chunky volumes. At their best books can be portable magic – the image, I believe, is Stephen King's – but they're not always very portable; sometimes the ones we need for work or some crazy self-imposed project possess not even a hint of occult charm, and instead of being succulent like a mango their contents are as tough as ashplant.

Sam's was indeed a *life* of reading. A young person 'should read five hours a day', he would tell Boswell, and the prescription was one he often exceeded. He devoured books in his youth, as a student at Oxford, and constantly thereafter, though he was increasingly inclined to berate himself for not reading enough – a sure sign of someone who reads a great deal. The books he consumed were fuel for his writing; he wanted to comment or expand on them. Many were rousing or inspiring, but sometimes they affected his mind in ways less immediately positive: 'Literature is a kind of intellectual light which, like the light of the sun, enables us to see what we do not like; but who would wish to escape unpleasing objects, by condemning himself to perpetual darkness?'

One might expect him to be an advocate of systematic reading, but his approach appears more relaxed, even capricious. It's fine to start a book in the middle, and you should read what you want, not what you feel you ought to read: 'If we read without inclination, half the mind is employed in fixing the attention; so there is but one half to be employed on what we read.' The flipside of this is, naturally, that 'What is read with delight is commonly retained, because pleasure always secures attention' – a statement that chimes with modern insights about the relationship between reading, pleasure and memory, not least the idea that when one reads with pleasure one's avidity has an erotic quality, a sense of being on the very edge of reality and of our cognition being a function not only of the mind, but also of the body.

In descriptions of his behaviour, the parallels between reading and eating are apparent: Sam consumed books hungrily, chewing and digesting their ideas, sometimes swallowing them whole yet sometimes pausing to savour their sweetest parts and perhaps to roll a particularly delicious phrase upon his tongue. But he had a taste for dry, bulky fare, and the list of his favourite authors includes figures whose works one is now unlikely to find outside a university library: Hugo Grotius, Angelo Poliziano, Joseph Justus Scaliger. His appetite for the more solid and juiceless sorts of literature was strong. He was capable of ignoring the scenery in the Hebrides because he was utterly absorbed in an obscure 1619 treatise about 'the nature and use of lots' (i.e. using objects such as sticks or paper slips to choose a person for a job or resolve a dispute), and he surprised his university tutor by breaking a long silence with a quotation from Macrobius, a far from well-known Roman writer of the fifth century. In fact, Macrobius, with his broad range of interests that included astronomy, geography and the importance of the number seven, was a model of the kind of reader Sam wanted to be: an omnivore who could participate with rigorous intelligence in the arguments of every work he ingested.

The truth is that he read in different ways for different purposes. We all do so, but tend to have a limited awareness of this divergence. Robert DeMaria distinguishes Sam's four approaches: he read curiously, entering into a 'dreamlike state of enjoyment' as he allowed himself to become completely engrossed in a book; perused texts for answers to specific questions that were preying on his mind; practised 'hard reading', the close and critical study of intellectually demanding material; and engaged in 'mere reading', which involved scanning a newspaper or some other ephemeral publication 'without the fatigue of close attention', for, as he remarked, 'the world . . . swarms with writers whose wish is not to be studied, but to be read'.[1] His attitude to reading is liberating and inspiring: he champions it, appreciates the range of forms it can take, and does justice to the truth of readers' experience.

Boswell recalled his uncle describing Sam as 'a robust genius, born to grapple with whole libraries', and the choice of verb is apt, for Sam handled volumes unsentimentally. On one occasion Boswell found him putting his books in order, wearing 'a pair of large gloves, such as hedgers use'. He certainly wasn't one of those book lovers who purr over exquisite bindings. Although he did care about the quality of the ink and paper, he concerned himself far more with what was inside books, and sometimes his urgency in seeking out their choicest parts became a churlish roughness. He surrendered a handsome copy of Demosthenes's speeches because he could see that it was 'too fine for a scholar's talons'. Garrick reported lending him a 'stupendously bound' volume of Petrarch and being horrified to see him toss it over his head onto the floor. In light of this, we might expect him to be addicted to inserting comments in his books, arguing with authors or their printers, but his marginalia are sporadic. Scribbling in the margin disrupts the flow of reading, and Sam usually prefers immersion to the herky-jerky progress of the chronic annotator. Or rather, he wants to do what he can to make immersion possible.

One of his liberating beliefs about reading is that you don't have to persevere with a book that's boring you. He drove home the point when asked about Elizabeth Montagu's *An Essay on the Writings and Genius of Shakespeare*, which he had not read all the way through: 'when I take up the end of a web, and find it packthread, I do not expect, by looking further, to find embroidery'. Hester Thrale recorded his exclaiming 'How few books are there of which one can ever possibly arrive at the *last* page!' One of the reasons for this was the abundance of hack work. When volumes are cobbled together in order to make money, the results are often tawdry. In the *Idler* he wrote, 'The continual multiplication of books not only distracts choice, but disappoints enquiry', and his distaste for hastily produced dross persists in a remark commonly attributed to him, which even if it's apocryphal captures his manner: 'What is written without effort is in general read without pleasure.' His ideas about pleasure will be the subject of a later chapter, but in the context of examining what he has to say about its connection with reading, I'm put in mind of one of the fictional correspondents he introduces in the *Rambler*. In the midst of a discussion not of books but of wit, this character makes a simple, sharp statement about the chancy alliance between writer and audience, reflecting Sam's profound experience of both sides of that relationship: 'The power of pleasing is very often obstructed by the desire.'

✿ 16 ✿

A chapter that reflects on the uses of Sickness,
and of Patrons

THE *DICTIONARY* was not only the culmination of a remarkable programme of reading, but also a treat for those who
shared Sam's sense that a reference book could be a work of
literature. Dictionaries are, to paraphrase Umberto Eco,
encyclopedias in disguise, and this one, besides its obvious
role as a guide to English vocabulary, is an anthology
of literary extracts, an educational primer, a history (or
museum) of learning, and a time capsule that enables us to
picture the age in which Sam lived. It is also full of hints
about the story of its own making.

No definition in the *Dictionary* tells us more about that
story than that of *patron*: 'One who countenances, supports
or protects. Commonly a wretch who supports with insolence, and is paid with flattery.' This was a dig at Lord
Chesterfield, who had neglected his role until shortly before
the volumes' publication. When at last he wrote the first of
two pieces in support of the *Dictionary*, in November 1754,
he explained that no one involved in its making had offered
him 'the usual compliment of a pair of gloves or a bottle of
wine'. Dodsley, he added, had not 'so much as invited me to
take a bit of mutton with him'. His tone was embarrassingly
trivial. 'I make a total surrender of all my rights and privi-
leges in the English language,' he condescendingly declared,
to 'Mr Johnson, during the term of his dictatorship'. Part of

the problem was that he was so used to his role as a paragon of polite learning – a man flattered by anyone with a product to push – that he had become a parody of graciousness. In private, Sam expressed disgust: 'I have sailed a long and painful voyage round the world of the English language; and does he now send out two cock-boats to tow me into harbour?' At length, in February, he responded to Chesterfield in stinging terms. The contents of his letter soon got out, generating welcome publicity. It remains a masterpiece of controlled anger:

I have been lately informed by the proprietor of the World that two Papers in which my Dictionary is recommended to the Public were written by your Lordship. To be so distinguished is an honour which, being very little accustomed to favours from the Great, I know not well how to receive, or in what terms to acknowledge.

When upon some slight encouragement I first visited your Lordship I was overpowered like the rest of Mankind by the enchantment of your address, and could not forbear to wish . . . that I might obtain that regard for which I saw the world contending, but I found my attendance so little encouraged, that neither pride nor modesty would suffer me to continue it. When I had once addressed your Lordship in public, I had exhausted all the Art of pleasing which a retired and uncourtly Scholar can possess. I had done all that I could, and no Man is well pleased to have his all neglected, be it ever so little.

Seven years, My Lord, have now past since I waited in your outward Rooms or was repulsed from your Door, during which time I have been pushing on my work through difficulties of which it is useless to complain, and have brought it at last to the verge of Publication without one Act of assistance, one word of encouragement, or one smile of favour. Such treatment I did not expect, for I never had a Patron before . . .

Is not a Patron, My Lord, one who looks with unconcern on a Man struggling for Life in the water and when he has reached ground encumbers him with help? The notice which you have been pleased to take of my Labours, had it been early, had been kind; but it has been delayed till I am indifferent and cannot enjoy it, till I am solitary and cannot impart it, till I am known, and do not want it.

I hope it is no very cynical asperity not to confess obligation where no benefit has been received, or to be unwilling that the Public should consider me as owing that to a Patron, which Providence has enabled me to do for myself.

Sam's letter is a trumpet blast: authors need no longer be subservient to vain benefactors. Yet it is also a more personal statement. When he tells Chesterfield that 'The notice which you have been pleased to take of my labours, had it been early, had been kind', he is dismissing not the whole principle of patronage, but specifically Chesterfield's failure to make good on his side of the bargain. Instead of being timely, his patron's notice has been delayed 'till I am known, and do not want it'. The key word here is *known*. When Sam signed the contract for the *Dictionary*, he was an obscure figure, but by 1755 he has a reputation and a public. He no longer needs to profess obedience to Chesterfield and to refer to himself as this lofty figure's 'delegate'. What's more, he no longer thinks of English as something that can be fixed (screwed in place, that is, and mended), and that makes

Chesterfield, with his enthusiasm for sending the language to school, seem like yesterday's man, priggish and unenlightened. The antipathy would cause Sam to remark, 'This man I thought had been a Lord among wits; but I find he is only a wit among Lords', and some twenty years later it would yield a memorably tart Johnsonian putdown: when Dodsley's brother James published Chesterfield's letters, which were meant to teach valuable lessons about self-reliance and the art of social success, Sam commented that they could inspire only 'the morals of a whore and the manners of a dancing-master'.

More immediately, Sam grasped that he was under an obligation not to his neglectful patron, but to the project's commercial backers and to the public, as well as to himself. Yet after seeing off Chesterfield, he wobbled. In the weeks preceding the *Dictionary*'s publication his letters referred to its appearance and possible reception with a mixture of coolness and pride. They included snippets of Latin that, while coming naturally to someone of Sam's erudition, still look revealingly pedantic. I'm reminded here of how I felt when waiting for the publication of my first book, which was in fact about the *Dictionary*. Waiting is a skill – one that I was then very far from having mastered (and something that in the fourteen years since I've in truth become only a little better at). Several emails from that time betray my fluttery state of mind and my need to make light of it. In one of them I refer to my book as a 'tome'. I suppose I was trying to mask my anxiety with a bit of jokey formality, but the email's recipient put me straight: 'Your use of the word "tome" can fuck right off.' Reviewing Sam's phrasing, I think I can hear the same effortful note. When he writes that the *Dictionary* is '*Vasta mole superbus*' ('Proud in its great bulk') and that 'My Book is now coming *in luminis oras*' ('into the realms of light'), one detects something other than ironclad confidence. In reaching for a grandiose phrase, he is caught between mocking authorial pomposity and subscribing to it.

Sam found, as countless others have, that the moment when he was expected to feel pride instead proved disappointing. A sense of anticlimax attends the completion of any large project, and this seems especially true of books. Some authors, adept at self-promotion, can pretend that the work they have just completed and now set before the public is the most important thing in their lives. Most are unconvincing. Reaching the shore, Sam could look back on the way in which he'd first approached the journey: 'I resolved to leave neither words nor things unexamined, and pleased myself with a prospect of the hours which I should revel away in feasts of literature.' These, he now knows, 'were the dreams of a poet doomed at last to wake a lexicographer'. He sounds like the PhD student of cliché, who imagines that before embarking on their thesis they can devour acres of books, write a novel and learn a couple of languages, but discovers that the reality of scholarship is a little less sexy.

The preface to the *Dictionary* is eloquent and poignant. 'I have protracted my work,' Sam writes, 'till most of those whom I wished to please have sunk into the grave, and success and miscarriage are empty sounds. I therefore dismiss it with frigid tranquillity, having little to fear or hope from censure or from praise.' Here we have the classic psychology of the envoi. Anyone who has toiled on a vast project will know that, no matter how much pleasure and relief they derive from its completion, self-doubt and despair accompany closure. For many people these will be dwarfish presences, easily brushed aside. But there is nothing strange about looking upon an achievement and thinking 'Was it worth it?', 'Is it good enough?', 'Couldn't I have got it done sooner?' and 'Will others care about this as much as I do?' There is nothing strange, either, in sending one's work out into the world frigidly rather than fervently – 'Do I still care about this . . . as much as I did, or should?' And of all the questions that shadow the end of a big task, none is more blue than the simple 'What next?'

For Sam, the answer was especially glum: he fell sick, wheezing his way through an eight-week bout of bronchitis. He was experiencing what we now call 'the let-down effect', the physical low that we plunge into not during a period of strain, but once it has ended. On his sickbed he learned of a rumour that he had died. He would live for another twenty-nine years, but would be plagued increasingly by rheumatism, gout and dropsy. Persistent difficulties with breathing were matched by a fear of being crushed, and his *Dictionary* definition of *nightmare* – 'morbid oppression during sleep, resembling the pressure of weight upon the breast' – is one of many images he conjures that relate psychological stress and the experience of physical stress. As his ailments multiplied, he waged an ever more furious campaign against them, dosing himself with all manner of purgatives and diuretics. Insomnia made him feverish by night and lethargic by day. He was bled for problems as diverse as flatulence, a cough and an eye inflammation.

That sickness makes it harder to be successful is no one's idea of a startling revelation. Yet its disruptiveness can add something to our self-knowledge and our insights into the world around us. A particularly striking statement on this theme occurs in *Ecce Homo* (1888), Friedrich Nietzsche's account of 'how one becomes what one is' – a work of self-justification dressed as autobiography. As a philosopher often labelled a nihilist, Nietzsche isn't someone we'd expect to find useful in this context, but long experience of ill health made it possible for him to reflect on the uses of adversity: 'It was as if I discovered life anew, myself included; I tasted all the good things, even the small ones . . . I turned my will to health, to *life*, into my philosophy . . . the years when my vitality was at its lowest were when I *stopped* being a pessimist: the instinct for self-recovery *forbade* me a philosophy of poverty and discouragement.'[1]

Even when ill health doesn't have this paradoxically elevating effect, it's an education in resilience, adaptability and hope. It makes us think that we are being punished, that we have an enemy within us, and that we are guests in this world, but it also obliges us to examine our priorities: what do we most want to achieve, and what would we like our legacy to be? In the *Rambler* Sam remarks that 'sickness shows us the value of ease' – with *ease* here signifying something more like 'neutrality' than 'comfort', and its value being the freedom to do all that one knows one can do. More strikingly, in his short life of Herman Boerhaave, a Dutch physician whose work he admired for its simplicity and rigour, he refers to the 'opportunities of contemplating the wonderful and inexplicable union of soul and body, which nothing but long sickness can give'. As so often in his writings, what appears to be a generalization is grounded in autobiographical truth; he has known long sickness and its opportunities, and his experience of navigating suffering can be an inspiration to anyone who's sick.

❧ 17 ❧

An essay, or 'loose sally of the mind', upon the methods
of a moralist, in which are considered prose style and
its higher functions

TODAY THE WORD *moralist* has unappealing connotations. I
find myself picturing a shrivelled martinet who takes grim
satisfaction in stamping out fun, or a fire-and-brimstone
politician who'll soon be caught with his pants around
his ankles. For a more mature perspective, I might quote
Francis Bacon's sixteenth-century observation that moralists
'appear like writing-masters, who lay before their scholars a
number of beautiful copies, but give them no directions how
to guide their pen or shape their letters'.

Sam is a moralist, but not of this kind. His idea of what
it means to lead a good life involves actions, not just feelings – and effort rather than dogma, beneficence as well
as benevolence. Although we are used to the term *benevolent*
being applied to acts of kindness, for Sam it was a 'disposi-
tion to do good' – a mere state of mind. Better benevolence
than malevolence, of course, but it was in *performing* good
works that one could be fulfilled, realizing one's potential.
This is why he disapproved of religious hermits, for private
piety 'like that flower that blooms in the desert, may give its
fragrance to the winds of heaven . . . but it bestows no assistance on earthly beings'. A recluse may have a stainless
character, yet accomplishes nothing.

Rather than pontificating about abstract notions of

goodness, Sam proposes a scheme of practical virtue. For instance, we should recall the times our commitment to doing the right thing brought success. If we reflect on past lapses, we should do so with regret rather than with a sneaking pleasure. We ought not to spend our days contemplating all the shocks and cataclysms that could befall us; an obsession with preparing for disasters, or really with preparing to prepare for them, diverts us from our responsibilities to others and to ourselves, increasing the chances of a more immediate kind of emergency. We mustn't allow ourselves to be paralysed by indecision under the pretence that we're awaiting the perfect moment to unfurl our plans: 'He that waits for an opportunity to do much at once, may breathe out his life in idle wishes' and will 'regret, in the last hour, his useless intentions and barren zeal'.

Then there were his more concrete commitments. Sam believed he had a duty to house the needy. Hester Thrale wrote of how by providing a refuge for poor wretches he 'shared his bounty, and increased his dirt'. In truth, his humanitarianism came at a stiffer price than this, for it meant that often, having gone out, he was reluctant to return. Hawkins depicts him wandering the streets giving 'loose money' to beggars and then heading home in a state of dread; in the biographer's opinion, Sam's waiting menagerie of 'distressed friends' consisted of 'undeserving people' who 'exposed him to trouble' and 'occasioned him great disquiet'.

In speaking of Sam's moral outlook, one has to understand that he was a Christian, solidly Anglican in childhood and then a doubter in adolescence, who renewed his faith while at Oxford, inspired by a single, recent book – William Law's *Serious Call to a Devout and Holy Life* (1729). Law, a fellow Midlander, shaped Sam's understanding of the need for self-examination and for keeping a record of his prayers. In the short term, the effect of reading Law seems to have been negative; he believed that the high standards counselled in the *Serious Call* were beyond him, and this made him anxious that in the end, when judged, he would not be saved. In the longer term, although fear persisted, the result was a faith of humility and patience, firm and meditative rather than elaborate or jubilant. The character of that faith is most evident in Sam's sermons. He wrote around forty of these for other people to preach; only two were published in his lifetime, and a total of twenty-eight survive. Their tone is one of elegant persuasion; these are works of practical divinity, concerned with ordinary human experiences such as friendship, suffering and the quest for domestic happiness.

Even in his sermons, Sam is mainly concerned with ethics and morality, rather than with unpicking knotty matters of theology. He discusses fraud ('it is generally an abuse of confidence') and defamation ('a false report may spread, where a recantation never reaches'), notes on one occasion that some taverns have to double up as brothels in order to survive, and writes astutely about the proud man who, thanks to 'an insatiable desire of propagating in others the favourable opinion he entertains of himself', 'tortures his invention for means to make himself conspicuous'. Elsewhere, when he ponders a religious question he remains mindful of the complexion of everyday life, and his personal struggles are palpable. Thus, in a theologically charged comment on John Milton's *Paradise Lost*, he reflects that 'we all sin like Adam, and like him must all bewail our offences'. The verb he chooses – *bewail* – may be intended to recall the *Book of Common Prayer* (the confession made at communion that 'We acknowledge and bewail our manifold sins and wickedness'). But it is vivid, and the total effect of the statement is immediate rather than abstract. It summons an image of Sam wringing himself out as he plumbs the depths of penitence. He treats the operations of sin and repentance as a drama to which anyone can relate.

The heart of Sam's moral writing lies in a work I have already mentioned, a journalistic venture that transcended its immediate circumstances and became art. The *Rambler* appeared in 208 instalments – two a week for two years, beginning in March 1750. Each Tuesday and Saturday he addressed a grave subject, avoiding topical matters in favour of eternal ones. The first five *Ramblers* are all to do with the difficulty of making a start on any large undertaking – reflecting the problems he had been having with the *Dictionary*. Later he wrote about marriage, the abuse of power, our competitive nature, self-control, the necessity of contemplating death, the dangers of flattery and dependency, the tyrannical behaviour of landlords, the barren career of someone who lurches from one job to the next. Many of the essays were concerned with writing, and his approach was bookish, yet he constantly tried to turn his reading and learning to quotidian purposes. Keen not to alienate a secular audience, he avoided theological issues and cited the Bible a mere seven times (by contrast, the poet Horace cropped up 103 times).[1] At the end of the final *Rambler* he spoke of hoping to be 'numbered among the writers who have given ardour to virtue, and confidence to truth'. It's a stirring statement about what he wanted to achieve – and a resonant one today, when so much journalism seems calculated to have the opposite effect.

Rather than working to a commission, he wrote about whatever he wanted and was able to put all of himself into the essays. The form is one we now take for granted; I have already referred to essays by several writers other than Sam, and haven't felt the need to explain what I mean. But it was only in the late sixteenth century that the essay became a recognizable genre. Michel de Montaigne, who published his *Essais* in 1580, is the father of the essay as we know it. The story of the word's etymology takes in the French verb *essayer*, 'to try', and further back the Latin *exigere*, 'to weigh': in its original conception the essay was a trial, a test, an act of weighing or sampling, an attempt to get a grip on a subject, a starting point for a conversation. In England, the form's outstanding exponent was Francis Bacon, whom Sam first read, with delight, while compiling the *Dictionary*; the first edition of his *Essays* appeared in 1597, and there were two enlarged editions in his lifetime. Bacon's style is more compact than Montaigne's, and his essays are less exploratory and personally revealing, but both make persuasive inquiries into the self.

Sam, writing for a periodical, had little room to be truly exploratory, let alone garrulous in the way Montaigne often was. Because he was required to knock out two pieces a week, deadlines were forever looming, and instead of losing himself in the maze of planning, he had to focus on getting his copy written. The result was immediacy: an idea, rather than being left to season on some high shelf in the mind's pantry, had to be served up quickly. A deadline is a challenge, and while not the prettiest kind of inspiration, it ensures that a writer doesn't get lost in the rigmarole of preparation – which is often no more than squirrelly fidgeting. Under pressure to produce essays swiftly, Sam would sent them to the printer without carefully revising what he had written; he felt the thrill of rapid production, and of its being followed by rapid circulation.

His sense of the form's possibilities is clear in his *Diction-*

ary definition of *essay* as a 'trial' or 'experiment', and as 'a loose sally of the mind, an irregular, undigested piece, not a regular and orderly composition'. It's too easy, I think, to get hung up on the word *loose*, and the word that interests me here is the next one: by *sally* he means a sortie or excursion, an audacious departure from convention. For Sam, the essay must put a belief to the test. It must be curious about the world, not least about the very processes of its own curiosity, and it must draw on deep reserves of experience. He values the essay's tolerance and the potential it affords to wander around a theme. Yet he brings to this 'irregular' form and its brisk execution a style that is memorably precise and rigorous.

The reading necessary for the *Dictionary* meant he was immersed in the ocean of English vocabulary, and he introduced into the *Rambler* some of the recondite terms he hit upon. For instance, he writes that certain feelings, rather than arising directly from our animal appetites, are *adscititious*, i.e. a supplement to them; a river serves as a source of water for a large region through its 'innumerable *circumvolutions*' (its winding course); butterflies are 'the *papilionaceous* tribe'; orators' best arguments should be at the end of their speeches 'lest they should be effaced or perplexed by *supervenient* images'.[2] The emphases here are mine, and the purpose of using these words wasn't to make himself look clever. Instead, he was intent on developing a style appropriate to painstaking moral thought. Working on the *Dictionary* made him alert to the differences between words that were commonly treated as synonyms. At the same time, he saw the degree to which familiar words were mired in ambiguity because they possessed so many shades of meaning. Abstract terms of Latin derivation, typically of a kind found in books on scientific subjects, were the building blocks of this experiment in analytical prose. Besides adopting words such as *adscititious* (from Bacon) and *supervenient* (from Sir Thomas Browne), he appears at this time to have coined words of his own, among them *colloquial, unimportance, symmetrical, evanescence, irascibility* and *disentanglement*.[3]

Phrasing of this kind has led to his writing being stereotyped as pompous. Macaulay claimed that it was sometimes monotonous and turgid, and an Edwardian critic, Walter Raleigh, spoke of its 'sonorous and ponderous rotundity'.[4] In fact, across his whole body of work his style varies a lot, to suit different purposes, and while some of his prose is grandly rhetorical, plenty is conversational or plain. It's when he is in deliberative mode, as in the *Rambler*, that it feels rigid. He loves setting up a contrast: it is typical that, instead of writing 'You may stop me accompanying, but not following you', he chooses a more ceremonious parallelism and writes 'You may deny me to accompany you, but cannot hinder me from following'.[5] This is something he does again and again. When he wants to construct a strong argument or dismantle a popular misconception, his vocabulary and sentence structure become more formal.

Boswell referred to the 'dignified march' of Sam's sentences and made a neat case for why they had to move in the way they did: 'Had his conceptions been narrower, his expression would have been easier.' The sheer lexical range of his writing reflects the diversity, incongruity and abundance of his reading and his experience. Yet at the same time he is keen to maintain a sense of proportion; in discussing matters where he thinks popular opinion is mistaken, he is performing a kind of adjustment, correcting distortions and errors of emphasis. As pros and cons are weighed up, his style, with its antitheses and parallels, feels like a meticulous putting-in-order of experience. This weightiness and vigilant balance are not exactly user-friendly. He is abrupt where we might prefer him to be fluid – a hammerer rather than a dulcet seducer. His fellow author Oliver Goldsmith aptly remarked, in his presence, that if he were to write a fable about little fishes for a young audience, the little fishes would probably talk like whales. But Sam was careful not to be abstruse. He remembered the conclusion of Swift's *A Tale of a Tub*: 'As to the business of being profound . . . it is with writers as with wells', for 'often when there is nothing in the world at the bottom besides dryness and dirt, though it be but a yard and half underground it shall pass, however, for wondrous deep, upon no wiser a reason than because it is wondrous dark'.

The best of the *Rambler* essays provided what Boswell called 'bark and steel for the mind'. Although bark and steel sound usefully sturdy, it's not immediately clear what Boswell is getting at. It seems that by 'steel' he meant iron in its medicinal use (as in the iron-rich waters found in spa towns), and by 'bark' the outer covering of the cinchona tree (which was at the time known to be effective against fever, and from which in the next century scientists would derive quinine). He may have been recalling a poem by a favourite writer of Sam's, Isaac Watts, who praised the substances' powers: 'when bark and steel play well their game / To save our sinking breath'. The bark and steel of Samuel Johnson's prose is not just fortification, then, but medicine. I can remember being persuaded as a child that the only medicines that work are ones that taste unpleasant, and while Boswell isn't saying that, he makes Sam's essays sound healthful or hefty, but not sprightly.

Sam saw them in a different light. Issues of the *Rambler* sold modestly (500 copies at most), and the printer lost money on the venture, but the essays were soon reproduced, and they drew argumentative responses that acknowledged their gravity and purposeful intelligence. When Sam viewed his achievement from a distance, he reflected that 'My other works are wine and water, but my *Rambler* is pure wine.' A red wine, I think we can safely say, full-bodied, rich and concentrated, spicy rather than jammy, chewy and well balanced, with plenty of grip. A Châteauneuf-du-Pape, perhaps. But it may be more useful to think of the *Rambler* as a whole cellar of wines with different bouquets: the essays show his range, and they also show us our range, our capacity to relinquish the comforts of cliché and to entertain, as he does, the contradictions and complexities of a life not merely examined, but re-examined.

With their fine sense of the layers of experience, the *Rambler* essays show that Sam the moralist has thought deeply, and one of their recurring subjects is the uses of literature. It is a commonplace that we read books for knowledge, enlightenment or escape, and apologists for literature may also point out that it teaches us the arts of concentration and absorption – or of vigilance, judgement, sympathy, awe. Yet Sam goes further, showing us that we turn to literature in order to engage in self-scrutiny and to intensify not only our powers of awareness, but also our contact with the textures of life itself. Sometimes this results in our recognizing who (and how) we are, sometimes it leads us to see ourselves in new ways, and occasionally we feel, as if for the first time, the density of existence, gaining access as we do so to the living palimpsest of human history.

❧ 18 ❧

Some further thoughts on the *Rambler* and the intricacies
of ordinary life

Rambler 68, published on 10 November 1750, is a good
example of Sam's peculiar range and his capacity for con-
structing a layered and surprising argument. There, after
some initial comments about how much of what we do and
feel passes unobserved, he writes that most of life is made
up of 'small incidents' and 'petty occurrences'. We spend
our days wishing 'for objects not remote' and mourning
'disappointments of no fatal consequence'; often we experience 'insect vexations which sting us and fly away' and
'impertinencies which buzz a while about us, and are heard
no more'. It is not just the irritants that are transitory, as
even compliments 'glide off the soul', leaving no mark.

His point is that at any given time we occupy ourselves
with matters that will soon seem unimportant. On one occasion, when Boswell was embarrassed by being unable to
offer hospitality to some guests, Sam remarked, 'Consider,
sir, how insignificant this will appear a twelvemonth hence.'
Boswell reflected on the usefulness of this precept: 'Were
this consideration to be applied to most of the little vexa-
tious incidents of life, by which our quiet is too often
disturbed, it would prevent many painful sensations.' And
yet, as Sam acknowledged, it's not our first instinct to apply
such a principle. In the moment when insect vexations
occur, they consume all our attention and appear immense.

The insect imagery feels apt: we tend to think of insects as pests, associating them with disease and destruction, and we often swat them away or kill them without a second thought, but we also marvel at their aerodynamic abilities and sheer abundance. Among those to whom Sam's image has since appealed, Thomas Jefferson stands out. In a long letter of August 1820 to Louis Hue Girardin, his neighbour in Virginia, he wrote of 'The thousand and one insect vexations which have, of late especially, buzzed about my ears'. Jefferson's choice of this Johnsonian language is piquant, because his letter is concerned with difficulties he had in his dealings with publishers, and also because he identifies procrastination as one of his habitual sins.[1] An admirer of Johnson's works, he claimed that his *Dictionary* was one of the books best able to 'fix us in the principles and practices of virtue', and he admitted that it was one of his favourite places to find quotable snippets from other writers. It is even possible that he owed his most enduring turn of phrase, the reference in the Declaration of Independence to 'the pursuit of happiness', to Johnson, who used it in print on several occasions.[2]

For Jefferson, as for Sam, life is a swarm of distractions. The buzzing presence of annoying concerns is enough to engross three of our five senses: taste and smell are usually unaffected, but we can see and hear and touch the vexation – not just its causes, but the effect itself, which vibrates a few inches out of reach. We're perhaps especially likely to think of vexation as having an acoustic signature, because we cannot close our ears and our appreciation of sound's great potential to soothe us means that we regard jarring sounds as particularly obnoxious. The modern reader will think here not so much of insects as of smartphones clicking, chirping and rumbling. A feature of all such disturbance is that we understand that it will end but can't be sure of when. I want it to go away, and in doing so I intensify its immediacy. Until it is over, my mind feels alien to me, as if a foreign object has taken up residence right in the middle of what was previously open, uncontaminated ground.

Rambler 68 captures the essence of this experience. But it does more than this – and takes a couple of unexpected turns. After referring to life being composed of small incidents and petty occurrences, Sam goes on to emphasize its essentially domestic character: 'Very few are involved in great events, or have their thread of life entwisted with the chain of causes on which armies or nations are suspended.' Home, he believes, is the heart of our lives, and 'To be happy at home is the ultimate result of all ambition, the end to which every enterprise and labour tends.' This is one of those Johnsonian statements that I greet easily but then review with less equanimity. Is it true? And if it is true, am I going about my life the right way?

The line 'To be happy at home is the ultimate result of all ambition' seems to be at odds with what we know of Sam's own domestic life, but the truth is that the difficulty he had in achieving domestic happiness made him more keenly aware of its rewards. Whenever he was hospitable to life's unfortunates, he was trying to provide them with comfort and stability, and when he found these elsewhere, as at the Thrales' pleasantly tranquil house in Streatham, it delighted him. Here was a promise of safety and seclusion. Consequently, anything that threatened the home was terrifying. 'The passions rise higher at domestic than at imperial tragedies,' he wrote in a letter to Hester Thrale, adding that 'What is nearest us touches us most.' He cherished the home's connotations of permanence and refuge

– the latter material, but also psychological, for domestic security could anchor one's identity.

In *Rambler* 68 he sustains the idea that our existence is shaped by small matters, and that 'a few pains and a few pleasures are all the materials of human life'. But he turns aside to make the case that our home lives, not our public ones, should ideally form the basis of people's estimate of our character: while there are lots of people whose existence is a 'continual series of hypocrisy', on their own turf they are true to themselves. For this reason, domestic servants are peculiarly useful witnesses; we betray our weaknesses to them, and we can do little to hide from them the reality of who we are. I can't vouch for this, but it feels right, and in the space of a few paragraphs Sam has moved a long way. At the start of the essay he claims that 'our pleasures are for the most part . . . secret', and that it is normal for people to be 'borne up by some private satisfaction, some internal consciousness, some latent hope, some peculiar prospect, which they never communicate, but reserve for solitary hours and clandestine meditation'. By the end, he is asserting that having servants is hazardous, because their knowledge of their masters' frailties gives them power: the fallible masters must keep buying their silence, but will find that in the end the truth bursts forth, in a moment of rage or drunkenness.

This kind of swerve is a feature of the *Rambler*. These essays don't tend to leave the reader with comforting certainty; instead the experience of following their intricacies is like going for a workout. Sam's arguments shift, ramify, and even appear to reverse themselves, not because he's indecisive but because the truth is complex. 'When we have heated our zeal in a cause,' he writes in an earlier *Rambler*, number

66, 'we are naturally inclined to pursue the same train of reasoning' and ignore 'some adjacent difficulty'. His own approach is to go against this natural inclination: if the argument of an essay meets adjacent difficulties, they become part of the essay, enlarging and enriching it. Sometimes the result is a trip to the mind gym, and sometimes it's nutritious even if less obviously a tonic. Yet either way it's a salutary alternative to the kind of essay that bulges with pride in its own unanswerable decisiveness – the kind that's all codpiece and no cod.

✒ 19 ✒

A short musing, upon exemption from oblivion
(or what is otherwise called Memory)

ONE OF SAM'S recurrent subjects in the *Rambler* is memory. His own was legendary, and there is a wealth of testimony to its calibre. Edmund Hector claimed that it was 'so tenacious, that whatever he heard or read he never forgot', and Boswell pronounced it 'eminent to a degree almost incredible'. Another, lesser-known biographer, William Cooke, commented that Sam possessed an active rather than static memory; having in his youth absorbed a great fund of learning, he could at any time 'draw bills upon this capital with the greatest security of being paid'. His friends commonly thought that his ability to retain and recall information underpinned his excellence in argument. In private he contemplated writing what he called a 'history of memory', which sounds more like a project for a modern literary theorist or the title of a band's unlistenable concept album. Yet his contemporaries would doubtless have thought him perfectly qualified, in both range of knowledge and mnemonic power, to attempt such a work.

In reviewing the plaudits above, we may well reflect that it's easy to attribute great powers of memory to people who can no longer be tested, and that even the best memory is faulty and mutable. We may note, too, the tendency to think that other people's memories are either very good ('She never forgets anything', 'His powers of recall are practically photographic') or very bad ('His brain's like a sieve', 'She can never remember my name'). I don't believe I've ever heard anyone described as having an average memory, or heard people describe themselves in such terms, whereas the unexceptional nature of other faculties draws comment ('I've got an okay singing voice', 'She's not a bad listener', 'Their spatial awareness is so-so'). It's also not unusual to think of superlative recall as a kind of trick: because there are little sleights we can perform to get facts lodged in our minds, a good memory must be a museum of such sleights.

Sam doesn't see memory this way. His fullest statement of its importance comes in *Rambler* 41 (in August 1750), where he characterizes it as 'the purveyor of reason'. It is 'the power which places those images before the mind upon which the judgment is to be exercised, and which treasures up the determinations that are once passed, as the rules of future action, or grounds of subsequent conclusions'. By making it possible for us to look beyond what's right in front of our noses, memory enables us to perform comparative judgements, equipping us to evaluate, consolidate or change our behaviours and beliefs. It therefore 'may be said to place us in the class of moral agents'.

In 1759, he returned to the subject in an *Idler* essay, where he represented memory as 'the primary and fundamental power, without which there could be no other intellectual operation', and in another *Idler* paper that year he declared, 'The true art of memory is the art of attention.' He was thinking in particular about our ability to remember what we read. Rather alarmingly, he went on to say that we must bring to a book 'an intellect defecated and pure'. It's hard now to see the word *defecated* without thinking of shit, but Sam is using it to mean 'cleared of dregs', a sense common among seventeenth-century authors he admired. The mind is continually being invaded by dregs – stray images and fragments of ideas, noise and the brief caress of other sensations – and the success of memory rests on the ability to direct it away from them.

But having a first-rate memory wasn't wholly rewarding. Not for Sam what Alexander Pope had called the 'eternal sunshine of the spotless mind', in which past traumas are forgotten and life is a state of blissful oblivion. Memory is dynamic, and its relationships with the imagination and self-esteem are complex and unsettling. Some of what we recall is inconvenient, and some of it disturbing. The ability to think of things in their absence is indispensable, but at times this faculty appears to dictate to us. Although the past has retired, it's still shouting instructions and can seem restlessly determined to impinge on our decisions; even when it's slumbering, some sensation in the present can jolt it awake.

One of Sam's best-known aphorisms, which occurs in the second instalment of the *Rambler*, is 'Men more frequently require to be reminded than informed'. Though this is mostly treated as straightforward, a statement about the porous nature of memory, the meaning is ambiguous; it hinges on how we understand the verb *require*. Is he saying that people *ask* to be reminded or *need* to be? On the one hand, he may be suggesting that the appetite for reminders is greater than that for fresh instruction: we desire something familiar more often than something new. On the other, he may be speculating that in many cases, when we seek the answer to a question, the information has already been vouchsafed us: when our memories are jogged we are reunited with facts of which we'd lost track.

Both are worthwhile insights. The former is relevant to questions of artistic taste. The latter seems especially applicable to education: a key part of teaching is activating ideas that have become submerged. But if we go back to the *Rambler* essay to see what Sam posits, the double meaning recedes. He is thinking of a specific problem that faces writers: 'What is new is opposed, because most are unwilling to be taught; and what is known is rejected, because it is not sufficiently considered, that men more frequently require to be reminded than informed.' So, while readers are likely to shun the efforts of a writer who produces something truly original, they also tend to ignore or undervalue established work because they fail to appreciate the rewards of being reacquainted with books and ideas they have seen before. The line about readers more frequently requiring to be reminded than informed isn't exactly thrown away, but Sam, rather than presenting it as a bright new perception, frames it as a familiar one that gets neglected – indeed, as something of which we need to be reminded, not informed.

Implicit in this statement are three linked arguments about the relationship between memory and the appreciation of books (and of art in general). First, he believes that criticism and commentary routinely deny the true tenor of people's tastes. Instead they are obsessed with originality. That this obsession existed, and continues to exist, is clear: a vast amount of energy is expended in claiming that ideas and products are revolutionary. It is not that he pooh-poohs originality, but he believes that the virtue of an original achievement lies in its usefulness rather than simply its distinctiveness. Something novel may be of huge value, yet isn't automatically so. To be great, it must open a fresh vista of understanding. Neophiliacs fail to grasp this and think that originality alone is enough. Addicts of newfangledness are keen to be cultural gatekeepers (and vice versa). Their influence results not only in a preoccupation with being first, but also in a quibbling concern over the ownership of ideas and images. Sam recognizes how unhealthy this obsession is. It fires up hype, obliges artists to become hucksters, and leads to a work's timeliness being regarded as more important than the intensity of its soul-effect.

Secondly, he suspects that what passes for originality is frequently nothing of the sort. Only because we are ignorant or forgetful does it seem pristine. When he read Edward Young's *Conjectures on Original Composition* he was, by Boswell's account, 'surprised to find Young receive as novelties what he thought very common maxims'. But of course he wasn't all that surprised. He thought that Young's excitability in the presence of the less than extraordinary was a symptom of what he described in the *Rambler* as 'the mental disease of the present generation', to wit 'impatience of study'. Such impatience had two aspects: it was a failure to stock the mind with information, and it was a failure to access whatever information the mind already held. It is normal to think of impatient people being easily bored, but here we encounter a different idea: the impatient are easily impressed. Impatience, poor memory and impressionability form an unholy alliance. We can perhaps make out its character by thinking of a rather mundane circumstance: when we are being reminded of something, we often believe that it's new to us – and that the reminder is a mistake, even an insult. If in this situation I ask myself 'Did I already know that?', there is a tremor of embarrassed self-doubt and, briefly horrified by the notion that my memory isn't airtight, I find it preferable to savour the newness of the not-actually-new.

Finally, in grasping that true originality is 'opposed, because most are unwilling to be taught', Sam gets close to a troubling truth: while the not-new is continually being acclaimed as splendid novelty, the genuinely original is misprized. It's identified as unpalatable, worthless or incomprehensible – and sometimes as not-new. Here the problem is not the failure of memory, but a failure of its prerequisite, attention, and of integrity and judgement. 'The learned are afraid to declare their opinion early, lest they should put their reputation in hazard', and 'the ignorant always imagine themselves giving some proof of delicacy, when they refuse to be pleased'. Whoever seeks acclaim for a bold new piece of work 'solicits the regard of a multitude fluctuating in pleasures' and 'appeals to judges prepossessed by passions, or corrupted by prejudices, which preclude their approbation of any new performance'.

Containing much to exercise the reader's thoughts upon
the questions of Fear and Sanity

BECAUSE MEMORY makes it possible for us to dwell on our
past mistakes and traumas, consolidating our ideas about
what might do us harm, it plays a role in conditioning our
fears. This is its dark side, the counterpart of its being 'the
purveyor of reason'. Yet while such a sense of memory's
ambivalence is common, Sam also – and more unusually –
finds grounds for thinking in much the same way about fear.
There is more than a hint of this in his *Dictionary* entry for
the word, where he quotes a sermon by John Rogers, a
preacher popular in the 1720s: '*Fear* . . . is that passion of our
nature whereby we are excited to provide for our security.'
It's an unexpected choice of illustration, indicative of Sam's
belief that fear has its uses.

Today, if we think about the utility of fear, we are likely
to picture the kinds of people who profit from increasing
society's anxieties: religious leaders, psychiatrists and the
suppliers of faintly palliative therapies, pharma companies
selling sedative drugs, providers of security services and
equipment, journalists who suppose that intensifying
readers' fretfulness is a means of making their reports and
commentary seem vital. We know, too, that fear can be
an effective political tool, an instrument of oppression and
coercion, used by many leaders to manipulate their people,
who live in terror of brutal physical and mental abuse,

although now we are more likely to think of the fear-inducing tactics of terrorists, who exploit the media's appetite for the sensational in order to gain maximum attention and heighten our sense of risk and vulnerability.

Yet fear can also perform a very different function – as an instrument of self-control, keeping our coarser urges at bay and obliging us to think of the consequences of what we do. In his *Introductory Lectures on Psychoanalysis*, Sigmund Freud distinguishes between two different kinds of fear. One is 'objective', 'a reaction to the perception of external danger' that expresses our instinct for self-preservation. The other is what he calls 'neurotic' fear, 'a general apprehensiveness . . . a "free-floating" anxiety . . . ready to attach itself to any thought which is at all appropriate, affecting judgements, inducing expectations, lying in wait for any opportunity to find a justification for itself'. Whereas neurotic fear is a handicap, objective fear is purposeful. It consists of alertness, a knowledge of danger's sources and harbingers, an awareness of the limits of our power, and may be useful to explorers or, say, prison inmates. It proves powerful but not ungovernable, for 'when dread is excessive it becomes in the highest degree inexpedient; it paralyses every action, even that of flight'.[1]

In the *Rambler*, Sam observes that there is widespread contempt for fear – for fearfulness itself, and for those who suffer from it. Yet no one is immune from its clutch: 'Fear is a passion which every man feels . . . frequently predominant in his own breast.' At root, 'Fear is implanted in us as a preservative from evil', and its role 'is not to overbear reason, but to assist it'. This chimes with the view of the historian Joanna Bourke, who in her book *Fear: A Cultural History* describes how it can 'stimulate attention, sharpen judgement and energize combatants'. She cites advertising campaigns that exploit our fear of death to discourage smoking and drink-driving, and argues that fear has played an important part in civilizing us, causing us to be more reflective and stimulating creativity (because we dread loneliness or being struck down in our prime). Bourke's conclusion that 'A world without fear would be a dull world indeed' differs from Sam's, but both understand fear as a response to those features of the world that make it interesting.[2]

Fear is not, of course, the same as worry, though it is common to narrow the gap between them. One is involuntary, the other a choice. Fear is electrifying, worry wearisome. Yet we tend to deny that our worries are manufactured. Many of us also treat worries as if they're a form of protection: to worry about something is to prevent its happening. Sam defined the verb *to worry* as 'To tear, or mangle, as a beast tears its prey' and 'To harass, or persecute brutally'. It is something done to others; he gives the examples of wolves worrying sheep and heathens using dogs to worry the Christians they wished to persecute. Only in the nineteenth century did *worry* start to be something self-inflicted, a state of anxious inner debate, a kind of literary criticism of the self in which the nuances of the ordinary are scrupulously parsed.

We worry *about* things, not *of* or *on* them, though we can worry *away* at an issue. The gesture here is fidgety and oblique rather than direct: instead of stepping decisively into view, worry encroaches, making the feelings that preceded the worry shrivel up. The psychoanalyst Adam Phillips writes that worries 'can be punishments for wishes, or wishes cast in persecutory form'; when we worry, we regret desires and reject our dreams, and our sense of life's potential narrows. 'All of us may be surrealists in our dreams,' notes

Phillips, 'but in our worries we are incorrigibly bourgeois.'[3] We worry about not having enough money, our status at work, how attractive we are, whether there'll be enough room in the suitcase for the vast number of things we need to take on a trip. All of which is prosaic. If I asked you to say what colour worries are, I'm guessing you'd say grey rather than purple. The grey army of worries, not so much soldier-like as bureaucratic, swarms around our plans and hopes and ideas, penning them in, causing them to starve.

Fear, on the other hand, is a response to an immediate threat, and the colour with which we're most likely to associate it is red – the red of warning, danger, anger, fire, blood and power. Yet for his first illustration of the word in the *Dictionary*, Sam chooses an extract from John Locke that doesn't evoke such a keen sense of scarlet passion or flaming hazard: '*Fear* is an uneasiness of the mind, upon the thought of future evil likely to befall us.' To a modern reader this sounds more like anxiety (which the *Dictionary* defines as 'Trouble of mind about some future event'), and Sam does not in fact distinguish clearly between fear and anxiety. But the quotation from Locke appeals to him because of the word 'uneasiness': though for us perhaps not very evocative, it makes him think of pain, disturbance, constraint and even cramping. Although Locke is referring to something that happens in the mind, 'uneasiness' captures some of the ways in which fear expresses itself through the body. 'All fear is in itself painful,' Sam argues in the *Rambler*. In one of his *Idler* essays he writes of how fear 'is received by the ear as well as the eyes' and can 'chill' the breast of a warrior, and in another he imagines a traveller who 'in the dusk fears more as he sees less' and 'shrinks at every noise'. These are a few examples among many. Again and again he pictures fear as something invasive, nagging, goading, physically oppressive – a state that takes control of both mind and body.

There was nothing that Sam feared more than insanity, which seemed proximate and hideous, and it was this that caused him to subdue his imagination, denying certain urges full access to his consciousness. In *Rasselas*, the philosopher Imlac speaks about what he terms the 'dangerous prevalence of the imagination' and refers to the need to 'repress' the 'power of fancy'. This choice of verb again brings to mind Freud, who wrote about the ego's rejection or censorship of 'unwelcome' impulses. Imlac is not identical with his creator and, unlike Freud, thinks of repression as straightforwardly beneficial, but the image is still an arresting one. Sam's other observations on the matter foreshadow Freud's notions about the mind's hinterland. Even if the language only a few times prefigures Freud's (in one of his sermons he refers to 'the repression of . . . unreasonable desires'), the connection deserves notice. In *Rambler* 29 he describes how anxiety fills the mind with 'perpetual stratagems of counteraction' – psychological defence mechanisms, like the ones Freud later identified. An especially potent statement on this theme comes in *Rambler* 76, where he observes that 'No man yet was ever wicked without secret discontent'; the last two words evoke the whole drama of muffled desire and neurosis. One of the most astute interpreters of Johnson's thought, Walter Jackson Bate, identifies his 'studied and sympathetic sense of the way in which the human imagination, when it is blocked in its search for satisfaction, doubles back . . . or skips out diagonally in some form of projection'. This, he argues, is probably 'the closest anticipation of Freud . . . before the twentieth century'.[4]

As he thought about the dangers of losing his mind, Sam sometimes pictured the poet Christopher Smart, sent to a madhouse in Bethnal Green at the insistence of his father-in-law John Newbery (Sam's sometime publisher). Smart was a whirlwind of religious fervour, frequently unstable, but to Sam he seemed a cautionary figure. Had he been locked up for his own good or for other people's convenience? At his lowest ebb, Smart could still claim that 'I am not without authority in my jeopardy', but his confinement denied him both his privacy – tourists came and gawped at him – and his access to public life and recognition. Sam saw how grotesque this was: 'I did not think he ought to be shut up. His infirmities were not noxious to society . . . Another charge was that he did not love clean linen – and I have no passion for it.' Those final words, replete with self-knowledge, invite laughter. But the possibility of being detained on grounds similar to Smart's was real and appalling.

Hester Thrale spoke of Sam's 'particular attention to the diseases of the imagination', and his understanding of that faculty was certainly complex. He believed in the power of the imaginary to activate our empathy, and, even though he tended to claim that the more inventive sorts of fiction were puerile and 'too remote from known life', he could revel in stories of adventure and romance. In his life of Milton, he proposed that 'Poetry is the art of uniting pleasure with truth, by calling imagination to the help of reason.' But the imagination could breed despair and shameful wishes – not the least of which was the urge to masturbate – as well as the overripe daydreams that he called 'this secret prodigality of being' and likened to 'the poison of opiates'. In *Rasselas*, Imlac voices the thoroughly Johnsonian anxiety that a solitary person can become fixated with a single idea and will feast on 'luscious falsehood' whenever 'offended with the bitterness of truth'. Indulging the imagination creates the impression of deliciously concentrated flavours, but it is only that – an impression. The result is a treacherous sense of the world's insufficiency.

At its best, then, imagination is a passport to enlightenment, and at its worst a route into madness. Sam thinks of it as a person, often 'licentious and vagrant' and capable of what he calls 'seducements' – yet with the potential to be 'bright and active' and to 'animate' one's knowledge. It can also be a cancer, 'a formidable and obstinate disease of the intellect' which 'preys incessantly upon life'; a vessel, which it is natural to keep trying to fill; a muscle, easily strained; or an appliance that overheats when charged with the 'blaze of hope' and needs cooling down with a dose of realism.

The double-edged nature of imagination means that the mind is in a state of perpetual turbulence. Sam writes in *Rambler* 8 of the need to 'govern our thoughts, restrain them from irregular motions', and in *Rambler* 125 of imagination's tendency to 'burst the enclosures of regularity'. But how to achieve regularity? He searched for means of keeping imagination under control, and in later years one of these consisted of carrying out small experiments. For instance, he shaved the hair on his arms, curious to see how long it took to grow back, and kept track of the weight of forty-one leaves he had cut from a vine and laid out to dry on his bookshelves. His interest in such matters chimed with a broader interest in science, but was a means of grounding himself, attaching his thoughts to exact details of reality when otherwise they might float off into fancy – or proliferate into frenzy.

In his diaries, Sam echoes the cries of Shakespeare's Lear – 'Oh, let me not be mad, not mad, sweet heaven! / Keep me in temper. I would not be mad.' He did not subscribe to the view, which has since been periodically fashionable, that madness is a form of protest or some kind of higher authenticity, an instinct for the poetic or an alertness to hidden truths. 'Reason is the great distinction of human nature', he wrote in *Rambler* 162, and in *Rambler* 137 he emphasized its capacity to 'disentangle complications and investigate causes'. In his view, whatever interfered with the powers of reason was dangerous, and insanity seemed always to be encroaching on them. But those powers often seemed most acute when he believed he was teetering on the brink of insanity; attending to their functions was a way to stop himself disintegrating.

His notion of reason was heavily influenced by his reading of Locke, who identified what he called 'the wrong connection in our minds of ideas' as a 'great force to set us awry'. In the *Dictionary* Sam cited Locke in his entry for *madness*: 'There are degrees of *madness* as of folly, the disorderly jumbling ideas together.' False associations can crystallize fanaticism and prejudice, and they have a tendency to persist stubbornly. In *An Essay Concerning Human Understanding* (1690), Locke gave the example of a young man who learns to dance in a room that contains an old trunk: he is able to dance only in the presence of this trunk, and being unable to dance in a public place (at least without lugging a trunk around) is a social handicap, perhaps not tragic but certainly insidious. Sam believed that by inspecting his thought processes he could identify and undo crippling associations of this kind.

But this was something to be done in private, when alone. He reserved commentary on his precarious state of mind for his diaries, or for discussion with his most intimate friends; in public, and especially in his published writings, he made a point of maintaining an impression of mental equilibrium. Though revealingly quick to express sympathy for people whose minds were in distress, he translated his own painful experiences of what he called the 'invisible riot of the mind' into wisdom. When he discussed with Boswell how to deal with upsetting thoughts, he was clear that diversion was the best remedy. Boswell wondered if it wasn't possible to combat them through the direct application of one's intelligence, and Sam replied, 'To attempt to *think them down* is madness.' Introspection is not its own cure.

At the same time, he wondered whether sanity was a substantive quality. The concept seemed vague – and still does. In his book *Going Sane* (2005), Adam Phillips writes that 'The language of mental health . . . comes to life . . . in descriptions of disability, incompetence and failure', whereas 'the rules of sanity that are being broken are never properly codified, or even articulated'. It is as though we think that 'if we look after the madness the sanity will take care of itself'. Maybe, in truth, we are 'unaccustomed to valuing things, to exploring things, that are not traumatic', and sanity 'has been invented as some fictitious vantage point from which the trauma that is madness can be observed'. The language of sanity is 'like propaganda for a world . . . that has never existed'.[5]

In the *Dictionary*, Sam defines *sanity* as 'soundness of mind'. The sole quotation he uses to illustrate this is from *Hamlet*, in which Polonius speaks of 'A happiness that often madness hits on, / Which sanity and reason could not be / So prosp'rously delivered of.' Polonius is referring to Hamlet's 'pregnant' utterances, full of wit and wordplay. It's an interesting choice of illustration, since it values madness rather than sanity. If we turn to the entry for *mad*, there are personal notes in Sam's defining it as 'delirious without fever', 'broken in the understanding' and 'overrun with any violent or unreasonable desire'. Under *madness* he cites Locke's statement that 'There are degrees of madness as of folly' – a view he certainly endorsed, though his contemporaries tended to disagree. The sole illustrative quotation for *madhouse* comes from a seventeenth-century collection of fables – in which an inmate in such a place explains that 'the mad folks abroad are too many for us, and so they have mastered all the sober people and cooped them up here'.

'Perhaps, if we speak with rigorous exactness, no human mind is in its right state.' So says Imlac, arguing that any moment when fancy gets the upper hand over reason is tinged with insanity. While it isn't safe to assume that a quotation from *Rasselas* represents Sam's views, Imlac is the closest thing in it to his mouthpiece, and the spirit of his creator is audible in this suggestion that we are all susceptible to inexplicable compulsions and the darker urgings of the unconscious. Humankind is fallible; even the most sublime mind will err, and all of us from time to time lose contact with our better judgement. In this view, which looks ahead to ideas developed in the twentieth century by such scholars of madness as Michel Foucault, unreason is simply one of the places that the strange pilgrimage of life takes us.

On his fifty-first birthday, Sam vowed to 'reclaim imagination', and the verb naturally makes one think about what it's being reclaimed *from*: benightedness, desire (he says that 'Every desire is a viper in the bosom'), thoughts of suicide perhaps, and twisted fantasy. It's worth noticing, too, that the verb *reclaim* was originally, in the fourteenth century, used of a hawk, and in Sam's time continued to be used in this way. The imagination, like the hawk, can glide gracefully, but there are moments when it slips beyond one's reach, when its violence and the drama of its flight can obliterate all other sensations. Here I'm reminded of Helen

Macdonald's *H is for Hawk*, a memoir in which training a hawk is a means of dealing with grief. 'Hunting with the hawk took me to the very edge of being a human,' writes Macdonald. 'Then it took me past that place to somewhere I wasn't human at all. The hawk in flight, me running after her, the land and the air a pattern of deep and curving detail, sufficient to block out anything like the past or the future.'[6] For Sam, it's essential to rein the imagination back in before it can take him past the edge of being a human – past it, over it, into the abyss.

An element of his heroism was a willingness to pay attention to any and every thought he had, no matter how unpleasant or painful. His choosing to look inside himself in this way feels unexpectedly modern, as does his urging the habit upon others. 'Make your boy tell you his dreams,' he instructed Hester Thrale, explaining that 'the first corruption that entered into my heart was communicated in a dream'. He would not tell her what this was, but clearly he had reflected on it, probing the source of a dark thought. Dreams seemed a particularly disquieting example of imagination's tyranny, continuing by stealth the mind's diurnal work, compensating for the steady hand of rationality, or dramatizing those conflicts and connections that lay low in his waking life. When he describes a dream as 'a phantasm of sleep' (his *Dictionary* definition) or 'a temporary recession from the realities of life' (in the *Idler*), he captures their fantastical quality and hints at their purpose: as a form of review, a solution to problems that under one's waking scrutiny seem insoluble, a means of correcting misperceptions or fulfilling socially unacceptable urges, a detox programme, and a repository for messages from the future.

✃ 21 ✃

A chapter one might, in a more facetious spirit, have
chosen to label 'Shakespeare matters'

THE IDEA OF JOHNSON the hero is bound up with the *Dictionary*, which, even more than the *Rambler*, has the potential to illuminate his character. As he translates his vast programme of reading into a work of encyclopedic scope, there is plentiful evidence of his curiosity and learning, his tastes and priorities, the rareness of his judgement. Yet that evidence is not readily discernible because the details of the *Dictionary*'s entries, though cumulatively revealing, disclose only a modest amount about his state of mind and personal qualities when read one (or a few) at a time – and that has always been how most of the *Dictionary*'s audience have consumed it: in small doses rather than great gulps. Indeed, most have consulted not the data-rich pages of the whopping folio volumes (which originally cost £4 10s.), but one of the 120 abridgements or 309 miniature versions that followed. It is one of these condensed Johnsons that Becky Sharp in *Vanity Fair* flings from the window of her carriage as she leaves Miss Pinkerton's academy. In having her do so, her creator William Thackeray means to show that this resourceful young woman is casting aside tradition and authority. For Thackeray, writing in the 1840s about events thirty years earlier, Johnson's magnum opus was the embodiment of both stout Englishness and its compiler's force of mind and personality.

From the moment the *Dictionary* appeared, and for the next hundred years, that was its prevailing image. But while it made Sam's reputation, it failed to solve his money problems. Those would continue until 1762, when George III granted him a pension of £300 a year. A reward for his literary achievements, the pension was dreamed up by Alexander Wedderburn, a Scottish lawyer and MP. Wedderburn had put the idea to the Earl of Bute, his fellow Scot, who was then prime minister (a role he occupied for a mere ten months). The intention was to relieve Johnson's financial distress, but the pension made him look like a docile servant of the monarch and the government. He knew he would be criticized for taking it, and soon enough the vitriol began to flow. The *Gazetteer* dubbed him 'Mr Independent Johnson' and sniffed at writers who 'feast on state pensions', while the *Public Advertiser* included in a list of spoof book titles 'The Charms of Independence, a Tale, by Sam. Johnson, Esq.'. This kind of comment would not abate and became a trope of lazy journalism; among the more striking examples are an item in the *London Evening Post* in April 1771 that calls him 'Dr Pomposo, Pensioner Extraordinary alias Extraordinary Pensioner' (the name Pomposo had been coined by the satirical poet Charles Churchill) and one in the *Morning Post* in March 1777 that refers in passing to 'the surly pensioned Dictionary-maker'.[1] Inevitably, and insistently, the sneerers drew attention to his *Dictionary* definition of *pension* – 'pay given to a state hireling for treason to his country'.

By the time the pension was offered, Sam longed to be free from financial anxiety. The years that followed the *Dictionary* were hard. In March 1756, he was arrested for a debt of £5 18s., and only when the novelist Samuel Richardson sent him six guineas was he spared a spell in a louse-ridden, fetid, violent debtors' prison. The indignity of having no money was all the greater because he was surrounded by evidence of wealth. Grub Street, it's true, was home to many penniless characters, and he had only to walk along Fleet Street to see droves of the down and out. But among his circle were people of means. An example was Sir Joshua Reynolds. Prolific and successful, he was able to collect the work of other artists – in 1756 he acquired a Rembrandt.[2] In the year he accepted his pension, Sam could report in a letter that Reynolds was earning £6,000 a year, which we might tentatively equate to £600,000 today.

Whenever Sam received visitors, they were astonished to find him dressed like a beggar, rising at noon and breakfasting at one, surrounded by papers but with little furniture and few comforts, coughing amid the dust. Lodgers traipsed in and out of his quarters, and would continue to do so for the rest of his life. They contributed little and stretched his meagre resources. He was, in any case, reluctant to demand much of them. Hester Thrale relates that, rather than send Francis Barber to fetch oysters for his cat Hodge, Sam would lumber off to do so himself; even when it was inconvenient for him, he feared injuring Frank's pride by sending him on an errand 'for the convenience of a quadruped'.

In June 1756, he signed a contract for another substantial project, which he had been contemplating for a long time: an eight-volume edition of Shakespeare. As far back as April 1745, Edward Cave had brought out Sam's *Miscellaneous Observations on the Tragedy of Macbeth*, accompanied by proposals for an inexpensive new edition, but within a week the scheme had collapsed. The Tonson family had published Nicholas Rowe's edition of Shakespeare in 1709 and Alexander Pope's eye-wateringly expensive edition in 1725 (£6 6s. a set); claiming that they still held the copyright in the plays, they warned Cave off, and he was daunted by the likely costs of a court case. Yet a decade on, after the remarkable achievement of the *Dictionary*, the mood was different. The Tonsons were now happy to be part of a group of booksellers backing his edition, who wanted the job done in eighteen months. The *Dictionary* had prepared him for this task, but, as before, he set out with too optimistic a view of how long it would require.

In an age when we tend to take for granted Shakespeare's primacy among authors who have written in English, it is easy to lose sight of how much less secure his reputation used to be. At the start of the eighteenth century, readers and theatregoers commonly expressed admiration for his plays, but not much more than they did for the best of his contemporaries, such as Ben Jonson. It was in Sam's lifetime that Shakespeare became a cultural icon. Beginning with Rowe's six-volume edition, which came out in the year he was born, scholarly attention to Shakespeare's works improved. Yet it was still far from unusual to believe that his phrasing could be tidied up. The same applied to his characters and plots; for instance, the conundrum-loving Fool was absent from productions of *King Lear* throughout the eighteenth century and did not return till 1838. Meanwhile, the appetite for staging Shakespeare owed something to expediency. The 1730s witnessed an increase in productions of his plays, partly thanks to the efforts of groups such as the Shakespeare Ladies Club, which urged theatre managers, in particular John Rich at Covent Garden, to promote him. But it was also because the Licensing Act of 1737, which meant that new plays had to be scrutinized by the censor, made older works easier to put on.

Nevertheless, by the time Sam embarked on his edition, talking up Shakespeare was a nationalist project. In 1753 the playwright Arthur Murphy could write of Shakespeare being 'a kind of established religion in poetry', and during the Seven Years' War (1756–1763), which pitted Britain and Prussia against France and Austria, that religion took on political colour. Pride in British culture solidified. The history of French critics writing about Shakespeare in patronizing terms now met with a revulsion that was part of a broader, flag-waving hostility to all things French. Around the time of Sam's edition, and boosted by Garrick among others, a Shakespeare industry was springing up. Its most dramatic moment of idolatry would be the Stratford Jubilee of 1769, and although that occasion, in no small part a celebration of Garrick, was ruined by bad planning and soggy conditions, subsequent Shakespeare festivities would ape its ritual silliness and cult of dubious relics.

Sam rose above such folderol. The context in which he interpreted Shakespeare was eternity, not the Seven Years' War. His edition is now remembered mainly for its preface, written only in the last couple of months of a project that occupied him on and off for nearly a decade. Less well-known are his 5,500 notes on the text, about 15 per cent of which engage with the work of previous editors. He sees himself as an improver of the public understanding of Shakespeare, building on others' endeavours, and in his many interventions to improve Shakespeare's grammar, amend his stage directions and sharpen his punctuation, he seeks to enhance the plays' immediacy. His approach is critical and informative, and his comments on individual plays contain smart insights as well as lucid explanations of tricky passages.[3]

He responded strongly to Shakespeare – to the plays, not the poems or the life. He likens them to a great forest, in which we can get lost, and one of the reasons he didn't care to see them on the stage was that they were so alive in the theatre of his mind. Reading *Hamlet* as a child, he was terrified by the ghost and rushed out into the street 'that he might see people about him'; the presence of real fleshly figures, some of whom he must have recognized, was enough to jolt him out of the spectral realm. Yet the play continued to transport him back there, and the ghost, he believed, always 'chills the blood with horror'. The murder of Desdemona in *Othello* was 'not to be endured', and the shock of his first experience of Cordelia's death in *King Lear* meant that 'I know not whether I ever endured to read again the last scenes of the play till I undertook to revise them as editor'.

In some cases, his reaction was curt and unfavourable. Some of the plotting in *Timon of Athens* was 'elaborately unskilful', *Julius Caesar* was 'cold and unaffecting', the final act of *Henry V* suffered from 'emptiness and narrowness', and *Cymbeline* was with minor exceptions a work of 'unresisting imbecility'. Sam is no one's idea of a hagiographer, and his judgements can strike a modern reader, used to Shakespeare simply being praised, as alarmingly negative (or excitingly so). For instance, 'He is not long soft and pathetic without some idle conceit or contemptible equivocation', and 'The plots are often so loosely formed, that a very slight consideration may improve them'. How about the claim that 'trivial sentiments and vulgar ideas disappoint the attention, to which they are recommended by sonorous epithets and swelling figures'? Or the statement that his puns are a seductive and ruinous distraction, 'the fatal Cleopatra for which he lost the world and was content to lose it'? Whether or not we agree, the attitude is instructive. Holding a writer in high esteem does not, in Sam's view, require one to gloss over their faults. Nor does it preclude cutting the knots when their arguments are impenetrable. Undiscriminating admiration is not loyal, but ridiculous.

Given Sam's personal take on his subject, it is no surprise that there are moments, as in the *Dictionary*, when a detail of his life intrudes. Sometimes this is a small matter, such as when his knowledge of Staffordshire dialect informs a note on a line of Edgar's in *King Lear*.[4] On other occasions he waxes philosophical, for instance prompted by a line in *Measure for Measure* to comment that 'When we are young we busy ourselves in forming schemes . . . and miss the gratifications that are before us; when we are old we amuse the languor of age with the recollection of youthful pleasures or performances; so that our life . . . resembles our dreams after dinner, when the events of the morning are mingled with the designs of the evening'. Writing about Falstaff, he comments that 'Every man who feels in himself the pain of deformity . . . is ready to revenge any hint of contempt'. Then there are times when he tells us more than he intends. In a note on *King John* about a character who muddles up his left and right slippers, he remarks, illuminating his own practices more than the rest of the world's, 'He that is frighted or hurried may put his hand into the wrong glove, but either shoe will equally admit either foot.'

More substantially, Sam's edition and especially its noble preface put forward arguments about why Shakespeare is worth our time. He makes confident claims about Shakespeare's whole body of work, rather than confining himself to a more gingerly discussion. His fundamental assertion is that the plays give pleasure because they contain 'just representations of general nature': although many of Shakespeare's characters behave unusually, we are struck by their human traits, and in even his most extreme characters and their most extreme behaviours we see traces of ourselves. Those who want to mock fusty old Dr Johnson pretend that this means he thinks all Shakespeare's characters are alike. In fact, he is quick to remark that 'perhaps no poet ever kept his personages more distinct from each other'. The people who appear in Shakespeare's plays are 'the genuine progeny of common humanity' – a common humanity, that is, teeming with weakness, folly and the potential for brutal, self-serving malignity.

Sam believes that the playwright's skill lies in making familiar psychology seem blazingly vivid. There's a rich understanding of behaviour in his observation that Lady Macbeth 'urges the excellence and dignity of courage, a glittering idea which has dazzled mankind from age to age', and in his picture of Polonius as 'a man bred in courts' and 'proud of his eloquence', who 'knows that his mind was once strong, and knows not that it is become weak' and is thus a perfect image of 'dotage encroaching upon wisdom'. A long note on the personality of Falstaff includes the following insight: 'At once obsequious and malignant, he satirizes in their absence those whom he lives by flattering.' Tell me that you don't know this person, and that these words don't illuminate a whole swathe of human conduct.

What's radical, then, in Sam's understanding of Shakespeare, is his conviction that the plays show us that the world is enough. As one modern account puts it, 'What he looks for in Shakespeare above all else is the power to deliver the mind from its restless desire to go beyond what life gives, the power to bring us home to our participation in that general human nature which unites us.'[5] Instead of satisfying himself with the platitude that the plays are timeless – a word that should immediately put one on high alert, ready to be sold a bucketful of Ye Olde Crappe – he finds in them a fecund timeliness, the quality of always being in season and always having something to say *to us*, whether about ambition, ageing, indecision, betrayal, love, conflict or transformation. At the same time, in treating the plays as if they are alive, he prizes their openness – not just a capacity to inspire new readings, but an endless soliciting of fresh interpretation.

✄ 22 ✄

In which Samuel Johnson idles, to some avail, not least
by enquiring into the soul of advertisement and our
artificial passions

EDITING SHAKESPEARE is now the preserve of professional
academics. But before the middle of the nineteenth century
it was mostly carried out by what we would now consider
amateurs – well-informed literati with an eye for commercial opportunity, or genteel antiquarians. Sam belonged to
the first of these categories and, like Pope and Nicholas
Rowe before him, could also lay claim to expertise as a poet.
Besides possessing a deep knowledge of the language of
Shakespeare's age, he sought to understand the plays, their
creation and their perspectives in the context of that age
and Shakespeare's 'own particular opportunities'. At the
same time, he saw producing an edition as a way of redeem-
ing from obscurity the phrasing and sentiments of an author
who had been dead for almost 150 years, and it is significant
that, when at last set before the public, Sam's eight volumes
were available for less than half of what Pope's six had cost
forty years earlier.

Although the impulse behind the edition was pragmatic,
the work proved demanding, and he soon found convenient
ways of diverting himself from the task. Among these was
contributing an essay each week, under the title of the *Idler*,
to a new newspaper, the *Universal Chronicle*. His first *Idler*
appeared in April 1758, and there was one every Saturday

for the next two years. The early numbers feel slighter and more topical than the *Rambler*, as well as less assertively moralistic. The tone of the whole series is brisker and less analytical. As if acknowledging the rhetorical exorbitance of the *Rambler*, he commented in *Idler* 70 that 'Few faults of style, whether real or imaginary, excite the malignity of a more numerous class of readers, than the use of hard words.' In another *Idler* essay he seemed to poke fun at the persona he had adopted in the *Rambler*, portraying 'my old friend Sober' who trifles with experiments, derives his greatest pleasure from conversation, and in empty moments bats away his own reproaches by persuading himself that he is always either teaching or learning something.

Yet there are moments when these essays, especially the later ones, show him at his most potent. 'Vanity inclines us to find faults anywhere rather than in ourselves.' 'However we may labour for our own deception, truth, though unwelcome, will sometimes intrude upon the mind.' 'Slavery is now nowhere more patiently endured, than in countries once inhabited by the zealots of liberty.' He frequently strikes a satirical note, for instance mocking people who endlessly scuttle from place to place in order never to be spotted in an unfashionable location, but he concludes that we shouldn't laugh too hard at such people's expense and should instead be merciful, for all of us are in some way absurd.

In the *Idler*, Sam is attentive to the fashions of the moment. He notes the topics under discussion in newspapers and coffee houses, and responds to recent events – such as the five inches of rain that fell in July of 1758. These essays show him living in a world of goods; though a man of few possessions, he knows the objects of other people's material cravings and is curious about the ways in which those cravings are stimulated. *Idler* 40, published in January 1759, reflects on 'the true pathos of advertisements', citing the example of mothers who feel they must buy special necklaces to relieve the discomfort of teething babies, having been told that they will never forgive themselves if they fail to do so. His comments on advertising were timely, as Britain had lately witnessed an explosion of commerce and consumption, as well as a surge in national prosperity. Controversies raged over luxury and the fickleness of fashion, yet all the while there was an eager, almost rabid promotion of *stuff*: toys and trinkets, household items, the wherewithal for comfort and self-indulgence – often sourced abroad. Fashions changed fast: the economist Adam Smith commented, in *The Theory of Moral Sentiments* (1759), that a man's coat might be in style for a year, and that notions of what furniture a polite home should contain changed a couple of times a decade. It's a pattern that still holds true.

Printed matter proliferated: newspapers and magazines, labels, tickets, certificates, receipts. Instead of an oral, courtly, amateur literary milieu there was now a market-driven, professional one; prose gained the upper hand over poetry, a formal understanding of copyright came into force (in 1710), and aristocratic patronage of literature faded. At the same time literacy increased, public libraries became more common, and the novel emerged as an important literary form.[1] To put that in perspective, between 1660 and 1800 about 300,000 books and pamphlets were published in England; in our own age, that many titles are published every two years. But Sam saw among the defining features of his age an 'epidemical conspiracy for the destruction of paper' and 'the itch of literary praise'. He was a creature of this new world – a serious and scholarly reader who nevertheless had a rare facility for producing journalistic copy. A master of the quick first draft, he prided himself on his versatility and could boast of being able, if required, to 'write the life of a broomstick'. Acutely conscious of the book as an object and a commodity, he was conscious also of authorship as a business. And, though he would not have used the word, he was conscious of the individual author as a brand.

Where there were goods to sell and an abundance of new means to talk about them, there was advertising. Britain's first daily newspaper was the single-sheet *Daily Courant*, which appeared in March 1702, with the news on one side and advertisements on the other. Soon there were plenty more publications of this kind. Joseph Addison, co-founder of the *Spectator* in 1711, said only half in jest that on days when news was in short supply he entertained himself by reading the advertisements, which were 'instruments of ambition' and allowed the purveyors of common goods or services to share space on the page with the rulers of nations. In 1712 the British government, seeking to curb the press, imposed a tax on such advertising – it would continue until 1853 – but in the 1730s, when Sam arrived in London, newspapers commonly devoted half their space to it. There one might find big talk of the benefits of fat from the carcass of a Russian bear, which was apparently good for nourishing the scalp, or of elixirs that could relieve one of bad dreams and writer's cramp; an advertisement might promise instruction in how best to use a snuff box, not least how to offer it to a stranger, or urge the attractions of attending a bull-baiting, at which a cat would be tied to the bull's tail.[2] Other promotional methods abounded, with posters, handbills, fancy catalogues and pattern books, extravagant shop signs and souvenir trade cards all used in order to create hype around goods and services.

Sam had witnessed a shift in advertising: from mere announcements, which told the public that articles or services were available, to acts of persuasion, which involved inflated claims about those articles and services and about the people responsible for them. He seems indeed to have been the first person to use the word *advertising* in its modern sense, writing in *Idler* 40 that 'The trade of advertising is now so near to perfection, that it is not easy to propose any improvement.' We may now laugh, since advertising has changed dramatically, but it's interesting that he thinks this. The key change in his lifetime was a move towards manipulation: of the facts, inasmuch as the benefits of products and ownership were overstated, and also of the customer's imagination. He saw it everywhere. An item in the *London Magazine* in 1732 explained that '*Puff* is a cant word for the applause that writers and booksellers give their own books &c. to promote their sale.' On entering the literary life of the capital, Sam was able to observe at close quarters the mushrooming of puffs. In the *Idler* he writes, 'Advertisements are now so numerous that they are very negligently perused, and it is therefore become necessary to gain attention by magnificence of promises.'

The science of manipulating image and taste was only just beginning. A latter-day Johnson would shudder at modern techniques in which products are endowed with personalities and subliminal messages are pumped into the air we breathe. He would balk, certainly, at the cynicism of the stories concocted by *Mad Men*'s Don Draper, that Gatsby-ish peddler of toxic products, who insists that 'Happiness is the smell of a new car', 'What you call love was invented by guys like me, to sell nylons', and 'People want to be told what to do so badly that they'll listen to anyone.' Yet Sam perceived the essence of the business:

'Promise, large promise, is the soul of an advertisement.' As an example, he cited the recent promotion of a particular type of duvet – yes, they had them in the eighteenth century – which was 'beyond comparison' with conventional eider-down and had 'many excellencies [that] cannot be here set forth'. He added wryly, 'With one excellence we are made acquainted, "it is warmer than four or five blankets, and lighter than one."' In similar vein, he mentioned a 'beautifying fluid' that 'repels pimples, washes away freckles, smoothes the skin, and plumps the flesh; and yet, with a generous abhorrence of ostentation, confesses, that it will not "restore the bloom of fifteen to a lady of fifty"'. The first time I saw this, I missed the twang of irony in his talk of that generous abhorrence of ostentation. How kind it is of the advertiser to tell us that the product will not achieve a huge miracle – and leave us to imagine that it will at least achieve a small one.

In an age when it was common to speak of 'good taste', Sam never used this form of words in his own writings. It appears in one of his translations, and Boswell once has him speak of 'good taste' when they are discussing differences of opinion about writers' style.[3] But Sam was unimpressed by the immediacy with which taste operated: there was no time for reason to arrest it. John Gilbert Cooper's *Letters Concerning Taste*, published in the same year as the *Dictionary*, described good taste as 'that instantaneous glow of pleasure which thrills thro' our whole frame, and seizes upon the applause of the heart, before the intellectual power, reason, can descend from the throne of the mind'.[4] Much of the contemporary discussion of taste invoked its force and irresistibility: taste draws people towards objects.

Sam was addressing this long before he started the *Idler*. In *Rambler* 49, he writes about the 'new desires and artificial passions' that spring up once our basic needs are answered: 'from having wishes only in consequence of our wants, we begin to feel wants in consequence of our wishes'. In short, 'we persuade ourselves to set a value upon things which are of no use, but because we have agreed to value them'. Here he identifies the imitative impulse that drives our behaviour as consumers. This is what the philosopher René Girard has since termed 'mimetic desire'. Writing about Girard in 2017, John Lanchester quoted his dictum that 'Man is the creature who does not know what to desire, and who turns to others in order to make up his mind'. Lanchester had fun translating this into the odious corporate motto 'Look around, ye petty, and compare.'[5] The tone may not be Johnsonian, but the argument is. In *Rambler* 49, Sam remarks on the folly of 'all those desires which arise from the comparison of our condition with that of others' and pictures the sad figure created by this hollow rivalry – 'He that thinks himself poor, because his neighbour is richer.'

Even as we tell ourselves that we hate viral marketing and product placement, decoy pricing and commercial propaganda, we are drawn to advertising. It has threaded mimetic desire into our lives. Tim Wu, author of a recent study of what he calls this 'industrialization of human attention capture', portrays a world 'cluttered with come-ons'. Thanks to smartphones having become 'technological prosthetics, enhancements of our own capacities', these come-ons are increasingly present in our private mental space, and we are subject to constant interruption. 'What an irony,' he comments, that this 'lamentably scattered state of mind' results 'from the imperatives of one particular kind of commercial enterprise that is not even particularly profitable most of the time'.[6] Modern consumers have surrendered control of their attention to advertisers. Now it is not just the promises that are magnificent, but also the means by which they find us: as we click and post, search and 'like', each of us is part of a giant network that powers the engines of commerce.

When Sam discusses advertising in *Idler* 40, he imagines the pioneer 'who first took advantage of the general curiosity that was excited by a siege or battle, to betray the readers of news into the knowledge of the shop where the best . . . powders were to be sold'. Later in the same essay he writes, 'as every art ought to be exercised in due subordination to the public good, I cannot but propose it as a moral question to these masters of the public ear, whether they do not sometimes play too wantonly with our passions'. In each of these quotations, there is one word that stands out: in the first *betray*, in the second *wantonly*. Sam's phrasing presages a world in which the false promises of consumerism, pseudo-science, religious extremism and sound-bite politics multiply ungovernably and colonize our souls.

Of tea and Abyssinia – a chapter about Choices, in
which we have chosen to include the word 'lumbersome'
(a curio you may reasonably think a mistake for
'cumbersome')

IF THE *IDLER* was one profitable diversion, another was
writing reviews, and Sam cast his eye over dozens of books,
on subjects as disparate as beekeeping, the history of
Jamaica, the national debt, techniques of bleaching, and the
Isles of Scilly. This was hack work that brought in a little
money and was completed while sitting in a three-legged
chair that had only one arm. Sometimes he fell into the
age-old trap of spending his fee three times – at the point
of commission, when he had executed it, and again after he
received the funds. When the rewards seemed too modest
or slipped too easily through his fingers, he could convince
himself on other grounds that a job was worth his while.
Reviewing books was an opportunity to test his knowledge
and his powers of analysis, to educate himself and highlight
other writers' achievements. He was drawn, here as before,
to works that dealt with practical matters: what it meant to
be a butcher or tanner, how cheese and butter were made,
the production of coinage. From 1756 to 1762 he was active
in the Society for the Encouragement of Arts, Commerce
and Manufactures, which existed to stimulate interest in
new solutions to problems such as how best to drain fields
and rotate crops, and many of the volumes he reviewed

were aligned with the Society's aims, publicizing innovative schemes and research.

It was against this background that Sam took exception to an attack on tea drinking by Jonas Hanway. A London merchant who had spent several years in Russia, Hanway shared some of Sam's enthusiasms, not least a concern for the welfare of prostitutes. But in 1756 he published *An Essay on Tea*, a trite criticism of the drink's various ways of 'obstructing industry'. Reviewing it, Sam described himself as 'a hardened and shameless tea drinker'. Reading those words, I recall Boswell's line 'I suppose no person ever enjoyed with more relish the infusion of that fragrant leaf than Johnson'. This is enough to make me brew a pot; I pour some, and it's reddish gold, at once delicate and assertive, grapey on the palate. Why even imagine that there might be any shame in taking a restorative cup? Sam's reference to being 'hardened and shameless' is joco-serious; he's laughing at Hanway, but also acknowledging the prevalence of the view that tea is a drug, dangerous to ingest. The practice had established itself in London by the 1660s, and the first tea shop in England opened three years before Sam was born, but mass consumption didn't start till the 1720s, and, as tea's popularity boomed, doctors worried that it increased flatulence, made the body weak and aggravated melancholy. *An Essay on the Nature, Use and Abuse of Tea*, published anonymously in 1722, claimed that it was 'very hurtful' and 'not less destructive . . . than opium'.

Hanway was resuming a familiar battle. This was not his only idiosyncratic mission; he campaigned against the practice of tipping, argued in favour of solitary confinement for difficult prisoners, talked about the health benefits of flannel waistcoats, and is often said to have been the first Londoner to walk the streets carrying an umbrella. According to

Hanway, tea destroyed the teeth, distressed the bowels and caused the hands to tremble. Striking a note that might have reminded Sam of his father, he claimed that women were apt to spend too much money on tea and imperil domestic finances. More seriously, he believed that the drink had weakened Britain's army. 'Since tea has been in fashion,' he insisted, 'even suicide has been more familiar amongst us' – it would be less common if less tea were consumed.

Sam was rather better than Hanway at telling the difference between correlation and causation, and his review makes it plain that he was unimpressed by its arguments and the style in which they were set forth. He portrayed himself as someone 'whose kettle has scarcely time to cool, who with tea amuses the evening, with tea solaces the midnight, and, with tea, welcomes the morning'. Yet on one point he could agree with Hanway: England had succumbed to a 'general languor'. Though in his eyes tea itself was not responsible, its popularity was an excuse 'for assembling to prattle', and such prattling was a symptom of society's love of idle self-indulgence.

The first illustration of *tea* that Sam provides in his *Dictionary* comes from a poetic tribute in 1662 to both the drink and new queen Catherine of Braganza, whose enthusiasm for it percolated through the court of King Charles II. The poem is the work of the enthusiastic royalist Edmund Waller, and identifies tea as 'The muses' friend', a substance which gives the imagination welcome aid and can 'repress those vapours which the head invade'. Yet shortly after this, Sam introduces a quotation from Jonathan Swift, which pictures young students of religion who are afraid of being thought drily pedantic and exchange their serious labours 'for plays, in order to qualify them for tea-tables'. Something of the atmosphere Swift had in mind can be seen in a popular print published around 1720, which celebrates the tea table but includes (on the table itself) an open book that identifies the taking of tea as an occasion for 'chit chat'.[1] For all his enjoyment of tea and his criticism of Jonas Hanway's essay about it, Sam understood that those who loved the drink most could end up drowning in the accompanying gossip.

Always confident in his approach to the books he reviewed, he brought a special zest to evaluating works of moral philosophy. In 1757 he examined the recently published *A Free Inquiry into the Nature and Origin of Evil*, which was the work of Soame Jenyns, a Member of Parliament. The dandyish Jenyns, who that same year sat for Joshua Reynolds, also had ambitions as a poet, and in *The Modern Fine Gentleman* pictured, with no little irony, a chancer who sits in parliament 'safe in self-sufficient impudence, / Without experience, honesty, or sense'.[2] His *Free Inquiry*, though a much larger undertaking, was a shallow treatment of a solemn subject, arguing among other things that evil is a necessary feature of any kind of government, and that it is foolish to encourage the poor to read, lest they become more aware of how wretched their lives are. Jenyns thought that all beings are connected in a universal system (the Great Chain of Being), with the result that one person's pain is beneficial to another. He believed that there are beings superior to us who 'may deceive, torment, or destroy us, for the ends, only, of their own pleasure or utility' (his words) and that 'the evils suffered on this globe, may by some inconceivable means contribute to the felicity of the inhabitants of the remotest planet' (Sam's paraphrase).

Jenyns was not the first or last MP to have little familiarity with the real world, but he was astonishingly incurious and complacent. In a remark about the necessity of poverty, he pictured it 'now and then pinching a few', and he claimed that all who are poor are compensated 'by having more hopes, and fewer fears' and 'a greater share of health'. Sam feared that Jenyns's arguments could be used to justify social inequality – not just to preserve it, but to increase it – and responded to his facile drivel with dramatic immediacy, mixing irony and contempt. For instance: 'That hope and fear are inseparably or very frequently connected with poverty . . . my surveys of life have not informed me.' He reproved Jenyns's ignorance, calling him 'this enquirer' and 'this great investigator'. Above all, he felt that Jenyns had failed as an author by being morally unserious. *A Free Inquiry into the Nature and Origin of Evil* was one of those books the reader suspects was written 'for the sake of some invisible order of beings', since they are 'of no use to any of the corporeal inhabitants of the world'. Jenyns had failed to grasp what seemed to Sam a central truth of authorship: 'The only end of writing is to enable readers better to enjoy life, or better to endure it.'

This is one of those statements that prompt either a nod of vague assent or blunt dismissal. Yet it is worth considering more closely. Looking at it a second time, one's reaction may well be 'The *only* end of writing . . . ?' Sam is ascribing to literature a pretty limited range of effects. Or so it seems. But his statement has a discreet power. It invites us to wonder why we write. Even when we do so with a view to satisfying our vanity, the act involves an affirmative gesture: we pass on secrets, share the truth, convey a lesson, add a brick to the mansion of knowledge, preserve something for posterity, honour the freedom of the mind, envisage a world somehow less preposterous than our own.

Hence Sam's suggestion to Samuel Richardson that *Clarissa*, his great novel about the darkness of desire and the rewards of virtue, should have an index, which would allow readers to consult it like a manual. In 1751 Richardson acted on this, appending to the seventh volume of his novel's fourth edition 'An Ample Collection of Such of the Moral and Instructive Sentiments interspersed throughout the Work, as may be presumed to be of General Use and Service'. Sam used this when compiling the *Dictionary*, welcoming its convenient array of bite-size precept.[3] Not long after the review of Soame Jenyns, he created a work of his own that provided a similar portfolio of useful principles.

At the beginning of 1759, Sam's mother Sarah fell ill. He received from his stepdaughter Lucy Porter a narrative of her failing health, and on 13 January wrote to his mother that 'The account . . . pierces my heart.' More letters, full of anguish, followed in the next few days. But he did not travel to see her, and she died on the night of 20 January. He could have done nothing to alleviate her suffering; they had long been separated, and he may have thought that his sudden arrival would be distressing, not calmative. The prospect of going back to Lichfield must have awakened bitter memories: of his melancholy father, his parents' tense marriage, his dead brother, and his own woebegone years there after prematurely leaving Oxford. Inevitably, there were memories of disappointing his mother; like his father and his brother, he had felt the force of her judgement and done what he could to avoid it.

While he had many times professed love for Sarah, it had seemed impossible to please her. Yet in London he had forged an identity that was entirely independent of her and not subject to her persistent disapproval, and it is telling, surely, that since settling there in the late 1730s he had not once returned to Lichfield – whereas after her death he went back at least thirteen times. In *Rambler* 148, a vision of despotism with a distinctly personal hue, he writes that 'The regal and parental tyrant differ only in the extent of their dominions' and notes that the abused child will, when its parent is dying, 'forget the injuries which they have suffered, so far as to perform the last duties with alacrity and zeal'. When it came to performing his own last duties, he found that he could not forget so easily. Being in his mother's presence was beyond him; even the thought of her was enough to link him to his losses and defeats.

When Sam had received the first news of her decline, he'd quickly considered how best to raise money for her expenses. The result, which he wrote in a single week, has come to be known as *Rasselas*; on the title page of the first edition it is billed as *The Prince of Abissinia. A Tale*. His biographers have tended to treat *Rasselas* as a sudden effusion of his creative genius, and it's not unusual for people to dismiss it as yet another European fantasy of the Orient, or as Abyssinian only in name. But the choice of Abyssinia as its location was not casual. In the twenty-five years since he'd translated Jerónimo Lobo's account of that country, he had kept abreast of works about the region, and although he wrote *Rasselas* quickly, it was the culmination of a long period of imaginative engagement with African history and travelogue.[4] It also marked the end of a ten-year period in which – the *Dictionary* aside – his published writings had dwelled on the practical problems of leading a moral life. Was it the publication of *Rasselas* or the death of his mother that ended that phase? Perhaps, rather than thinking of Sam's writing it in the shadow of his mother's death, we should think of his now emerging from the shadow of his mother's life.

Rasselas depicts an Abyssinian prince of that name, twenty-five years old and living in the wide and fruitful Happy Valley, a place where 'the blessings of nature were collected, and its evils . . . excluded'. Frustrated by the blandness of his existence, he withdraws from the mushy routines of this utopia – where piped music plays on loop to heighten its occupants' opinion of their bliss – and contemplates his escape. He meets an engineer who makes wings that he believes will enable them to fly beyond the mountains that enclose the Valley. Rasselas suspects that this is wishful thinking – or, as he puts it, 'you now tell me rather what you wish than what you know'. Sure enough, the engineer's aeronautical career lasts a matter of seconds; the first time he uses the wings, he bellyflops into a lake, and Rasselas has to drag him to safety, half-dead and wholly disillusioned. A while after this, though, the prince meets the poet Imlac. Keen on philosophy, but not on a world that has little respect for intellectualism, Imlac has retreated to the Happy Valley. The conversation that passes between the two men invigorates both of them, and Imlac becomes 'the companion of my flight, the guide of my rambles, the partner of my fortune'. Inspired, Rasselas heads off in search of experience, never to return. Plausibility is sometimes stretched – one chapter is headed 'They enter Cairo, and find every man happy' – but the journey is revelatory.

The book has been interpreted as gloomily pessimistic or a fable of Christian redemption, as an attempt to create a philosophical novel or as a misshapen comic squib. What's for sure is that it has an air of the Old Testament, a splendid tone of legislative seriousness that makes one travel through it at tortoise pace. It seems fitting that in *Jane Eyre*, when Charlotte Brontë imagines Jane arriving at Lowood, the charity school where she spends eight grim years, she has her catch sight of a girl sitting on a stone bench, absorbed in what she's reading; it's *Rasselas*, and Jane thinks it sounds strange and attractive, but on inspection it disappoints her, because there's nothing about fairies or genies and 'no bright variety seemed spread over the closely printed pages'. Many modern readers share her reaction, and it is true that Rasselas, his sister Nekayah, her maid Pekuah and his tutor Imlac don't have the psychological richness we now expect of major characters in a novel.

Yet *Rasselas* imparts important truths. For instance, melancholy people are almost always superstitious. Pilgrimage doesn't necessarily improve us, and retreating into solitude is no guarantee of being devout. Undertakings that are hard to plan, or even contemplate, often transpire to be easy once we try to carry them out. Integrity without knowledge is weak and useless. The greatest teachers, no matter how celestial the beauty of their lessons, are human. We can recognize inconsistencies in our attitudes and still feel that they are authentic. People in authority must do what they can to allow those they govern to cultivate their intellectual faculties. You'll never get anything done if you insist on overcoming all possible objections (but objections still need to be raised).

One of the more uncomfortable truths of *Rasselas* is hinted at in the title Sam originally had in mind – 'The Choice of Life'. That phrase appears eight times in the text, and without the definite article another three times. The words, as they're repeated, take the reader further into the limbo of ambivalence. Although it retains some connotations of hopefulness, *choice* is associated here with disappointment and undecidability. On one level, *Rasselas* recommends the questing spirit we might urge upon a student taking a gap year: the pilgrims must inspect various ways of life – learning from direct experience, rather than at second hand. But it also reflects on the complex, anxious business of choosing.

This, we gather, is a time-consuming process. It means examining alternatives, evaluating and comparing them, and finally making a commitment. In *Rambler* 178, Sam discusses choice:

> Of two objects tempting at a distance on contrary sides, it is impossible to approach one but by receding from the other; by long deliberation and dilatory projects they may be both lost, but can never be both gained. It is, therefore, necessary to compare them, and when we have determined the preference, to withdraw our eyes and our thoughts at once from that which reason directs us to reject.

His description of how this feels is suitably lumbersome. Yet this is just choosing between two objects; the more abundant the alternatives, the more time the choice can potentially take. That may be obvious, but what is less obvious – to the person making the choice, even if not to someone observing it – is that the greater the abundance of alternatives, the more reductive we need to be in our appraisal of each of them, with the result that the process feels absurd. A world dense with alternatives is one in which we either stall hopelessly as we wrestle with the complications of choosing or make abrupt decisions – not necessarily bad, but mechanical, cavalier or offhand, and not *alive*.

The tyranny of choice is the tragedy of prosperity. Not, admittedly, the sort of tragedy that is certain to make a bystander feel compassion, yet the sort that confronts us with our vulnerability and fallibility. The problem of choice is one of scale – at my local supermarket there are 206 varieties of yogurt, 118 different fruit juices and 37 kinds of gin – but also one of attitude, because we come to think that all life's choices are consumer choices, and we thus shop for a lover the way we might shop for a pair of shoes. What's more, the expansion of choice creates the illusion that we are the masters of our destinies, perpetually capable of self-fashioning and self-improvement. Yet in reality, both the choice and the deliberation that results from it are alienating and isolating. Ashamed of the selections we have made, or exhausted by the process of making them, we are twitchily curious about the road not taken. Overwhelmed by information, we turn to authorities (in a broad sense, including both apps and real-life gurus), but judging their merits becomes yet another entanglement.

Rasselas, which has achieved its own kind of giddy plurality in attracting so many different critical interpretations, speaks to this feeling. When Imlac contemplates the difficulty of reaching decisions, especially ones that are informed by mere impressions of what's being selected, he comments that 'while you are making the choice of life, you neglect to live'. It's a mordant observation, a caution to anyone who believes it's possible to navigate a perfect path through the dizzying bazaar of goods, services and experiences.

❧ 24 ❧

In which the definition of *network* provides an opportunity
to appraise certain marvels of the twenty-first century,
not least the inventions of Mr Mark Zuckerberg

RASSELAS is rooted in a specific moment in the life of Samuel
Johnson and draws on remote inspirations, such as Lobo's
Voyage to Abyssinia, yet yields insights that are shapely and
prescient. It confirms the impression that Sam's works are
simultaneously antique and alive. Here, in essence, is the
Johnsonian spirit that excites each generation of his devotees – rational but full of feeling, stern but compassionate,
orthodox in many things but unenamoured of conformism.
Often he is most incisive when his phrasing looks most difficult; as he articulates himself in ways that demand our
close attention, he is aiming for precision, for economy and
durability of expression. Although the language may seem
idiosyncratic and obscure, its condensed power becomes
apparent when we try to come up with a more efficient
alternative, and it is when we think we have caught him in
the act of archaism that his words, re-examined, instead
appear far-sighted.

We see this in one of his most celebrated *Dictionary*
definitions, of the word *network*: 'Any thing reticulated or
decussated, at equal distances, with interstices between the
intersections.' This isn't a triumph of simplicity. *Reticulated*
and *decussated* don't crop up every day: there's the reticulated
python, a popular zoo exhibit, but one of the few other

places I've found the first of these words is in a Sherlock Holmes story ('There, criss-crossed upon the man's naked shoulder, was the same strange reticulated pattern of red, inflamed lines which had been the death-mark of Fitzroy McPherson'), and *decussated*, meaning 'formed with crossing lines like an X', is an even rarer term, which Sam seems to have encountered in a book by Sir Thomas Browne. Yet part of this supposedly anomalous definition survives in the *OED*, where one of the senses of *network* is 'A piece of work having the form or construction of a net; an arrangement or structure with intersecting lines and interstices resembling those of a net.' Early critics of Sam's *Dictionary* complained that the definition was too abstract. But even if it's not much help to someone who doesn't have a sizeable vocabulary, it has an oddly satisfying technical integrity, and while Sam was undoubtedly trying to describe a physical object, he evokes a more general form, a kind of lattice or matrix that doesn't have the immediate tangible quality of, say, a fishing net.

This now seems quite apt, since today a network is likely to be a complex system of relationships that we can't necessarily see or touch – between computers, people or neurons. The word and its definition suggest a link between our own era, with its network of networks, and Sam's, in which a technology – print – created new channels of communication. Printing with movable type had been possible since the second half of the fifteenth century, but now it had come of age. The result was a cultural explosion, changing both public and private life. Books, images and ideas could travel further and more freely. Authors began to think of their works as being infinitely reproducible, rather than having a limited circulation; as the presentation of those works was standardized, and as their readership expanded, so they felt a greater need to express their individuality, the idiosyncrasies of self. Memory played less of a role in the transmission of texts, information and opinions. Readers' literary diets became more varied. Teaching changed. Preaching changed. The mechanisms of politics changed. The production of literature (in the broadest sense of that word) became a playground for entrepreneurs. Yet the growth of opportunities for sharing knowledge, keeping records and doing business created anxieties about privacy, piracy, the precariousness of social order and the very stability of truth itself.

All these concerns are resonant today. The last of them, apparent in the ubiquity of the word *post-truth*, feels especially troublesome and seems to fester among the reticulations and decussations of social media. It's natural to think of social media as a creation of the twenty-first century, but it is much older than we tend to imagine. The ancient Romans got their news from papyrus rolls – the stories copied, filtered and amplified in ways that feel modern. If we focus specifically on Britain, we see in the manuscript culture of the sixteenth century something more than a little like Twitter, with wannabes promoting themselves and drawing attention to publications they rated, as one might now retweet something amusing or admirable. Starting in the seventeenth century, coffee houses functioned in ways that foreshadowed the tumultuous topicality of internet discussion forums.[1] As so often, a phenomenon that appears novel is more like a rebirth.

In the realm of social media and post-truth, one of Sam's most to-the-point remarks is this, from *Idler* 80: 'We are inclined to believe those whom we do not know, because they have never deceived us.' Here he anticipates a pestilential feature of life online, the widespread willingness to put faith in wholly unproven sources. The social-media-savvy Samuel Johnson is an odd conceit, arguably as chimerical as the 'alternative facts' of post-truth politics, but he is present in the pages of *Dr Johnson's Dictionary of Modern Life*, published in 2010 by advertising executive Tom Morton, who originally launched the project on Twitter. 'Samuel Johnson . . . lives again within the pages of this book,' wrote Graham Linehan, creator of such cherished sitcoms as *The IT Crowd* and *Father Ted*. In truth, the tone of Morton's book is often closer to Ambrose Bierce's satirical *The Devil's Dictionary* than to anything Sam wrote. But many of the definitions are very funny, and although most focus on ephemeral phenomena – *PlayStation*, 'wondrous Obsidian Obelisk that does dominate both the Room &, more oft, the Life of its Owner' – some have more scope to endure – *Spin Doctor*, 'Showman task'd with th'impossible Endeavour of lowering the Esteem in which the Publick do hold Politicians.'

Sam's real *Dictionary* definitions are rarely this playful, but there are moments when he is enjoyably caustic, as in the entry for *excise*, part of which I cited in Chapter 15: 'A hateful tax levied upon commodities, and adjudged not by the common judges of property, but wretches hired by those to whom excise is paid.' His definitions can pack a great deal of worldliness and insight in a small space, and in some there's a single verb or adjective that stands out like the wagging finger of judgement: a *fortuneteller* is 'one who cheats common people by pretending to the knowledge of futurity', a *pressgang* is 'A crew that strolls about the streets to force men into naval service', and *suicide* is 'The horrid crime of destroying oneself'. Given his ability to sum up a whole swarm of society's ills in a handful of words, the idea of transporting him into the twenty-first century is appealing, and it's more than just a frivolous gimmick to imagine him casting a discerning eye over the trashier trappings of modernity.

Somehow I don't think Sam would have been keen on posting selfies, but a lot of people would have wanted him to appear in a selfie alongside them, looking grave while they gurned for the camera. He would have grasped immediately that in the arena of social media, people present an embellished version of themselves. It is easy to look at the evidence they broadcast and believe that their lives are more glamorous and interesting than ours. But they are omitting all the dullness of their existence (or, if they acknowledge it, exaggerating for comic effect), and though we imagine that they are likely to regard our lives as flat, they find plenty to envy. This may not be the case right across the board, but it's one of the more perturbing truths of social media: we feel bad because we believe we don't have what others have – a superb physique, a beautiful home, a wide circle of cool friends, perfect children, idyllic holidays – yet in fact they don't have those things either, or have a much less rosy relationship with them than we infer. We waste our lives fretting about some sorry inadequacy when in fact we're in the grip of a delusion. All the while, our lives look different (and better) to other people from the way they look to us. What we may see as deficits – our not having children, perhaps – others may see as a lack of encumbrances. What we see as encumbrances – our untameable hair, a job that entails huge amounts of travel, a vast extended family – they may see as glorious gifts.

In saying this, it's essential to point up a further truth: other people spend less time thinking about us than we imagine. Sam identified our inability to see this as an adolescent trait, easily carried over into adulthood: 'He that has not yet remarked how little attention his contemporaries can spare from their own affairs, conceives all eyes turned upon himself, and imagines every one . . . to be an enemy or a follower, an admirer or a spy.' Yet there will usually be a few people who spend a lot more time thinking about you than you're likely either to suppose or to find comfortable. Social media illustrates both these points very well. Those of us who use it become experts in the art of ignoring and over-looking (or so we think), but are also at the mercy of silent obsession and covetous resentment.

So what would Sam have made of Facebook? Some readers may hold the question cheap, but Facebook is used by about a third of the world's population and has altered the landscape of, among other things, advertising, politics and journalism. In the process it has achieved a degree of scale and influence that make it not only an almost inescap-able object of interest, but also, as Sam would have noticed, a hostage to the risk of massive disenchantment. Besides, as an archive of the self and of relationships, it could scarcely have failed to fascinate someone so keenly concerned with memory and biography. He would have seen it, I think, as a space for vanity and self-deception, as an opportunity for selective attention at its most febrile, and above all as envy's playground. 'All envy would be extinguished,' he wrote in the *Idler*, 'if it were universally known that there are none to be envied', and in the *Rambler* he remarked that life will always 'incline us to estimate the advantages which are in the possession of others above their real value'. Envy is 'a stubborn weed of the mind', he wrote in another *Rambler* essay, and it ensnares those who 'propose no advantage to themselves but the satisfaction of poisoning the banquet which they cannot taste, and blasting the harvest which they have no right to reap'. These last images are especially sug-gestive; they sum up two of the besetting vices of those social media users who seem able to type faster than they can think.

ᴥ 25 ᴥ

On the business of a Club – being not 'a heavy stick; a staff
intended for offence' but rather 'an assembly of good fellows'
(where the staff may cause offence, without intent)

THE MECHANISMS of sociability were, of course, very different in the eighteenth century. Letters played an especially
important role and were the best substitute for face-to-face
conversation. Besides being a vital means of maintaining
individual relationships, they were often shared around,
with the result that they bolstered social networks and stimulated debate. Like so many of his contemporaries, Sam was
a frequent correspondent, though not on the whole a jaunty
one. He favoured a blunt epistolary style and demurred
from the common view that a personal letter was a guileless
expression of intimacy. It seemed to him not wonderfully
revealing of hidden truths, but instead 'a calm and deliberate performance', and he believed that 'no transaction . . .
offers stronger temptations to fallacy and sophistication'.

Still, beginning in the second half of the 1760s his correspondence becomes noticeably less functional and more
artful. Although the letters he writes to Hester Thrale are
his richest, plenty of others show him nurturing relationships, and in even the most perfunctory we find him
hatching plans or making himself useful, whether it's looking forward to drinking tea with the shy and scholarly
Thomas Warton or picturing the cake he'll eat with his
Lichfield friend Elizabeth Aston, sharing a book with

Edmund Burke or seeking help with getting an old acquaintance's son discharged from the navy.

He had a broad sense of what letters could achieve, differentiating between those that were plain and purposeful (containing 'business' or 'intelligence') and uninformative ones that existed in order to preserve contact (and were heavily decorated, since 'trifles always require exuberance of ornament'). Here as elsewhere, his understanding of style was more flexible than tends to be claimed, for he thought that every item of correspondence should be tuned to its recipient and occasion. He also differed from most of his contemporaries in thinking of a conversational style not as the natural mode of letter-writing, but as one of several options – and as easy enough to aspire to, yet difficult to achieve.

The main reason for this was his unusually elevated idea of conversation, which he regarded as a source of good health. After the mental invigoration accomplished by physical exercise, it was 'the most eligible amusement of a rational being'. What was more, conversation wasn't something that could be simulated. Proceeding from gregarious closeness, it was more like an atmosphere than a technique – a communing with others that could also be a communing with oneself. Today we are inclined to think of conversation as something that needs lubricating (perhaps with alcohol or jokes), but Sam thought of it as the lubricant, akin to trust in its capacity to foster sociability.

At the heart of social activity Sam saw 'the general desire of happiness' – and happiness was, he believed, 'the only thing of real value in existence'. The means by which he cultivated it are worth examining. Any credible account of his life, no matter how much it insists on his pains and dreads, will be full of meals and visits, conversations and storytelling, evidence of friendship and camaraderie. In his later years, having no family of his own besides his step-daughter Lucy Porter, he acquired alternative families (at the Thrales', and in his own domestic space), and the time he spent among them, for all its melancholy moments, was rich with laughter.

The sociable Samuel Johnson was fond of clubs. The first in which he played an active part was the Ivy Lane Club, which, beginning in the winter of 1748, met each Tuesday evening at the King's Head, a steakhouse near St Paul's cathedral. Its more famous successor, now often simply called Johnson's Club, first met in 1764 at the Turk's Head, a pub in Soho on a site where today there is an Asian supermarket. The founder members included Burke, Sir Joshua Reynolds and Oliver Goldsmith, the last of whom proved a nuisance, always trying to ride the surf of discussion and prompting Sam to comment that 'he goes on without knowing how he is to get off'. Among those who joined later were Adam Smith, the father of free-market economics; Edward Gibbon, author of the *History of the Decline and Fall of the Roman Empire*; Charles James Fox, who was three times Foreign Secretary; and the playwright Richard Brinsley Sheridan, best known for his comedies *The School for Scandal* and *The Rivals*. When Sam died, membership stood at thirty-five. There were no women, and Reynolds succeeded in keeping out any other painters; as in most institutions of its kind, noble talk of equality and accord didn't put a stop to internal politicking.

At the time Johnson's Club began, there were around 2,000 societies in London that met his *Dictionary* definition – 'an assembly of good fellows meeting under certain conditions'. That sounds vague, and Henry John Todd, who updated the *Dictionary* in the early nineteenth century, noted that 'a club is not always "an assembly of good fellows" in Dr Johnson's meaning; but an association of persons subjected to particular rules'. Todd's point was twofold: membership was restricted, and some clubs were a home from home for those hung up on gambling, political agitation or unorthodox sexual practices. Certainly they came in different shapes and sizes, and some clubs' preoccupations were weird – a tendency satirized as early as 1709 by the poet Ned Ward. In *The Secret History of Clubs*, Ward wrote about groups that didn't exist but very well could have done; these included the Farting Club, whose members met to 'poison the neighbouring air with their unsavoury crepitations'.[1]

In reality, while there were mixed clubs and all-female ones, the vast majority were exclusively male, and they indulged a male enthusiasm for odd little ceremonies, customs, fines and toasts. It is easy to dismiss such coteries as realms of fantasy, as breeding grounds for pettiness and snobbery, as mechanisms for reinforcing elitism or sexism. They can be cradles of criminality, and often they're places of debauchery. Behind closed doors, members indulge in gossip or grease the wheels of nepotism. But clubs offer a refuge from the workplace and an alternative to the familiar tone of family life. They play a role in nurturing local identity or other kinds of solidarity (intellectual, political, artistic, and so on). For Sam and his contemporaries, they were a sphere in which to discuss new ideas – scenes of communion, not conspiracy.

The growth of these institutions, most of which were voluntary and secular, began in the seventeenth century and rocketed in Sam's lifetime, reflecting the increasingly urban nature of Britain. Much of their activity happened at night. Street lighting had arrived in London in the 1680s; in the decades that followed, the night, instead of being a time for inertia or fear, became a social space, a scene of what the philosopher Lord Shaftesbury called 'amicable collision'.[2] Often fuelled by invigorating and newly fashionable coffee and tea, rather than by soporific wine, club life was, above all, dense with talk.

It is not hard to imagine what Sam's fellow clubmen got from him. By the 1760s he had become the sort of elder statesman who routinely dispenses wise advice. In the press he was 'voluminous Mr Johnson', Chief Justice of the Court of Criticism, a 'walking library'; to one of his critics he was Old Atlas, who imagined that he was carrying the world on his shoulders, and to one of his admirers, aware of such snarks, he was a lion surrounded by chattering monkeys.[3] For those who had direct access to his powers of counsel and judgement, rather than merely hearing about them, he was a modern Solomon.

What, though, did Sam get from his clubs? He enjoyed their competitive buoyancy, and enjoyed eating good food. There was the pleasure of access to other people's intimate thoughts, though when the scatterbrained Goldsmith argued that bringing in new members would spice up the debate, since all involved 'had travelled over each other's minds', Sam was indignant – 'You have not travelled over my mind, I promise you.' For most people, regardless of the subjects discussed and the productive differences of opinion, the reward of membership is at root the simple pleasure of togetherness. Contact, and a sense of belonging, of being endorsed by others. But for Sam it was conversation that mattered most in the life of the club. He needed it. He needed to exercise his talent for it, which prompted Boswell to claim that 'his language was so accurate, and his sentences so neatly constructed, that his conversation might have been all printed without any correction'. But, more than that, he needed its presence: to engage in dialogue was to escape introspection.

In *Rambler* 89, he observes that people who are in the business of serious thought are likely to spend a lot of time on their own. They must compensate for this, banishing self-scrutiny through 'that interchange of thoughts which is practised in free and easy conversation'. Here he may be recalling Michel de Montaigne, who in his essay on the art of conversation described it as a kind of exercise, invigorating the mind after the 'languid' and 'feeble' study of books. For Montaigne, 'This world is but a school of inquiry', and it is through talking wisely and in an orderly fashion that one learns most.[4] Sam's facility for such conversation is apparent in Boswell's *Life of Johnson*. As Fanny Burney noted when the *Life* came out, its record of his talk kept 'filling all sorts of readers with amaze, except the small party to whom Dr Johnson was known'.

But of course, not all conversation is good. Sometimes it can be trite, hurtful or dishonest, and sometimes it can simply be awkward. Montaigne deplored conversation that was defensive or blandly compliant. He felt the same way about pushful cleverness – exhibitionism was a way of masking meagre content. Sam was similarly averse to meek agreement and pretentiousness, as well as to mere chitchat ('we had *talk* enough, but no *conversation*; there was nothing *discussed*'). In *Rambler* 14, he noted that many writers are poor conversationalists, and in the *Life of Savage* he applauded his old friend's powers of listening ('He mingled in cursory conversation with the same steadiness of attention as others apply to a lecture'), thereby hinting at a common social problem – the listener whose concentration wanders like smoke.

At the same time, he understands that in some conversations the fact of engagement is more important than its terms. 'It is commonly observed,' he wrote, 'that when two Englishmen meet, their first talk is of the weather.' The English are not alone in doing this, but it is a habit that amuses visitors to England, since English weather, while changeable, is less extreme than that of most other places. Yet the truth is that while talking about the weather may be an attempt to master its peculiarities, mostly it's a means of overcoming inhibitions in unfamiliar company: the weather, for all its fluctuations, is a safe subject, unlikely to lead to confrontation, and a stranger's attitude to it can be a good indication of their mood.

What Sam recognizes is that weather chat isn't obsessively precise. When we embark on the subject, we are 'in haste to tell each other, what each must already know'. That element of obviousness is key – a means of establishing common ground. Compare with this the way people converse about their cars, minutely commenting on engine size, acceleration, torque and fuel economy. At the time of writing, I've within the last twenty-four hours had a conversation in which a friend mentioned that his car has a boot capacity of 1,851 litres with the rear seats down and torque of 273 pounds per foot. By contrast, in talking about the weather I've never known someone refer to anything more technical than temperatures and (occasionally) wind speed. Considering we're fixated with the subject, we're remarkably ill equipped to discuss it, and that's because doing so is a performance of rapport, not meteorology.

When Sam defined *rapport*, signifying 'relation; reference; proportion', he commented that the word had failed to catch on. Since then it has gained ground, but when we use it today it's with a nod to Freud: rapport is the sympathetic connection between a patient and therapist, though its sense has broadened – it's now any kind of close mutual understanding. Even if Sam wasn't keen to adopt the term (too French), he cherished the concept, and his model of how not to socialize was a writer whose failures of rapport were legendary. This was Jonathan Swift, sardonic and twisted, addicted to hoaxes yet unable to laugh, permanently disgusted by the world. 'He seems to have wasted life in discontent,' wrote Sam; his chief pleasure lay in 'depravity of intellect', an enjoyment of the sort of thoughts 'from which almost every other mind shrinks with disgust'. Crucially, and disastrously, Swift was fond of 'singularity', a vice analysed in the *Adventurer*. What Sam called singularity consisted of an arrogant contempt for the normal way of doing things. When Swift was sick, he insisted that his ailments, despite their familiar symptoms, were unique. And when visitors turned up expecting dinner, he would give each of them a shilling, so that they might provide themselves with food.

Sam abhorred singularity because 'voluntary neglect of common forms' – the conviction that one 'is an odd fellow, and must be let alone' – involves excessive pride. It suggests a disdain for the rest of society and an assumption that one's merit is exceptional. In moral questions, he concedes, one must 'hold no consultations with fashion'. Here, certainly, it is noble to stand alone:

> To be pious among infidels, to be disinterested in a time
> of general venality, to lead a life of virtue and reason in
> the midst of sensualists, is a proof of a mind intent on
> nobler things than the praise or blame of men, of a soul
> fixed in the contemplation of the highest good, and
> superior to the tyranny of custom and example.

But in the usual course of life, compliance with the broad norms of behaviour is prudent. Many people make the mistake of thinking that such amenability is somehow inauthentic, a failure to be true to oneself. They misunderstand complaisance as insincerity and think of conventionality as mere performance – a kind of barrier rather than a form of emollient.[5]

Intriguingly, this is one of several points of connection between Sam's ideas and those of Confucius. We might assume that he knew nothing of this Chinese sage, born more than two millennia before him, but in fact he wrote about him in the *Gentleman's Magazine*, applauding his 'philosophical dignity'. In the eighteenth century, accounts in English of Chinese thought were often garbled, but Sam's was lucid even if necessarily limited. While Confucius's manner was cryptic and far more didactic than his own, Sam shared his interest in thinking seriously about social matters, and was naturally struck by his statement that, if called on to govern a country, his first act would be to rectify the names of all things. Besides having a Confucian talent for giving memorable advice, he shared his understanding of the importance of ritual – the very kind of procedures practised in clubs, where ceremony and protocol existed to avert the risk of disorder. For Sam, *ritual* was most of the time an adjective, and where we would use it as a noun he tended to refer to *rite*, *solemnity* or *observance*, which he characterized in terms of respect, reverence, attentiveness and dignity. These qualities, present in his private devotions, were ones he hoped to carry over into his public life. We know that he didn't always manage to achieve this, but he understood that in adapting himself to the rituals of sociability he had an opportunity for self-reform.

We are now inclined to see ritual as stifling, even to dismiss it as jejune nonsense. Yet ritual can liberate us from the constraints of the everyday and adjust our perception of the world around us. Worship is one way to achieve this, but the transformative effect of ritual need not be confined to religious practices, or even to quasi-religious ones such as yoga or a therapy session. Ritual removes us from the frictions of our familiar reality. In doing so it enables us to see the extent to which our lives are full of routines and compulsive behaviours that are hollow. It heightens our awareness of habit, the mechanisms of our ordinariness, and it inspires us to think about how we might change those mechanisms and change that ordinariness. By observing the frameworks of ritual, we pay new attention to all the other framing devices that shape our lives, many of which are pointless or counterproductive.

26

A chapter upon Samuel Johnson's lawyerly inclinations,
in which we may wonder at the conduct of Signor Giuseppe
Baretti and the philosophy of Dr George Berkeley – of
whom, we can be sure, only the latter was fit to
be a bishop

OF ALL THE PEOPLE with whom Sam socialized, none was more mercurial than the linguist and travel writer Giuseppe Baretti. Known for his strong prejudices and prickly manner, he was ten years Sam's junior. He had grown up in Turin and since his twenties had made it his business to alienate people with heated outbursts and a litany of contemptuous opinions – about the playwright Carlo Goldoni, the study of archaeology, and many of his fellow linguists. One evening in October 1769, Baretti was walking along London's Haymarket when, near the junction with Panton Street, he was accosted by a couple of prostitutes. Apparently one of them asked him to buy her a glass of wine. He took exception to her grasping at his crotch and struck her companion. Three pimps then lurched out of the darkness and tried to shove him into a puddle. In the ensuing scuffle, Baretti stabbed one of them, Evan Morgan, with a fruit knife that he habitually carried (a custom of his people in Italy, he would later explain). The wounds were fatal, and Baretti was accused of murder. When he stood trial at the Old Bailey, Sam's character evidence was crucial to his acquittal, and the Italian's own arguments were shaped by Sam's understanding of the law surrounding provocation and self-defence, as well as showing signs of carefully measured Johnsonian phrasing.

This was far from being the first occasion when Sam displayed an interest in the law as a profession and intellectual discipline. As a young man he seriously considered a legal career, and his decision not to pursue one would later haunt him. Many who encountered the mature Samuel Johnson thought him perfectly suited to the law – by his acuity, fine understanding of subtle points of language, wide range of knowledge, moral seriousness and capacity for taking up cases that were not his own. His familiarity with important books about the law was impressive, and the eminent modern jurist Lord Bingham of Cornhill comments that his library was 'a remarkable treasure-trove of legal knowledge for a literary man' and that 'he would have been a brilliant advocate and a wise, erudite, compassionate and constructive judge'.[1] We get a flavour of Sam the judge-who-never-was in *Rambler* 79, when he writes that 'Whoever commits a fraud is guilty not only of the particular injury to him who he deceives, but of the diminution of that confidence which constitutes not only the ease but the existence of society'. We also discern it in Hester Thrale's report of his saying that 'The law is the last result of human wisdom acting upon human experience for the benefit of the public.'

Boswell, who practised as an advocate (barrister) in Scotland, often sought his opinion on questions of law. Sam was directly involved in several other cases, and his most significant contribution to the field came in the 1760s, when he collaborated with Robert Chambers, the newly appointed Vinerian Professor of Law at Oxford. Chambers struggled to draft the lectures he was required to deliver; his sure grasp of jurisprudence was not matched by an ability to write clearly and briskly. The help that Sam provided, though mostly editorial rather than technical, included some trenchant thoughts on the triple benefits of punishment, which secured the public from criminals, made a form of reparation to the victim and held out the promise of rehabilitation for the offender. The collaboration was at the time unknown and potentially embarrassing, with only Hester Thrale having an inkling of what they were up to. It fortified Sam's sense of the need for what in Chambers' lectures is called 'public wisdom' – a governing power that, as he put it to Boswell a few years later, 'gives every man a rule of action, and prescribes a mode of conduct which shall entitle him to the support and protection of society'. 'That the law may be a rule of action,' he explained, 'it is necessary that it be known', and 'it is necessary that it be permanent and stable'. This enables 'the deficiencies of private understanding . . . to be supplied' and creates laws 'not . . . for particular cases, but for men in general'.

Sam's friends enjoyed calling upon his legislative powers, not just because they admired his legal knowledge and incisiveness, but also because doing so yielded anecdote. When delivered in person, rather than on the page, his pronouncements were likely to have a special degree of brio, and for reasons that will be obvious, no one was keener than Boswell on getting him to hand down zippy judgements. One of the most famous examples occurred in 1763, when Boswell was heading to Holland and said goodbye to Sam at Harwich. He was off to study law in Utrecht; though his time there would be unhappy, he would draw comfort from reading the *Rambler* ('several papers seem to have been written just for me') and from being able to have newsworthy encounters with eminent Europeans. After he quit Utrecht in the summer of 1764, he travelled to Germany, where he hoped to meet the Prussian king, Frederick the Great. This didn't happen, but there were compensations; before the year was out he met two of the most famous people in Europe. When he ventured to the tiny Swiss village of Môtiers, he was granted an audience with Jean-Jacques Rousseau, who disconcerted him with the information that 'Only by doing good can you undo evil'. Not long after that he was in Ferney, close to Geneva, to visit Voltaire, with whom he argued about the immortality of the soul (something in which Boswell was keen to believe).[2] Both encounters shaped his understanding of literary fame – the degree to which authors craved renown, and the ways in which they manipulated public curiosity.

But that day in August 1763, he had another redoubtable thinker on his mind. As he and Sam strolled to the beach in Harwich, they discussed what Boswell took to be the philosopher George Berkeley's belief that matter does not exist. (In fact, Berkeley, a pious and scholarly Irish bishop, argued something a little different: that the attributes we ascribe to objects exist only in our perceptions.) Boswell reports that 'though we are satisfied his doctrine is not true, it is impossible to refute it'. Then: 'I shall never forget the alacrity with which Johnson answered, striking his foot with mighty force against a large stone, till he rebounded from it, "I refute it *thus*."' The last four words are the bit that people remember: plenty have regarded this as an example of Sam's common sense, and plenty have seen it as absurdly pudding-headed.

The way the story is repeated, especially by incredulous philosophers, it's as if Sam thought that by seeing the stone move he'd proved that it existed. But he knew more than the episode, as commonly reported, makes it appear. He was aware that Berkeley had attributed a special importance to our sense of touch, and he was familiar with the writings of David Hartley, who had argued that the contraction of our muscles, when we exert ourselves against resistance (whether it's a dumb-bell or a large stone), delivers the essential properties of matter to the mind. A different reading, then, is that the stone moved Sam, and the proof for him of its independent existence was its power to repel his foot. His response to Boswell will always be cherished by people who think of philosophy as disingenuous sophistry, and others will see in it a peculiarly English refusal to engage in abstract thought.

The phrase 'I refute it *thus*' is indelibly associated with Samuel Johnson, and its appeal lies in its vim, the impromptu snap and vigour of defiance. Though this is only one of his modes, it has defined his posthumous reputation because it produces such quoteworthy lines, so many of which are put-downs. For instance, there's the more obviously flippant remark he is supposed to have made to a fan of Berkeley's ideas: 'Pray, sir, don't leave us; for we may, perhaps, forget to think of you, and then you will cease to exist.' Of a tiresome person he could say, 'That fellow seems to me to possess but one idea, and that is a wrong one'; of a poor piece of roast mutton, 'It is as bad as bad can be: it is ill-fed, ill-killed, ill-kept, and ill-drest'; of the witty, shy politician Dudley Long, 'He fills a chair'; of two poets whose merits were being compared, 'There is no settling the point of precedency between a louse and a flea'; and of the Giant's Causeway, 'Worth seeing? Yes; but not worth going to see.'

For some, comment of this kind is rudely dismissive and warrants no analysis. Yet for many it's attractive, because it deals succinctly and decisively with matters we're used to hearing discussed in a long-winded or woolly fashion. This is the legislative Johnson, who closes down a debate not because his mind is narrow, but because he knows that humanity's great enthusiasm for discussion is matched by a great desire for finality. We can make any of his 'closing' judgements our own, recycling or modifying it, pretending that it's something we've invented or making a show of having encountered and remembered it. Utterances of this kind are most enjoyable, I think, when they come from a person and a time far removed from us. Vividly durable, they function like a bridge: we not only see a remote moment, but find ourselves in it, laughing, observing. My hunch is that everyone who reads the story of Johnson kicking the stone pictures him doing so, pictures being present (the image is a little hazy – details of attire and hairstyle remain vague), and hears in 'I refute it *thus*' – specifically in Boswell's italicized *thus* – another word, *ouch*, or perhaps, in the idiom of the day, *hegh*. The episode may not help us understand the intricacies of philosophy, but it makes us feel close to him.

✎ 27 ✎

In which at last we attend to the life and loves of
Hester Thrale, a foisonous fund of Anecdote

THOSE CURIOUS about Sam, in his own lifetime and ever
since, are nourished by the impression of his being a
person remarkable in his humanity and in the breadth of
his achievements. Yet there is also a nagging sense of his
strangeness – his being not just Mr Oddity, a living anthology of mannerisms, but also more than a little weird about
family and friendship, women and sex. For anyone interested in Sam's stranger aspects, the place to look has long
seemed to be his close friendship with Hester Thrale. When
she documented their relationship, it was under the title
Anecdotes of the Late Samuel Johnson, and alert readers would
have been reminded of Sam's definition of *anecdote* as 'secret
history'.

Samuel Johnson is a figure wrapped in anecdote. He
lived in an age when it was in vogue as a form of entertainment, an accessory of smart conversation, and stories about
him circulated widely because he was a celebrity. Not in
quite the modern sense, admittedly, since he was renowned
for his accomplishments, rather than as a result of frenzied
self-promotion or being the child of someone famous. But
people who knew him wanted to tell stories about him –
partly for the sheer pleasure of doing so and basking in the
warm light of his vitality, and partly because the very fact of
their having such stories to tell was proof of their intimacy

with the great man. Meanwhile, those who didn't know him delighted in these stories, which gave them access to his mystery and spoke vividly of life's charm and peculiarity. So the stories multiplied, and, as Sam commented, their effect was inhibiting: 'I am prevented many frolics that I should like very well, since I am become such a theme for the papers.'

When *Anecdotes of the Late Samuel Johnson* came out in 1786, readers pounced upon the book, for it was widely understood that he had bared himself to Mrs Thrale as to no other. The public's expectations of an intimate portrait, containing major revelations as well as a fresh instalment of Sam's sharp remarks and wise observations, meant that within six weeks of publication the *Anecdotes* had sold around 5,000 copies – a high figure at a time when a season's leading bestseller would sell 10,000. The *Monthly Review* in May 1786 commented that 'The name of Thrale had been long made known to the public' and readers were therefore likely to 'expect great entertainment'. In the opinion of its critic, the *Anecdotes* contained 'much that ought to have been suppressed' and risked leaving the reader 'disgusted with egotisms'.[1] Frankly, this is the kind of bad review that prompts sales rather than discouraging them, and it reinforced the impression that Hester Thrale had had unusually privileged access to the private Sam.

Besides the *Anecdotes*, there is ample evidence of their closeness. More than 370 of his letters to her survive, whereas we have a record of only one of his letters to Tetty (in which he speaks of her being 'exposed by my means to miseries which I could not relieve'). Their exchanges bear out the truth of John Donne's delicious line that 'more than kisses, letters mingle souls'. Though some of what passed between them was banal, he would often write to her warmly, in a relaxed and affectionate style, and she responded volubly. 'Your letters,' he could say, 'give me a great part of the pleasure which a life of solitude admits.' Once, when he felt she had gone too long without writing to him, he prodded her about this 'omission' before launching, half in self-pity and half with an appropriate sense of the absurd, into 'the history of one of my toes'.

In person, as on the page, Hester Thrale was lively. Petite (she stood just 4'11"), with a birdlike angularity and oddly large hands, she combined wit, attentiveness and practicality. When Arthur Murphy introduced her to Sam in January 1765, it was just fifteen months since she had wed Henry Thrale, a rich brewer with twin weaknesses for food and philandering, but already she was eager to compensate for the frustrations of her marriage. Sam was the remedy – entertaining, knowledgeable, appreciative. Soon he was a frequent visitor to the Thrales' townhouse. This stood next to the brewery in the ominously named Dead Man's Place in Southwark, a district for which Henry that year became the MP. But it was at their villa six miles south-west of town that he found a sanctuary. Streatham Park, built in 1730, stood in 109 acres lined with English elms, and there was room enough for him to be assigned his own apartment there, complete with large bed and mahogany bidet.[2]

For all his quirks, Sam was a reassuring presence. While Henry appreciated his guest's varied conversation and would eventually find him an ally in both politics and business, Sam thought Mr Thrale skilful in trade and sound in understanding, a man of some scholarship and firm principles. On the last point he was wrong, but their friendship burgeoned, and all the while he and Hester could share their secrets, in the course of which he proved particularly good at listening to complaints that her husband preferred to brush aside. The Thrales' children came to think of Sam as a most welcome component of the household; in the words of his biographer Walter Jackson Bate, they treated him as 'a combination of friend and a sort of toy elephant'.[3] He was also a project, a grand charity case in which Hester could invest her energies. Despite being more than thirty years Sam's junior, she was as much a mother figure to him as a surrogate daughter, taking responsibility for keeping him in good health and entertaining him. That could mean supplying him with pineapples and strawberries or providing mental stimulation. Towards the end of his life he reflected on her kindness and with raw emotion thanked her for having 'soothed twenty years of a life radically wretched'. His true mother had done less.

Hester Thrale was his confidante and supervised him in his more man-childish moments of helplessness, but that was not all. Rumours circulated that they were sexual partners, with one newspaper reporting that 'an eminent brewer' had grown 'very jealous of a certain author in folio, and perceived a strong resemblance to him in his eldest son'.[4] Sam shrugged aside this scurrilous chatter, but the letters that passed between the two of them contained hints of an unusual rapport: he called her his 'dear mistress', and she referred to him as 'my inmate'.

During a spell spent at Streatham Park, he entrusted her with a padlock. When her effects were sold in 1823 this was among them, along with a note reading 'Johnson's padlock, committed to my care in 1768'. Did she have to chain him up, or was the padlock a symbol of his slavish devotion, of passions best kept out of sight? If she shackled him, was it to satisfy masochistic cravings? The subject has attracted speculation. In June 1773, Sam wrote a letter to her in French – the language of both love and diplomacy, as cliché

would have it, and also of course one that the family servants weren't likely to understand. In it he showed sensitivity
to her difficult domestic circumstances (her mother was
dying at the time), while also expressing unhappiness about
having to spend so much time in a state of '*solitude profonde*'.
The letter can be read as an elaborate piece of politesse, but
it is a key document for anyone looking for the suppressed
eroticism in their relationship, and some of his imagery is of
a kind that excites the literary historian's inner Freudian
analyst, especially when he refers to her holding him '*dans
l'esclavage*' (in a state of slavery). Her reply is disconcerting,
too, informing him that 'If we go on together your confinement will be as strict as possible' and ending with the
injunction 'do not quarrel with your Governess for not using
the rod enough'. One recent biographer has offered the
tame theory that Sam may have thought he needed to be
restrained with a padlock and fetters because he was afraid
of sleepwalking. Another concludes, less cautiously, that it is
'not surprising . . . that a man tormented by lifelong sin and
guilt would seek penance and want to be gently whipped', a
performance that 'both satisfied and punished his sexual
urges'.[5]

Purchasers of *Anecdotes of the Late Samuel Johnson* didn't
know about the padlock, but they expected some special
matters of the heart to be unclasped by Mrs Thrale. In fact,
by the time the book came out, this was no longer her name.
Henry Thrale died in 1781 of a stroke ('I never had such a
friend,' declared Sam), and in July 1784, having secured her
future by selling his brewery for £135,000, Hester married
again. Her new husband was Gabriel Piozzi, a musician
from Brescia who had lived in London for around eight
years. She had originally met Piozzi through Charles Burney,
and soon afterwards recruited him to give singing lessons to

her daughter Hester Maria (known as 'Queeney', much admired by Sam, and later the wife of a distinguished Scottish admiral). The relationship with Piozzi deepened, and though she knew that marrying him would be controversial, she believed she could introduce him into polite society.

Sam was appalled by her choice of second husband. Besides being a singer, Piozzi was a Roman Catholic, which by the prevailing standards of the day made him a thoroughly unsuitable match. Since he was an Italian, malicious observers also assumed that he was oversexed and that the widowed Mrs Thrale's enthusiasm for him was shamefully sensual. Sam made his feelings plain in a letter written on 2 July, accusing her of having 'forfeited your fame, and your country' as well as having 'abandoned your children and your religion'. 'You are ignominiously married,' he thundered, and many others agreed, with her rival literary hostess Elizabeth Montagu declaring, 'I am myself convinced that the poor woman is mad.' Yet even as Sam condemned her choice, he tried to give her practical counsel, and near the end of his final letter to her, six days later, he revealed his vulnerability, writing that 'The tears stand in my eyes.'

Once it became clear that she was not going to be persuaded, Sam was done with her. The rupture was complete and irreversible. If he chanced on one of her old letters, he destroyed it. 'I have burnt all I can find,' he told Fanny Burney – though a few that he didn't immediately discover he later deliberately preserved. 'I drive her quite from my mind,' he insisted, and Burney was struck by his vehemence. She had often been at Streatham when Sam was in sportive mood and the company feasted on venison, pineapples, nectarines and ices. But now he was dining on bitterness: 'I drive her, as I said, wholly from my mind.'

This turn of phrase, tellingly in the present tense rather

than the past, will be familiar to all of us from conversation with people who are not in fact able to expel their past loves from their thoughts. His letters to Hester Thrale are his record of what he called 'a little paradise' – of Streatham Park and its peaceful rural atmosphere, but also of the idyllic nature of his conversation with someone who understood him, got his references, and appreciated his ironies and wordplay. 'A friendship of twenty years is interwoven with the texture of life,' he had written to her in November 1783; now, in his disappointment, he could not simply shake off something that was part of the fabric of his existence. In truth, her marriage to Piozzi may have hastened his death. He had nursed a fond hope of being her second husband, and she had shocked him by preferring a simple man to a complicated one.

These events, seen from a distance, naturally lend themselves to the sympathetic novelist or dramatist, and in the 1930s another Sam, Samuel Beckett, researched and began work on 'Human Wishes', a play he never completed that took its name from Samuel Johnson's best-known poem. The idea was to start with the death of Henry Thrale and end with the death of Johnson. Beckett, who said half-jokingly that one could write fifty plays about Sam's life, was not the first person to hit upon the idea of dramatizing episodes from it. In 1923, the Philadelphia book collector A. Edward Newton had published *Doctor Johnson: A Play*, in which Fanny Burney refers to Hester Thrale as 'licentious' and Johnson corrects her – 'Why no, Fanny, do not say so. That she should prefer the company of Signor Piozzi to that of a very sick old man is but natural, as it is perhaps but natural that the sick old man should have resented it.'[6]

If Beckett was aware of Newton's efforts, they could hardly have deterred him. *Doctor Johnson: A Play* is the overegged confection of an excitable bibliophile. Beckett was drawn to Sam for less quaint reasons. It is no great surprise that such a chronicler of failure and resilience – later the author of the line 'Ever tried. Ever failed. No matter. Try again. Fail again. Fail better' – should have been attracted to a writer so ravaged by ailments and so eloquent about bleakness and yet also about hope. He was particularly taken with Sam's statement that 'Life is a progress from want to want, not from enjoyment to enjoyment', as well as with his remark, of Brighthelmstone Downs in Sussex, that it was a place 'so truly desolate that if one had a mind to hang one's self for desperation at being obliged to live there, it would be difficult to find a tree on which to fasten the rope'. This looks ahead to *Waiting for Godot*, in which Beckett's characters Vladimir and Estragon, rough-hewn counterparts of Johnson and Savage, contemplate hanging themselves from the one sad tree that's available to them.

'It's Johnson, always Johnson, who is with me,' said Beckett several decades later. 'And if I follow any tradition, it is his.' What he had in mind was the solitary misery of a writer plagued with unwelcome thoughts, able to admit his susceptibilities, bent on self-analysis and stunningly articulate about his doubts and pains. For Beckett, 'doped and buttoned up in sadness', the author of *Rasselas* and the *Rambler* was the poet laureate of death and despair, as well as a master of language, balance and paradox, able to make art out of equivocation.[7] There could be no better inspiration for Beckett's devastating brand of tragicomedy, summed up in his play *Endgame*, where one character remarks that 'Nothing is funnier than unhappiness' and another that 'You're on earth, there's no cure for that.'

In the surviving fragment of 'Human Wishes', Beckett depicts the fractious mood among Sam's fellow lodgers at

Bolt Court, north of Fleet Street, one April evening in 1781. The subject of death is uppermost. Elizabeth Desmoulins accuses Anna Williams of 'the peevishness of decay', and the retired prostitute Poll Carmichael (whose habits of thought Sam once described as 'wiggle-waggle') quotes a sermon on the theme that 'Death meets us everywhere'. Neither Sam nor Hester Thrale appears. It is clear from his notes that Beckett regarded these two as horribly and fascinatingly mismatched, and that he wished to portray Sam caught between the clamour of sociability and the torment of solitude. It's hard to guess, on the basis of only a chunk of the first act, exactly how the play might have developed, but his notes indicate that he was interested in Sam's final decline and the notion of a great man suffering at once an excess of other people's attention and a dispiriting neglect.[8]

Beckett referred to his fascination with the subject as 'my Johnson fantasy'. One of his most astute readers, Frederik N. Smith, suggests that the preparatory work done for 'Human Wishes' heightened the playwright's sense of the tragic nature of Sam's life, with the result that 'the declining Johnson became for him a sort of metaphor of Western man, academic and witty, alone, afraid of dying and yet intrigued by his own physical deterioration'. Unusually, Beckett was interested in Samuel Johnson the writer before he became interested in Samuel Johnson the man, but when he latched on to details of the life he responded to the image of a 'learned mind fastened to a body plagued by physical ailments', and, even as he was abandoning 'Human Wishes', he could write of beginning to grasp how his research 'coincides . . . fundamentally with all I shall ever write or want to write'. Although he never put Sam onstage, many of the characters in his plays and novels feel Johnsonian: intellectually and morally powerful figures who are skilled conversationalists yet also dishevelled and even grotesque, liable to have trouble with their legs or their hearing and to be afflicted with other unfashionable illnesses.[9]

While occupied with 'Human Wishes', Beckett wrote to the poet Thomas McGreevy of his sense that Sam was 'rather absurdly in love' with Hester Thrale. He went on to say, 'It becomes more interesting, the false rage to cover his retreat from her, than the real rage when he realizes that no retreat was necessary, and beneath all, the despair of the lover with nothing to love with.'[10] The last words here reflect Beckett's belief that Sam was impotent – an 'aspermatic colossus' like Lord Gall in his 1933 story 'Echo's Bones'. For Beckett, the presence of Henry Thrale had made this impotence irrelevant, but Henry's death changed that, and Sam, in protesting that he was driving the widowed Hester from his mind, was like a man embarrassed to find himself flexing a muscle that he knows doesn't work.

For Hester Thrale, now Hester Piozzi, there was no question of trying to drive Johnson from her mind. She began the *Anecdotes* a few weeks after his death, while still on a continental honeymoon. It was a project for which she had long been preparing. One wonders how Mr Piozzi felt about her being so involved in transcribing memories of a man who had plainly thought he was a piddling nonentity. But he seems not to have taxed her on the subject, and their trip ended up lasting more than two years: she wrote that living in Venice was akin to visiting the moon, but the months she spent with Piozzi were more like an escape into sunshine.

This was just as well, because Sam's friends shunned her, believing she had treated him shabbily, and when they later ventured into print she appeared in an unfavourable light. Hawkins's biography was explicit about the anguish her second marriage had caused, and hostilities intensified in

March 1788 when she published her correspondence with Sam. Boswell was aggrieved, but the most accusatory voice was that of Giuseppe Baretti. Her relationship with him had long been strained, and now he attacked her in the press, suggesting for instance that one of her sons had died because she'd insisted on his being dosed with quack medicines. In private he was even more outspoken, spattering his copy of the Johnson correspondence with marginalia such as 'You lie' and 'Impudent bitch!'

Yet while Hester Piozzi capitalized on her deep knowledge of Sam with a less than ideal degree of tact, and while her editorial practices were sometimes geared to making herself look as good as possible, the rancour directed at her was tinged with envy. Her enemies were shocked to discover that someone had known their friend better than they had. Though they damned what they claimed were mistakes and fanatical acts of self-justification, the truth was that the letters revealed a relationship both playful and profound. Arthur Murphy, writing in the *Monthly Review*, declared that they 'are often in the language of the heart' and 'We here see Dr Johnson, as it were, behind the curtain . . . retired from the eye of the world, and not knowing that what he was then doing would ever be brought to light'. In short, 'We see him in his undress.'[11] This wasn't the slovenly undress of a person confused by ardour or madness. Rather, it suggested openness and trust, respect and intellectual sympathy. Sometimes it is hard to digest the idea that another person has had such special access to a friend of ours, and in this case there was an added element of professional rivalry, with Sam's biographical legacy not just a matter of honour, but a gold mine.

28

Some ruminations upon scepticism, amid which appear the
names of both Sir Thomas Browne and Scratching Fanny

THE MYTHIC JOHNSON, a creature established in the
popular imagination by the 1770s, is assertive, fond of generalization and capable of dismissing things with a rugged
forcefulness – an idea because it is a 'violation of established
practice', a companion because 'there is nothing *conclusive*
in his talk', the novel *Tristram Shandy* because 'Nothing odd
will do long.' But the 'assertive' Johnson is also the sociable
Johnson, keen on debate, eager to challenge others and to
be challenged. When he issues what looks and sounds like a
cast-iron edict, it is in the hope of further discussion.[1]

As he engaged in debate or brooded over some fashionable new idea, he often hesitated to accept what others were
blithely willing to embrace. With this in mind, Hester Thrale
recalled that 'Mr Johnson's incredulity amounted almost to a
disease'. She makes it sound as though he refused to accept
all but the most basic facts of life; in reality, he was simply
inclined to prefer hard evidence to enthusiastic reports.
In the *Dictionary* he defines *incredulity* as 'hardness of belief'.
By this he means a disinclination to believe things readily,
although he manages to make it look more like a position of
adamantine conviction. The same term occurs to Boswell,
who on one occasion complains that 'He did not give me
full credit when I mentioned that I had carried on a short
conversation by signs with some Esquimaux, who were then

in London'. Continuing his account of Sam's unconvinced-ness, Boswell writes, 'No man was more incredulous as to particular facts, which were at all extraordinary,' adding that no one was 'more scrupulously inquisitive, in order to dis-cover the truth'. What begins as a snapshot of the wounded pride of a young man not given credit for his accomplish-ments ends up as a vision of Sam's rigorous concern with veracity.

Perpetually striking a note of scepticism can make one pretty bad company. No one enjoys talking to a person whose default mode is to challenge every statement they make. (I'm reminded of a fellow student when I was at uni-versity, who would face down even the most humdrum observation with a self-satisfied 'Can you justify that?' This was bearable when debating points of politics, but not when you were saying you preferred brown toast to white.) Yet scepticism is an instrument for finding the truth. It functions like a scalpel: it pierces the flummery of careless assertion and probes the adequacy of our grounds for belief.

People often speak of cynicism when what they are describing is an instance of scepticism. To be cynical is to insist on finding the worst explanation; Sam defines it as 'having the qualities of a dog; currish; brutal'. By contrast, scepticism is a wish to have things explained. The cynic thinks that everything is rotten; the sceptic sees a shiny exte-rior, is aware that it may be a facade masking rottenness, is aware that it may be nothing of the sort, and wants to know more. That scepticism gets folded into cynicism, as if some poky subset of it, seems to be a sign that it is out of fashion. It's seen as an insult to the 'Can do' mentality – as a mech-anism for blocking positivity, a retrograde influence. *Sceptic* suffers from the company it keeps: I most often encounter it in stories about climate change sceptics, and the term is surely worth reclaiming from this degrading collocation. But it is the activity of scepticism that really matters. A world in which one can't ask questions and check how things work (or if they work) is a place of real danger.

A complicating factor here is the existence in philosophy of a specialized meaning for scepticism. It is the doctrine that we cannot attain real knowledge of any kind, a school of thought initiated in Greece nearly 2,500 years ago by Pyrrho, who argued that, since we can't know the truth and our senses are untrustworthy, we should suspend our judgement about all things. Sam encountered the arguments of Pyrrho through later writers, including Sextus Empiricus and the Swiss theologian Jean-Pierre de Crousaz. He has these in mind when he writes his *Dictionary* definition of *sceptic* (or as he prefers, with an eye on the word's Greek root, *skeptick*): 'One who doubts, or pretends to doubt, of every thing.' His own interrogative scepticism differs from this agnostic stance. It has as its motto not the bleak 'No one knows anything', but a more urbane 'Are you sure?' He is suspicious of received wisdom, and he often questions the adequacy of his grounds for holding the beliefs that he does. 'Human experience,' he told Boswell, 'is the great test of truth.' Time and again it is at variance with bloodless theory, and as we seek a richer appreciation of life we have to embrace contradiction, seeing it as a vital instrument of our quest for understanding.

This was one of several points of intellectual kinship with Sir Thomas Browne, a writer whose language and experiments fascinated him. Browne was a medical man, a moralist and natural historian. He was also the originator of many useful words – among them *amphibious*, *anomalous*, *electricity*, *hallucination* and *medical*. In his most intriguing book, *Pseudodoxia Epidemica*, he examines the 'vulgar errors' of his contemporaries. Among these are some laughable popular beliefs about animals: elephants have no joints, peacocks feel shame when they see their own legs, storks will live only in countries that don't have a monarchy, hares are hermaphrodites, and badgers have legs shorter on one side than the other. Browne seeks up-to-date testimony about matters he is unable to examine personally, but aims to scrutinize whatever he can – he keeps a deathwatch beetle in a little box in order to hear the ticking sound it makes, and is intrigued to see what happens when he puts a mole, a viper and a toad in a single glass (the mole comes off best). His methods are patient, and when he finds that a common belief is wrong he is civil and witty about it, rather than gloating.

Sam wrote a short life of his fellow sceptic, published in 1756 as a preface to a new edition of Browne's *Christian Morals*. In portraying him, he seems to shed some light on his own character, as when he refers to the 'troublesome irruptions of scepticism, with which inquisitive minds are frequently harassed'. In admiring *Pseudodoxia Epidemica* as a work that emerged 'not from fancy and invention, but from observation and books' and 'arose gradually to its present bulk by the daily aggregation of new particles of knowledge', he sounds as though he is recalling the labour involved in his own recently completed *Dictionary*.

Other details of Browne's life and work call forth pointed comment. Struck by Browne's failure to write about the years he spent studying abroad, he notes that 'those who are most capable of improving mankind, very frequently neglect to communicate their knowledge'. In another apparent dig at the torpid culture of universities, he observes that 'scholastic and academical life' is 'very uniform' and affords 'more safety than pleasure'. Discussing Browne's style, he commends his having 'augmented our philosophical diction'

– as he too had done in the *Rambler* and the *Dictionary* – and he identifies the fearlessness required to write distinctive prose, describing Browne's 'forcible expressions', verbal flights of fancy 'which would never have been reached, but by one who had very little fear of the shame of falling'. He also applauds his 'exuberance of knowledge', but notes that it sometimes 'obstruct[s] the tendency of his reasoning', and when he turns to Browne's highly unusual exploration of cosmic geometry, *The Garden of Cyrus*, he remarks on the profligacy of writers who channel their energies into producing *jeux d'esprit*: performances of this kind are the 'sport of fancy', and 'It seems to have been, in all ages, the pride of wit, to show how it could exalt the low, and amplify the little.'

This last statement puts me in mind of Sam's rather obtuse line on *Gulliver's Travels* – 'When once you have thought of big men and little men, it is very easy to do all the rest.' What others find ingenious he dismisses as mere tricks of perspective. In the case of *The Garden of Cyrus*, where Browne writes about the 'quincunx' that he again and again finds in art and nature, the problem is that the author has become so obsessed with observing this pattern (⊡) that he sees it in everything. The mixture of scholarly digging and freewheeling, meditative prose is even more eccentric in *Urn Burial*, a survey of funerary customs which elicits the splendidly blasé judgement that 'Of the uselessness of these inquiries, Browne seems not to have been ignorant'. Sam is unimpressed by 'speculatists', over-elaborate philosophers 'who strain their faculties to find in a mine what lies upon the surface'. He prefers the less arcane manner and matter of *Pseudodoxia*, in which the rhetoric, though elaborate, less often eclipses the scientific curiosity.

At the heart of Johnsonian scepticism is a sense of both the ubiquity of falsehood and the limits of what we know. When he writes in the *Lives of the Poets* that 'The basis of all excellence is truth', he is making a specific point about the empty mediocrity of love poetry that's not actually occasioned by love. But it is a broadly revealing statement. Sam knows how many professions of love are made by people who feel none of love's power, and he knows as well how high a proportion of them convince their recipients. In more general terms: the world is full of suave falsity, and it's easy to drift along in its current. Yet to achieve anything of consequence we need to anchor ourselves on solid ground, and we must be vigilant to tell the difference between solidity (which can seem dull) and bullshit (which can appear comfortably fluid or deceptively substantial). To sustain the metaphor, perhaps a bit parlously: we should look to see what's below the waterline.

Sam is especially suspicious of systems and schemes that relieve people of the need to think for themselves. Extreme philosophical positions belong in this category; they strike him not as courageous, but as affected and absurd. 'Of the numberless projects that have flattered mankind with theoretical speciousness,' he writes in *Adventurer* 45, 'few have served any other purpose than to show the ingenuity of their contrivers.' To Boswell he observed, of philosophers whose ideas seemed a mixture of wilful cleverness and vanity, 'Truth, Sir, is a cow which will yield such people no more milk, and so they are gone to milk the bull.'

In fact, the philosophical aberration that drew this pleasantry was scepticism, but it was a particular brand: that of the philosopher David Hume, who argued that our experience of the world is only a series of impressions. Sam regarded Hume as a destructive writer, obsessed with the fallibility of our faculties and the incoherent nature of the mind (to Hume a mere 'bundle or collection of different perceptions'). Although Hume actually rejected the more hardcore forms of scepticism, Sam was troubled by his readiness to cast a shadow of doubt over basic principles such as our understanding of cause and effect.

His own version of scepticism was moderate and localized. One occasion when it served an immediately practical purpose was in 1762. In January of that year a London newspaper, the *Public Ledger*, published several items that mentioned the activities of a poltergeist known as Scratching Fanny – and later more widely known as the Cock Lane Ghost. According to the paper, a young Norfolk woman called Fanny Lynes had fallen for a certain William Kent and, after they moved to London, had been persuaded to represent herself as his wife; Fanny soon became pregnant, and the couple's deception was identified by their Clerkenwell landlord, Richard Parsons, who argued with his lodgers over money matters and later, when Fanny died, supposedly of smallpox, spread the rumour that Kent had murdered her. Excitement around the story arose from one particular detail – Parsons claimed that since Fanny's death his property had been haunted. Fanny's ghost made strange knocking and scratching sounds, and at several seances held there had communicated with his young daughter, conveying the information that Kent had indeed poisoned Fanny. People curious about the phenomenon flocked to the house. Eventually, under the leadership of a local clergyman, a commission investigated, and Sam was part of this. The commission discovered that the ghostly noises were made by Parsons's wife Elizabeth, who was surreptitiously knocking on a wooden board.[2]

Sam was proud of his involvement in exposing the

deception. His approach here was similar to one he had often adopted as an essayist: to confront the seductions of facile or fantastic explanations, to challenge scaremongering and the hysteria of the press. As he had commented in a book review as far back as 1742, 'Distrust quickens . . . discernment of different degrees of probability' and 'animates' the search for evidence. The reference to different degrees of probability is key; he was conscious of how many people were terrible at estimating the likelihood of events, and had observed occasions on which unscientific credulity made it easy for criminals and charlatans to succeed. His awareness of these problems never let up. One of his reasons for being interested in biography was that it is an education in what's probable: learning about other lives improves one's understanding of what might happen in one's own. In thinking about people and what it's plausible they may have seen or done, a constructive scepticism is a corrective to the hyperbole, presumptuousness and spiralling caprice of public opinion.

✥ 29 ✥

A short chapter on politics and public life, wherein
the radical John Wilkes does rear his head

ONLY IN THE 1770s did Sam turn to writing the sort of political pamphlets that his £300-a-year pension had, in many
people's eyes, been designed to encourage. The publications
that resulted were by his own standards undistinguished,
written 'with a fraction of his mind'.[1] *The False Alarm*, scrib-
bled down in the space of twenty-four hours in January 1770,
defended the government's decision to eject from parliament
John Wilkes, the MP for Middlesex. Wilkes was a daring
radical and crackerjack self-publicist whose writings had
been condemned as seditious and obscene, and the 'alarm'
was the result of his supporters persuading voters that his
expulsion was an assault on their liberties. *Thoughts on the Late
Transactions Respecting Falkland's Islands* (1771) argued that there
was no need for a war with Spain to decide the question of
who should be 'the undisputed lords of tempest-beaten
barrenness'. *The Patriot* (1774) was an election pamphlet, written at the urging of Henry Thrale. It contrasted Thrale's
authentic patriotism with the gestures of political agitators
who, like Wilkes, used professions of how much they loved
their country to mask darker purposes. *Taxation No Tyranny*
(1775) condemned the American colonists who were staging
protests – notably the Boston Tea Party of December 1773 –
against the imposition of taxes by a British parliament in
which they were unrepresented. Here Sam would turn out to

be on the wrong side of history, but the pamphlet contains one of his most memorably acerbic lines, as he notes the hypocrisy of people who complain of being oppressed while still feeling able to keep slaves. 'How is it,' he wonders, 'that we hear the loudest yelps for liberty among the drivers of negroes?'

Traditionally he has been represented as a royalist and a conservative, and in adverse accounts as a blindly dictatorial reactionary – which is still how many people picture him. Beginning in the 1960s, the Canadian scholar Donald Greene offered a very different reading: Sam was an instinctive rebel with a deep mistrust of authority. Greene's version proved influential, but its validity has been debated, sometimes with that rancid ferocity that's a common feature of scholarly argument. One aspect of this controversy is the reluctance of some Johnsonians to accept that in the course of a fairly long life their hero might have changed his political outlook. Such a shift hardly seems implausible, but it undermines Sam's image as a figure of unswerving consistency, and there are diehards who insist on his adherence to a strict party line, rather than seeing him as either a realist whose attitudes never quite settled or as a complex individual whose political and personal journeys were equally tortuous.

During his childhood, Sam was surrounded by people who questioned the legitimacy of the Hanoverian succession to the throne. Why was Britain ruled by George I, a German who could speak no English, rather than one of the large number of people more closely related to his predecessor, Queen Anne? The answer, of course, was that George was Anne's nearest Protestant relative; all those with closer ties to her were Catholics, disqualified from inheriting the throne by the 1701 Act of Settlement. Staffordshire, though, was a bastion of support for Anne's Catholic half-brother James, the Prince of Wales.[2] Favour for the cause may have thrived even in Sam's own home – his early biographers identify Michael Johnson as a Jacobite – and the general political mood of Lichfield made a keen impression on him. Yet equally he had friends who were emphatically pro-Hanoverian, such as Gilbert Walmesley.

There is evidence of Jacobite sympathies in some of Sam's early writings. Among these is the pamphlet *Marmor Norfolciense* (1739), a spoof of clodhopping scholarship that was in fact an attack on the German king (George II) and the venal premiership of Robert Walpole. According to Sir John Hawkins, the government reacted so badly to its satire that Sam, once fingered as its author, had to go to ground for a while in 'an obscure lodging in a house in Lambeth marsh'. After the fall of Walpole in 1742, and with Richard Savage no longer in his life, Sam became noticeably less interested in overt politicking of this kind. Later he concentrated on developing a less jarring identity as a judicious non-partisan thinker. When he returned seriously to political writing in the 1770s, his prose was vigorous, but by this time he was prepared to concede that there was no credible alternative to the Hanoverians, reflecting that 'the long consent of the people' meant that 'the family at present on the throne has now established as good a right as the former family'.

'Faction seldom leaves a man honest,' he wrote in his life of John Milton, and in another of the *Lives of the Poets* he identified 'composure' as a desirable alternative to the political sphere's 'tumult of absurdity and clamour of contradiction'. Though he was referring to the instability of the seventeenth century, when 'every man might become a preacher, and almost every preacher could collect a congregation', he was clear that such conditions persisted, imbuing political and religious differences with an ugly emotionalism. In the *Dictionary* he treated *faction* as a synonym for 'discord'; *factious* meant 'Given to faction; loud and violent in a party; publicly dissentious; addicted to form parties and raise public disturbances'. For present purposes, it is less important to identify his (shifting) factional allegiances than to recognize his commitment to certain political causes: the end of slavery, the advancement of women, strong government and renouncing the violent excesses of colonialism.

Reflecting on the subject of reputation, Sam told Boswell that 'A man, whose business it is to be talked of, is much helped by being attacked.' The conversation had begun with Boswell remarking that David Garrick kept a written record of all who had praised or abused him. Sam thought this a good idea, but believed that 'it could not be well done now, as so many things are scattered in newspapers'. He continued: 'A man who tells me my play is very bad is less my enemy than he who lets it die in silence.' It seems that for a moment here (in 1773) he recalled the reception of *Irene* and grasped the sour half-truth that all publicity is good publicity: 'Every attack produces a defence; and so attention is engaged.'

There is a lot to elucidate in this exchange. To begin with, Garrick's book of praise and abuse seems a recipe for self-harm, and keeping a list of people who'd talked him up was potentially just as bad for him as maintaining an archive of grudges. What did Sam like about this? Quite simply, I think, it appealed to his taste for documenting life's shifts and novelties; he thinks we should keep accounts, registering highs and lows and in-betweens. His diaries are the closest he comes to this, a ledger of debits and credits (mainly debits); he uses them as a means of 'studying little things'.

For Sam, a book like Garrick's would serve as a form of therapy more than an aide-mémoire. For Garrick its purpose was different; Sam could see that he had been 'perpetually flattered in every mode that can be conceived', and 'So many bellows have blown the fire, that one wonders he is not by this time become a cinder.' A written record of his acclaim was an appurtenance of vanity.

As for the notion that all publicity is good publicity, the phrase itself is a twentieth-century coinage, but the principle is an old one. In essence, negative impressions fade faster than awareness; in the short term, a bad story stimulates interest in a product, person or issue, and in the longer term the very fact that there was a story becomes more salient than the exact nature of that story. Such, at least, is the wisdom of PR. It's easy to think of bad stories that would permanently damage one's image, not to mention one's self-confidence. It's also easy to think of other people or products permanently disfigured by unfavourable exposure. But attacks that miss the target are useful. They become, as Sam says, opportunities for self-defence, which may be robust or rude or eloquent but will enhance the sense that you're substantial, resilient, serious . . . and not going away.

Public figures adopt inflammatory attitudes in order to make themselves memorable. This is especially true in politics and the media. Vitriol and outrageousness catch the eye and ear; carefully developed arguments and initiatives do not. Often politicians strike provocative poses in order to divert attention from the shoddiness, shabbiness or sheer ordinariness of their achievements and plans. Each of us, I'm sure, can think of an apt example; Sam's was Wilkes, who campaigned with rare efficiency, drilling into the electorate the idea that he was a 'patron of liberty', and at all times acting as if his prosecution was really persecution.

Wilkes's inheritor is the rabble-rouser who fires up both his fans and his haters with crude un-jokes, slathering his false assertions in a hot chilli sauce of zingy adjectives. On some issues he is as bland as white bread – best to keep them out of sight. For in his mind, as long as there's a commotion he is winning. It's when the noise dies down that he's in trouble. His supporters feel the same, and the uproar attracts more of them, on the grounds that anyone so rowdily controversial must be authentic – and must pose a danger to the shopworn hubris of the political establishment.

✥ 30 ✥

Containing a sketch of Dr Johnson's visit to the Caledonian
regions – and matters pertinent thereunto

WHEN SAM RECEIVED his pension, he declared that if it
had happened twenty years earlier he would have gone to
Constantinople to learn Arabic. At various points in his life
he nursed fond notions of visiting Poland, India and China.
The purpose of such travel was the study at first hand of
people, customs and manners, and this required a daunting
total immersion. In the *Idler* he wrote scathingly about mere
tourists, whose 'method of travelling' equipped them only to
be bores:

> He that enters a town at night and surveys it in the
> morning, and then hastens away to another place, and
> guesses at the manners of the inhabitants by the enter-
> tainment which his inn afforded him, may please himself
> for a time with a hasty change of scenes, and a confused
> remembrance of palaces and churches; he may gratify
> his eye with a variety of landscapes, and regale his
> palate with a succession of vintages; but let him be con-
> tented to please himself without endeavouring to disturb
> others.

Were he to travel much himself, he thought, it would be to
enlarge his mind and make useful discoveries; he hoped
he might be able to bring back some wisdom that would
benefit his compatriots.

The idea of his going to China to see the Great Wall was received by others with amused enthusiasm, for they knew, as he did, that it would be a momentous achievement – and that it would never happen. Less adventurously, he thought of a trip to Scotland, which he mentioned to Boswell as early as the summer of 1763, a couple of months after their first meeting. He was particularly keen to see the Hebrides, having as a child read *A Description of the Western Isles of Scotland*, an account published in 1703 of a trip made in 1695. Its author, Martin Martin, had revelled in describing 'isles . . . but little known, or considered . . . even by those under the same government and climate'. The resulting book was informative and sometimes fascinating, though also sometimes hard to follow – a sample sentence being 'There is another coarser scurf called crostil, its of a dark colour, and only dyes a philamot.'[1]

Boswell was amused, if not entirely convinced, by a proposal that struck him as a 'very romantic fancy'. But for Sam the point of travel was precisely, as he had written in his preface to Lobo's *Voyage*, to correct 'romantic absurdities': one could improve on the information picked up through reading, anecdote and rumour. Going to the Hebrides was an opportunity to remedy misconceptions, replacing received images with immediate ones. Which is not to say that Sam's interest in this trip was untouched by yearning. Islands have an intriguing doubleness: are they the last remains of a broken landscape or the seeds of a new culture? To visit an island is to indulge one's fantasies of escape while also containing them, and for Sam, who mostly found such fantasies unsettling, islands seemed manageable and knowable, possessing both observable boundaries and rich possibilities. His vision of island life was, of course, coloured by his reading – Shakespeare's *The Tempest*, Sir

Thomas More's *Utopia*, and *Robinson Crusoe*, a portrait of self-sufficiency that was one of a handful of books he believed readers wished were longer.

Ten years after first discussing a Scottish trip, he and Boswell finally made the journey. As we have seen, they both wrote about it, and the difference between their accounts is illuminating. Their chosen titles are subtly different: Sam's book, published in 1775, is *A Journey to the Western Islands of Scotland*, and Boswell's, published a decade later, is *The Journal of a Tour to the Hebrides*. If we turn to these two volumes, we find that Sam's *Journey* gives very little indication of time and is instead structured by place, whereas Boswell's *Journal* is a day-by-day narrative; Sam is reflective, a social and cultural historian, often disenchanted, whereas the comparatively well-travelled Boswell resembles a busy choreographer. 'I am, I flatter myself, a citizen of the world,' writes Boswell, the phrase not really covering up how callow he still is. He is half-aware, but no more than that, of the ridiculousness of promising an 'account of the transit of Johnson over the Caledonian hemisphere' – Scotland is huge, Johnson is a planet, the trip is an epic and recalls Captain James Cook's recent observation of the transit of Venus. When he tries to muffle his boastfulness, he ends up sounding more boastful, and when he excitably claims that a mountain is 'immense' – proof that Scotland has some impressive sights – Sam corrects him, enjoying his own pedantic polysyllables, 'No, it is no more than a considerable protuberance.'

There were differences from the moment Sam arrived in Edinburgh, on 14 August 1773. He and Boswell met at Boyd's Inn at the head of the Canongate, where he took exception to a greasy-fingered waiter who plopped a sugar lump into his glass of lemonade. He threw the drink out of the window, and it fell to Boswell to keep the waiter from being hurled in the same direction. The English visitor would need some mollifying on other counts: he complained of the city's stench (Boswell's, too) and, even once persuaded that there was no need for the pair of pistols he had brought north with him, insisted on being armed with a mighty stick carved from oak.

They set out four days later – Sam in a roomy brown coat that had huge pockets like panniers, giving him the appearance of a collector expecting to accumulate a great many oddments. Travelling north, by carriage, the two of them followed the coast – St Andrews, Arbroath, Aberdeen – and then headed west to Inverness. From there they proceeded on horseback, and where necessary by boat. They were in the Hebrides for seven weeks, four of which were spent on Skye, before returning to the mainland, to Glasgow and the Boswells' family home at Auchinleck in Ayrshire, and at last back to Edinburgh.

In the course of a tour that lasted until late November, Sam examined the landscape, its ruins and inscriptions, the country's past conflicts and traditions. Along the way, he took in the heath where Macbeth met the weird sisters, admired caves and waterfalls, paused to appreciate the clear water of Loch Ness (full of salmon, trout and pike), and slept in a bed once occupied by Bonnie Prince Charlie as he fled after the Battle of Culloden. Wherever he could, he spoke with prominent locals, including Flora MacDonald, who'd aided the Bonnie Prince in his escape. Sometimes he had to make do with less rewarding company; on the island of Raasay he met a woman who seemed so inert it was as if she had been 'cut out of a cabbage'. At least he had Boswell, 'whose gaiety of conversation and civility of manners' were 'sufficient to counteract the inconveniences of travel'. But there were days when the younger man, prone to pouty homesickness, needed reminding that these were the qualities expected of him. There were also spasms of rivalry. When they were on Skye, Sam raised eyebrows by saying that he had often thought of keeping a seraglio, adding that his companion, 'if he were properly prepared', would make a very good eunuch – a ludicrous notion, given Boswell's priapic urges, and an embarrassing one.

A Journey to the Western Islands of Scotland contains the sort of particulars that devotees of travel writing adore: a woman near Loch Ness boiling goat's flesh in a kettle, the detail that candles on the island of Coll have wicks made from tiny shreds of linen, Sam describing brogues as 'a kind of artless shoes . . . that though they defend the foot from stones . . . do not exclude water', and the taste of Hebridean labourers for whisky, with each of them swallowing 'the morning dram, which they call a *skalk*'. It is also an account of disappointment. In a letter he sent from Skye to Hester Thrale, Sam reflected that 'The use of travelling is to regulate imagination by reality, and instead of thinking how things may be, to see them as they are.' He had headed north expecting to see 'a people of peculiar appearance' and 'a system of antiquated life'. But he had got there too late. Since the Act of Union in 1707, and especially since the second failed Jacobite uprising of 1745, English influence had penetrated Scotland, dissolving its ancient culture. Legislation passed in 1746–47 had weakened the old clan system, replacing it with a market economy; now the Highland Clearances were under way, and many Scots were seeking better prospects in America. Sam found a society in the midst of upheaval, and acted like a conservationist. He speaks with feeling about the importance of community, the threat posed by rapacious landlords, the dangers of rapid social change and of meeting it with nothing more than apathy. In addition, he recognizes that reform, especially in the realm of law-making, tends to be fumbled.

Sam emphasizes the decline of Scotland's monuments and its people's learning. He claims that illiteracy and anti-intellectualism are rife, and refers to the 'wide extent of hopeless sterility' that has superseded the land's ancient dignity (and the edifices that were once its markers). Skipping over the sights of Glasgow and Edinburgh – the latter 'a city too well known to admit description' – he is drawn to less familiar terrain, commenting that 'to the Southern inhabitants of Scotland, the state of the mountains and the islands is equally unknown with that of Borneo and Sumatra'. Here, as when he comments on his 'delight in rarity', he draws a link between his activities and the endeavours of Captain Cook and other contemporaries whose voyages opened a new age of discovery. He is curious about rough and obscure places, and in the extent to which their barrenness is the result of neglect, ignorance, poor record-keeping and an addiction to myth. At the same time, he is interested in disappointments of another kind: the traveller's risk of feeling trapped or in peril, the scarcity of food and shelter, the impossibility of taking precise measurements, the obstructions and disruptions that prevent him from enjoying 'extensive views', and the constant challenge of being scientific while also identifying universal themes in what he sees. He thinks of travel writing as, in two respects, a literature of omission: a report of local deficiencies, struggles and errors, and an account of the traveller's own failings. Although his trip was no washout, he articulates the travel writer's vexing sense of mobility-as-futility – how hard it is to render the genuinely alien in terms that are both vivid and accessible, and how constrained one is by a narrative form that typically consists of departure, adventure and return.

The sensitivity he brings to all of this, and indeed his enthusiasm for the journey in the first place, seem odd in light of his reputation for making pungently negative statements about Scotland. He was known for these before he went there, added plenty to the canon during his travels with Boswell, and continued in this vein for the rest of his life. The result is that one of the things he is most known for today is anti-Caledonian sentiment. Sometimes this was jocular, sometimes more combative; when the latter, it could feel like an exercise in demonstrating his candour. He told John Ogilvie, a Church of Scotland minister who went into rhapsodies over the majesty of the Scottish landscape, that 'The noblest prospect which a Scotchman ever sees, is the high road that leads him to England!' When the soldier Sir Allan Maclean boasted of Scotland's abundant rivers and lakes, he shot back that 'Your country consists of two things, stone and water.' The treelessness of Scotland was a recurrent theme, and when he lost his oak stick he rejected Boswell's assurances that it had not been stolen, saying that 'it is not to be expected that any man in Mull, who has got it, will part with it. Consider, Sir, the value of such a *piece of timber* here!' Discussing the achievements of Lord Mansfield, a legal reformer who had been born in Perth but received most of his education in England, he joked that 'Much may be made of a Scotchman, if he be *caught* young.' Most famously, in the *Dictionary* he defined *oats* as 'A grain, which in England is generally given to horses, but in Scotland supports the people.'

The disputed *Dictionary* definition was not inaccurate – after all, haggis, porridge and oatcakes are prominent features of Scottish cuisine. It also wasn't original, deriving from Burton's *The Anatomy of Melancholy*. But Sam's continual needling of the Scots seems oafish; or rather, it seems like an oaf's idea of what might pass for incisiveness. In common with many of his English contemporaries, he thought the Scots were an intrinsically savage race, remote from them in character and lifestyle, and yet believed that when they travelled south, as Boswell had, they were outrageously successful in fields such as law and medicine. In the 1750s, tensions increased as more and more Scots assumed positions of influence in England, and especially in London. Anxiety peaked when the Earl of Bute, a native of Edinburgh, held the office of prime minister in 1762 and 1763; his role in securing Johnson's pension was, to his detractors, simply further evidence of his guile. This was a climate in which casual abuse could multiply. To many English people, if not most, the Scots were clannish, crafty, on-the-make, rude and prone to violence – the same charges levelled by twenty-first-century xenophobes at incomers of all nationalities.

What differentiated Sam from most of his fellow Scot-bashers was the tendency for his statements to be recorded, and unsurprisingly it was Boswell who did most to note them down. He also harboured a specific grievance against the Scottish world of letters, which hardened his antipathy. In the early 1760s James Macpherson, a young teacher with handy connections in Edinburgh literary circles, presented what he billed as a translation of Gaelic ballads by the medieval bard Ossian. These poems attracted huge interest, at first mostly positive. Sam considered them a fraud. Among those he regarded as having being ingloriously duped was the Scottish scholar Hugh Blair, who had been moved by their 'vehemence and fire' to compare the poems favourably to both Homer and Virgil; when Blair wondered if it was truly possible for any man in the modern age to have written them, Sam allegedly replied, 'Yes, sir, many men, many women, and many children.'

Although his private comments about the Ossian poems got around, it was only in *A Journey to the Western Islands* that he went public with his views on the matter. Macpherson complained, belligerently, and Sam did not take this lightly. After all, Macpherson was physically imposing and nearly thirty years his junior. Sam tried to make peace through his friend William Strahan, who had recently printed a revised two-volume *Poems of Ossian*, but Strahan's diplomacy failed, and when Macpherson continued to make threats, Sam wrote back sharply. 'I received your foolish and impudent note,' he began, and he carried on in that vein – 'I will not desist from detecting what I think a cheat, from any fear of the menaces of a ruffian', and 'what I have heard of your morals disposes me to pay regard not to what you shall say, but to what you can prove'. Sam was disgusted by what he took to be the circulation of counterfeit antiquities – a crime against history. Modern accounts of Ossian vary, but it appears that about three-quarters of the poems are Macpherson's fabrication. When Sam's debunking of Macpherson met with anger and contempt, he had reason to be angry himself, as it seemed clear that anyone who blithely accepted the poems' authenticity would draw false conclusions about Scottish history and identity.[2] Yet he was nervous enough about Macpherson's desire for violent revenge that he kept by his bedside a new cudgel, the head of which was as big as an orange.

On this occasion Sam, rather than intending insult, was trying to halt the spread of a fantasy. But posterity has treated his skirmish with Macpherson as a straightforward example of his hostility to Scots. He saw that this would happen: amid the Scottish excitement over the Ossian poems, criticism of any aspect of them, no matter what its grounds, was regarded as an attack on indigenous Gaelic culture. By the time he travelled to Scotland with Boswell, his anti-Scottish sentiment was proverbial, and *A Journey to the Western Islands*, read against this background, compounded the image of him as a smiter of all things Scottish, whether ancient or modern.

Sir John Hawkins pointed out that 'If he stigmatized Scotland as a country, and the Scots as a people, his compliments to individuals in some measure atone for it . . . and express the sense of gratitude proportioned to the favours he experienced.' But stigmatizing the Scots could seem like one of his cherished pastimes, and his more generous observations – such as that Scotland would be any epicure's choice as the best country in which to have breakfast – didn't compensate for the ungracious ones. Boswell's account of the 101 days that he and Sam spent together on their Scottish tour does little to dispel this impression of churlishness. He depicts himself educating Sam out of his prejudices, reforming the great man's insularity with his own sophistication. In reality, he had another agenda: to show Sam off, as if to say 'Look at this strange beast I have almost tamed.' 'To see Dr Johnson in any new situation is always an interesting object to me,' he writes, sounding a bit like someone who parades a pet (or a child, or a gadget) with a view to testing what it can do. Johnson scholar Pat Rogers suggests that Boswell was looking for 'interesting confrontations rather than scenes of harmony' – good material for his account of the trip.[3]

Although the younger man undoubtedly enjoyed Johnsonian wit for its own sake, he also saw that there was a potentially lucrative public appetite for it. The first volume to be billed as *Johnsoniana* appeared in 1776, selling well and drawing Sam's condemnation, in part because it attributed to him some lewd jests that certainly weren't his. Boswell received further evidence of that appetite, as if he needed any, in 1781, when a volume called *The Beauties of Johnson* appeared, and then in 1785, when Stephen Jones published a volume with the title *Dr Johnson's Table Talk*. Although the genre was an old one, Jones's compendium had a particular seventeenth-century model, the polymath John Selden's *Table Talk* (1689). The relish for this kind of book – for portable entertainment, like highlights from a dream dinner party – would continue for a couple of centuries after Selden, and one of its leading Victorian exponents, the campaigning journalist Leigh Hunt, would in 1851 summarize its spirit and appeal: 'Table-talk, to be perfect, should be sincere without bigotry, differing without discord, sometimes grave, always agreeable, touching on deep points, dwelling most on seasonable ones, and letting everybody speak and be heard.'[4] While this doesn't perfectly describe what either Stephen Jones or Boswell collected, or what Sam served up, it captures some of the appeal of Johnsonian utterance.

It was to Boswell's advantage that each day they spent together was like a hatchery of aphorism, and during their Scottish travels Sam reflected on the way this appetite for the nuggety and the sententious was becoming a trend among writers and their audience: 'I love anecdotes. I fancy mankind may come, in time, to write all aphoristically, except in narrative; grow weary of preparation, and connection, and illustration, and all those arts by which a big book is made.' In the age of social media, his prediction is at last borne out. On Twitter, for instance, bumper-sticker wisdom abounds, to the extent that aphorisms are now regarded as 'the Twitter of philosophy' (the phrase occurs in *The Philosopher's Toolkit*, a book by Julian Baggini and Peter S. Fosl). The pace of life – or the perception that life's pace is constantly increasing – makes us susceptible to the allure of witticisms and pat answers.

The remark about writers of the future stringing together anecdotes and aphorisms can be taken as another little dig at Boswell, who, after all, was eager to construct a big book about Johnson along just such lines. But while that ambition, together with pride in his roots, explains Boswell's desire to go on this lengthy trip, one of Sam's particular motives for it is easily overlooked. The most detailed analyst of the two men's journey, Pat Rogers, has the theory that it was 'a sort of fugue, an act of wilful self-withdrawal', which allowed Sam to reflect on large questions, and 'the sparseness and remoteness of the landscape forced him to confront his own physical . . . inadequacies, as London seldom did'.[5] When he set out for Scotland he was sixty-three – he reached his sixty-fourth birthday on Skye, and was keen to play the occasion down. We don't now attach significance to that specific age, preferring to celebrate round numbers, but it was then common to think of sixty-three as the 'grand climacteric', an ominous waypoint in the journey of life. Herman Boerhaave had written about it, and Sir Thomas Browne had commented on the irrational suspicion of its 'considerable fatality'. The notion persisted that it was a dangerous moment, and Sam, conscious of popular beliefs even if also dubious about them, thought of this as a time for taking stock. Among his journey's purposes, one with which all travellers can identify was the wish to transport himself to a place where he could view with some detachment the usual patterns of his life.

❧ 31 ❧

On the fleeting nature of Pleasure and the state of Felicity

NOT LONG AFTER Sam's return, Boswell decided that he would like to make an extended visit to London. He particularly fancied celebrating Easter at St Paul's cathedral, which struck him as 'like going up to Jerusalem at the feast of the Passover'. But he was having money troubles, and his wife Margaret, always uneasy at the idea of being separated from him, was pregnant. Sam wrote to him, arguing that he should not come, since his reasons were not good enough to answer the obvious objections. After all, he and Boswell had just spent more than three months rambling around Scotland; Margaret had permitted this, and now she should be permitted to keep her husband at home. While he was sympathetic to Boswell's desire to 'come once a year to the fountain of intelligence and pleasure', he reflected that 'both information and pleasure must be regulated by propriety'. That propriety was partly a question of marital responsibility. It was also a matter of financial prudence. If pleasure is achieved only at unaffordable expense, it 'must always end in pain', and if 'enjoyed at the expense of another's pain, can never be such as a worthy mind can fully delight in'.

Underpinning Sam's arguments here was an awareness that pleasure is, as he writes in *Idler* 18, 'seldom such as it appears to others, nor often such as we represent it to ourselves'. We exaggerate its possibilities, fixate on its power to transform us, pursue it selfishly, and yet are rarely more pleased with our own critical faculties than when explaining why the quest for it has failed. One of the things he admired about Confucius was his ability to resist pleasure, which seemed to guarantee that he would also be able to withstand pain. He was impressed, too, by Confucius's judgement that no one is as ardent in the pursuit of virtue as pleasure-seekers are in the pursuit of thrills.

Pleasure is fleeting. I cannot write those words without being reminded of an incident when I was in my early twenties: as I helped myself to a large serving at a buffet, while on holiday in Egypt, a stranger sidled up to me and said, 'A minute on the lips, a lifetime on the hips.' At that moment I resented what seemed an unhelpful and intrusive remark. But since then the hips have broadened and the lips (or what lies behind them) have become no less voracious. Pleasure is fleeting, and our attempts to prolong it come at a price – one we keep paying.

Today we have an idea of the neuroscience of pleasure. Sam of course knew nothing of the brain's circuitry and hedonic hotspots, of dopamine and its release in the region of the basal forebrain called the nucleus accumbens, but he instinctively understood how pleasure works. His most sustained discussion of the subject was in *Idler* 58, which opens with the large claim that 'Pleasure is very seldom found where it is sought.' He goes on: 'Our brightest blazes of gladness are commonly kindled by unexpected sparks.' Pleasure, in this view, isn't something that can be programmed, the way I might today devise an iTunes playlist, and 'Nothing is more hopeless than a scheme of merriment.' For someone organizing a birthday party or a hen weekend, that's a discouraging maxim. But it's true that the deepest pleasures are spontaneous, and that minutely scheduled amusement soon starts to feel like a series of chores. In the same essay he argues that 'Merriment is always the effect of a sudden impression' and 'The jest which is expected is already destroyed.'

Sam also grasps that our pursuit of pleasure is often so frantic that we miss the highlights as they occur; we hurtle past them, blind to everything except the vague penumbra of the big sensation we are chasing. This tunnel vision is a pipeline to disappointment, because whatever we go after so unswervingly becomes a fetish, and the reality of attaining it can't match the glamour with which we have invested it. The pattern I'm describing is one that afflicts addicts to an unbearable degree. Addiction can be thought of as nostalgia for the first heady experience of what I'll for convenience's sake call a stimulant (alcohol, heroin, gambling), but it's more useful, I think, to imagine that for the addict every time is the first time, and if it fails to be as vivid as they hope then there is the next first time, which will come along soon, and the total hunger for the next first time propels life, gives it shape, shrinks the universe into the prison of compulsion, the narrowness of one's cell, one's bed, the needle in the vein.

In his short account of the life of Joseph Addison, Sam observes that 'In the bottle discontent seeks for comfort, cowardice for courage, and bashfulness for confidence.' Addison was a writer acclaimed for his rich comedy yet often guilty of cheap facetiousness, and he seems to have wrecked his already fragile health by knocking back too many supposedly restorative alcoholic cordials. For Sam, he was a cautionary illustration of drink's twin tendencies to create a phoney self-certainty by reducing one's field of vision and to amplify the pains it is supposed to dampen. He told Sir Joshua Reynolds that alcohol did nothing to improve talk and made people blind to their own defects – a state he called 'self-complacency'. Religious scruples, illness and the embarrassment that occasionally resulted from his friends' drunken antics combined to make him feel that he was wise to forswear alcohol.

Yet his attitude to drink demands more scrutiny. This, after all, is someone who could claim that 'he who aspires to be a hero must drink brandy' (leaving wine and port to lesser mortals) and who said in the hearing of his biographer Hawkins that a tavern chair is 'the throne of human felicity'. Perhaps what he enjoyed most in a tavern was the company and atmosphere – he revealed that on entering such establishments 'I experience an oblivion of care'. But when he went into more detail about the freedoms of tavern life, he mentioned that 'wine there exhilarates my spirits, and prompts me to free conversation . . . I dogmatize and am contradicted, and in this conflict of opinion and sentiments I find delight'. The problem, he saw, was that this exhilaration was also disorganization; drinkers know how much they can take, but by the time they've taken it they've forgotten. Eventually he concluded that he was one of those people for whom the price of overindulgence is too steep. On one occasion, asked by the poet and philanthropist Hannah More if he would have a little wine at dinner, he replied that 'Abstinence is as easy to me as temperance would be difficult.' Not everyone feels this way, but it's far from unusual to do so. Temperance is an ability 'to set the mind above the appetites', and finding it difficult means that one lurches between extremes.

Cultivating temperance sounds dull. It's not a virtue that brings praise or admiration, and it is sometimes mistaken for prudish incuriosity, perhaps because the nineteenth-century temperance movements that flourished in Britain and its colonies, as well as in America, resulted in teetotalism, which came to be associated in the popular imagination with fanaticism and a joyless faddiness. Teetotalism has a better reputation now, but it's still common to think of it as a monochrome solution to a manageable problem. Temperance is different from this, necessitating not insensitivity to pleasure, but a keen awareness of one's sensitivity. While it doesn't preclude our trying the fruits of every tree, it argues for leaving something on the branches for tomorrow.

In *Rambler* 178, Sam notes that 'the future is purchased by the present', before pronouncing with flinty authority that 'It is not possible to secure distant or permanent happiness but by the forbearance of some immediate gratification.' Here, crucially, he identifies happiness as something distinct from pleasure. He also addressed the issue in conversation with Boswell, who was inclined to treat them as the same thing, and during one of his sermons noted gravely that 'As we extend our pleasures, we multiply our wants'.

In fact, pleasure is to him almost the opposite of happiness. This may strike us as strange, yet it's a powerful idea. While a neuroscientist might explain pleasure with reference to the mesolimbic dopamine pathway or medium spiny neurons, I'm more likely, if I choose to focus on my awareness of the experience of pleasure, to think of it as a concert of the intellect and the emotions. It's a subtle collaboration, but also a routine one, with the result that we rarely try to unpick its complexity – perhaps for fear of wrecking it. What's also apparent is that our pleasures are particular. When we say 'I like music' or 'I enjoy cooking' we mean 'I love early Miles Davis' or 'I enjoy following recipes from *Mary Berry's Christmas Collection*', not 'Everything in the Top 40 is fabulous' or 'I'd be delighted to fry up some breakfast for you and your fourteen friends'. In the moment of experiencing the pleasure, we are aware of what is causing it, and we can usually see it coming. Sometimes the anticipation of pleasure is more pleasurable than the pleasure itself.

Most of us can think of things that give us pleasure: winning a bet, scoring a goal, quenching our thirst, reminiscing, having an orgasm, looking at a great painting, eating cheese (in my case probably Comté). Some of us derive pleasure from sources that would tend to be considered repellent or bizarre – being spanked, sniffing dirty laundry, inflicting cruelty, cycling up hills – though they aren't so very different from the more orthodox ones. In these cases, and indeed in almost all cases, pleasure derives from an activity, and the repetition of the activity will ultimately exhaust its rewards. Pleasure is specifically and externally stimulated, and we can think of it as involving gain – something is added to our lives, however briefly, and that something is in the foreground of our experience. Whereas the experience of pain demands that we act to reduce it, the experience of pleasure is not a call for action. It is also affected by how it's framed: such pleasure as I get from drinking a £5 wine you've picked up at the local corner shop will be increased if I don't see the label and believe it comes from your personal vineyard in Provence.

Happiness, on the other hand, is not fixated on a specific object. Whereas we know where pleasure can be obtained, we have an imperfect understanding of how to make ourselves happy. Anticipation isn't a part of it, and we can be happy without knowing precisely why. More than 2,300 years ago, Aristotle identified three kinds of 'goods' (as in 'beneficial circumstances') that contribute to happiness: 'goods of the soul', such as a sense of being morally or intellectually virtuous; the goods of the body, such as being strong and in excellent health; and external goods, among them friendship and esteem. There are, it's true, *moments* of happiness, in which we feel ourselves greeting experience with a particular bounce and brightness, but in broad terms happiness is a quality of existence, a tone rather than an event.

In the *Dictionary* Sam defined *happiness* as a 'state in which the desires are satisfied', but when he discussed it with Boswell in 1766, he arrived at a different formula – 'Happiness consists in the multiplicity of agreeable consciousness.' This needs some unpacking. First, what is agreeable consciousness? Is the agreement within oneself – my feelings are in perfect harmony – or with others – my feelings are in step with yours? Is it both? Second, what is this business of 'multiplicity'? It could mean that happiness requires several different stimuli; that it consists not of a single bright emotion, but a constellation of them; that it depends on the good feelings one has right now being maintained; that it comes alive only if the mood is shared, with multiple positive feelings boosting one another and the whole upsurge of affirmative energy proving greater than the sum of its parts; that it somehow involves broadening our repertoire of personal resources, our capacity to act and to have ideas; or that it depends on feeling good all at once about the past, the present and the future.[1]

Each of these readings is suggestive. But above all, Sam's talk of the multiplicity of consciousness makes happiness sound like a property of sociability. He says in *Idler* 41 that 'Happiness . . . is perceived only when it is reflected from another', and this is one of several indications that he believes happiness involves a special attention to those around us: we step outside our selves and the petty cravings of egocentricity, blossoming by enabling others to blossom, treasuring the expressive aspect of our relationships rather than their instrumental features. Here I can't resist quoting the comedian George Burns's line that 'Happiness is having a large, loving, caring, close-knit family – in another city.' Though this is flippant, it hints at an important idea: the things that do most to make us happy are ones that can touch the very marrow of our lives, but we appreciate them more when at a slight distance from them. The sense of satisfaction and well-being that we derive from our engagements, with family or community or ideas, resides not so much in the moment when those engagements are most intense as in their afterglow.

Aggressively pursuing happiness is a sure way not to achieve it. But happiness is now big business. Perhaps America's Declaration of Independence is partly to blame, since it enshrines the notion that the pursuit of happiness is an inalienable right. Thomas Jefferson was borrowing from John Locke when he wrote of the rights to life and liberty, yet substituted 'the pursuit of happiness' where Locke had the word 'property'. He meant something different by *happiness* from what we now tend to understand – something closer to Aristotle's concept of *eudaimonia*, namely 'flourishing' and the resources that enable one to flourish. But the idea that we have a right to pursue happiness has become a staple of English-speaking culture, and it is often confused with a somewhat different idea – that happiness itself is an entitlement. It's the latter that has made mechanisms and therapies for achieving happiness into an industry. Among the more benign manifestations are books that prescribe exercises for making oneself happier. One such volume, Gretchen Rubin's *Happier at Home* (2012), has the gratifying subtitle 'Kiss More, Jump More, Abandon a Project, Read Samuel Johnson, and My Other Experiments in the Practice of Everyday Life'. Publications of this kind treat happiness as an art and argue that like any other art it can be learned. Many of them embody the wisdom – a catholic term here – of healers and coaches who promote neuroplasticity or reveal why zebras don't get ulcers. Businesses, governments and swindlers promise to boost our spirits. They profit from the cult of positive thinking, wellness and mindfulness. According to the gurus of industrial beatitude, happiness is a commodity and can therefore be tracked, measured and regulated.

One pernicious effect of this industry is to entrench the belief that unhappiness and negative thoughts are a crime – a toxic aberration for which we need to apologize, rather than a natural part of life. Another, in the end even more sinister, is to foster the idea that each of us is secretly omnipotent, if only we can master the art of perpetual positivity; rather than liberating us from self-loathing, this philosophy makes us self-obsessed, deadens our powers of empathy and turns us into robotic goons, unable to tell the truth about our disappointments or venture criticism of those around us. Sam has a more realistic understanding of happiness. We cannot expect it to be total; as he says in his life of Addison, 'Human happiness has always its abatements; the brightest sunshine of success is not without a cloud.' We do well to focus on the happiness we have, rather than some other chimerical form of it that's been shoved in our faces: 'Every man may grow rich by contracting his wishes, and by quiet acquiescence in what has been given him supply the absence of more.' And we should try to find ways to multiply agreeable consciousness, for 'That kind of life is most happy which affords us most opportunities of gaining our own esteem.'

✄ 32 ✄

In which thought is applied to an awkward question: whether
Dr Johnson subscribed to the doctrines of S****ism

As OTHERS TOOK more responsibility for entertaining
him, and after his pension permanently removed the risk of
poverty, Sam was able to indulge his appetite. He enjoyed
plum pudding with oyster sauce poured over it, salted flank
of beef, hot chocolate with lashings of cream or melted
butter, veal pie with plums and sugar. In Scotland he
savoured roast kid and, on Skye, complained that the local
goose was not to his taste, since the birds 'by feeding in the
sea, have universally a fishy rankness'. Hester Thrale reports
that he was so fond of peaches that he would sometimes
devour seven or eight large ones as a prelude to breakfast.
But episodes of gluttony alternated with periods of carefulness, and eventually the carefulness prevailed. Sometimes he
cut meat out of his diet or restricted himself to spinach and
potatoes. Sometimes, too, he fasted, though mainly as a
preparation for receiving the sacrament, which most years
he took only at Easter. 'I mind my belly very studiously,' he
said, adding that 'he who does not mind his belly will hardly
mind anything else'.

When he refers to minding his belly, the image that
comes to mind is of his attending to it, nurse-like, even
parental, ministering to its needs yet now and then exercising discipline. The adverb 'studiously' makes me think of
a critical analysis of the belly's talk, whether it's the early

rumble of hunger or the growls of digestion, and the overall impression is of a conversation, dense with nuance, between the belly and its supervisor. As someone who occasionally scoffs too much and has tried to be a more circumspect eater, I recognize in Sam's talk of very studious belly-minding the sound of a person wishing he didn't have to be so careful.

Like anyone else, he found that certain foods held no appeal. Boswell recalls visiting the Isle of Coll and chancing there on a stone shaped like a small cucumber, and this reminds him of Sam's explanation of a reference in John Gay's *The Beggar's Opera*, where the pragmatic Mrs Peachum pictures her trusting daughter Polly: 'And when she's dressed with care and cost, all tempting, fine and gay, / As Men should serve a cucumber, she flings herself away.' Sam told him that 'it has been a common saying of physicians in England, that a cucumber should be well sliced, and dressed with pepper and vinegar, and then thrown out, as good for nothing'. There's no indication of how Sam came by this impression, but he may have had in mind the words of Sir Thomas Browne, who argued that 'cucumbers are no commendable fruits' on the grounds that they were 'very waterish', causing wind and inhibiting the functions of the stomach.

Some of Sam's ideas about diet can be traced back to *The Anatomy of Melancholy*. This vast work was not so much an account of melancholy as a collection of strange information about humankind that its author Robert Burton had picked up during his very extensive reading. Published in 1621 and ransacked by several generations of writers and medics, the *Anatomy* was full of contradictions, but it established a lot of culinary prejudices: that cabbage causes bad dreams, venison 'begets bad blood', pork is 'moist' and can cause fever, cheese is unsuitable for anyone prone to headaches.

In the eighteenth century, melancholy was regarded as an illness. True, it was sometimes à la mode, and Bath doctors had to treat patients who thought that it made them seem interestingly artistic. But Sam inherited the idea that it was an affliction of the spleen and the liver, the common symptoms of which were wakefulness, convulsions, vertigo and a ringing in the ears, as well as fear, lasciviousness and paranoia – a list he would have read with grim recognition. Hoping to find ways to alleviate the condition, he turned to George Cheyne's *The English Malady* (1733). This took a broad view of nervous diseases – hysteria, hypochondria and depressive 'lowness' – and stressed the relationship between mind, body and spirit. Without referring to madness, Cheyne made it clear, through an account of his own melancholy, that he understood just how debilitating it could be and the extent to which it could impinge on one's relationships. Sam found his discussion of spasms and convulsions especially pertinent, and went along with the argument that the causes of chronic illness included variable weather, heavy food and a sedentary lifestyle.

Cheyne recommended a diet containing lots of 'soft, mild, sweet, or at least insipid things'. He also encouraged exercise, though some of the examples he gave wouldn't satisfy today's personal trainers: hunting, billiards, bowls, and even riding in a chariot.[1] Sam was bothered by Cheyne's belief that this 'malady' was confined to the educated elite, and warned Boswell, 'Do not let him teach you a foolish notion that melancholy is a proof of acuteness.' But, like many others, he was impressed by the author's forthrightness about the roots of his own ailments. Cheyne had arrived in London from Scotland in 1702 and had immediately become a hard-drinking, gluttonous man-about-town. Even after embracing a more austere regime he relapsed – at one point ballooning to thirty-two stone. In *The English Malady* he drew on a history of personal failings to set out a doctrine of self-improvement. With his emphases on well-being, detoxification, the mental struggle involved in being slim and the opportunity for repairing the soul by reconditioning the body, he anticipated the vast modern literature of dietetic self-help.

Inevitably, Sam was struck by the connection Cheyne drew between disorders of the nerves and 'corruptions in the habit'. For him, 'habit' meant 'bad habit'. He thought of habits as tyrannical; one needs to guard against them, for if they are not subdued they will stymie all one's powers of reason. In 'The Vision of Theodore', an allegorical tale published in 1748, he pictured Habit as a creature, a monstrous enemy enforcing 'sordid bondage'. It restricted movement with chains 'so slender in themselves, and silently fastened, that while the attention was engaged by other objects, they were not easily perceived', but 'each link grew tighter as it had been longer worn, and when by continual additions they became so heavy as to be felt, they were very frequently too strong to be broken'. Here Habit appears at once stealthy and brawny; when opposed, it gets bigger and more potent (like a battle-hardened Pokémon) unless one manages to defeat it completely.

'Corruptions in the habit' is at once a catchy phrase and a vague one, but it was a form of words that could serve as an umbrella for Sam's melancholy, his tics and other nervous disorders – the gesticulations and see-sawing, his anxiety about masturbation, his urge to scrape the joints of his fingers with a knife till they were raw. As he searched for means of controlling these behaviours, of driving out the corruptions, his approach was combative. Yet patience and endurance were necessary, too. The pursuit of personal virtue was something that, as he wrote in the *Rambler*, called for a 'constant and determinate' mindset, and indeed a failure to believe in the value of perseverance was guaranteed to 'enchain the mind' (to sluggish mediocrity). It is through what he calls 'gradual accessions' and 'accumulated labours' that one masters any subject, not least one's self.

The word that comes to mind here is *stoical*. Sam would have shuddered to find it being applied to him, as he disapproved of large portions of Stoic philosophy. He considered most of the ancient Stoics – men such as Chrysippus and Zeno of Citium – haughty in their pretence of 'exemption from the sensibilities of unenlightened mortals' and being 'above the reach of those miseries which embitter life to the rest of the world'. There was something absurd in their refusal to admit being pained by poverty, exile or the end of friendship; for his own part, he preferred to engage with life's hazards and vicissitudes. Yet he did concede that the Stoic philosophers were 'very useful monitors'. They were capable of insights that could, with a certain caution, be applied to modern life. Of all these thinkers, the one who most appealed to him was Epictetus, and his appreciation deepened as a result of reading a translation by one of his friends, the poet Elizabeth Carter. This appeared in 1758, and Sam was one of 912 subscribers to the handsome edition; in her introduction Carter expresses reservations about the Stoics' 'great arrogance', but applauds their 'excellent rules of self-government, and of social behaviour'.[2]

Born in what is today Pamukkale in southern Turkey, Epictetus moved as a child to Rome, where he was kept as a slave. According to popular myth, his master on one occasion tortured him by twisting his leg, and Epictetus coolly pointed out that if he kept twisting the leg would break; his master ignored him, the leg snapped, and Epictetus responded, 'There, did I not tell you that it would break?' This makes him sound insanely unyielding rather than admirably tough, but he's a practical philosopher, preaching the gospel of resilience. Those of Epictetus's reflections that survive, after nearly two millennia, do so because they were noted down and published by one of his pupils, Arrian. His *Discourses*, which appeared around 1,600 years before Sam was born, begin with some thoughts about what is in our power and what is not. He points out that you can't control the weather or your friends, and that there are limits to how far you can control your body. But you can control what you believe. Most of us spend too much time trying to exercise control over things that are beyond our power, or feeling frustrated about our inability to do so – and not enough time taking responsibility for what we think.

Sam wrote approvingly in the *Rambler* of Epictetus's notion that one should try 'often to think of what is most shocking and terrible'. When I put this to a friend, in the bleak winter of 2016, she responded, 'Aleppo? I don't want to think about Aleppo.' After a little consideration, she added, 'But perhaps I ought to.' Sam, after Epictetus, holds that we should, not least because in being aware of what's truly terrible we improve our sense of perspective. Thinking of something shocking stops us wallowing in the morass of what often get called 'first-world problems' – the local deli's having run out of quince jelly, the squirrel droppings atop the barbecue, the momentary skipping of our Collector's Edition DVD of *Scarface*. Sam was of course familiar with Alexander Pope's poem *The Rape of the Lock* ('the most attractive of all ludicrous compositions'), in which the theft of a fashionable young woman's lock of hair provokes an almighty tantrum, and with the serious point of Pope's poem, which is that our perception of offence is determined by context. A cosseted Hollywood star may be no less upset by a grey hair on his chest than a starving child in Yemen is by the death of one of her siblings. The Hollywood star could do with being less self-obsessed, but this requires him to change his frame of reference.

Epictetus's appeal for Sam, as for those readers who study him today, lies in both his subject matter – integrity, happiness, sociability, the nature of how we act and what we feel – and his style, which is conversational. Philosophy, according to Epictetus, is a cure for adversity. It teaches us to have authority over ourselves. One of his key beliefs is that our relationships and roles commit us to certain responsibilities. In particular, we have relationships we did not choose, such as with our parents, and a life of virtue involves attending to the duties those relationships entail, however mundane they may be. If we step aside from these duties in order to pursue what we claim are higher purposes, we are guilty of both negligence and self-importance. For Sam, fitful in his devotion as both son and brother, this was a chastening doctrine.

❧ 33 ❧

Upon Charity – whether it be cold, and how it is performed

IN A LETTER of April 1776, Sam tells Hester Thrale about V. J. Peyton, who had been one of his amanuenses when he was at work on the *Dictionary*. 'Poor Peyton expired this morning,' he writes, and the adjective *poor* looks formulaic. But if we read on, we see that he uses it with some force. Peyton's wife had long been sick, and he was 'condemned by poverty to personal attendance' – unable, that is, to get help with looking after her. Moreover, he was 'by the necessity of such attendance chained down to poverty'. He was thus one of those trapped in the vicious cycle of hardship, which is unbreakable without some intervention from outside. Sam regards his 'fortitude' as heroic, yet is appalled to think that his quiet forbearance kept him from achieving anything of note. He paid for Peyton to be buried, but believed he ought to have done more for him.

The question of what we do for those in need was one that preyed on his mind. He argued that 'the true test of civilization' is 'a decent provision for the poor'. Ideas of decent provision vary, but it is striking that he thought this. He believed that in England the poor were better served than in most other places, yet he lived in an age where it was common to treat them with contempt and to imagine that their alleged privations were a fiction concocted by sanctimonious busybodies. As he commented in *Rambler* 48, 'those who do not feel pain, seldom think that it is felt', and Hester

Thrale was one of the people he upbraided for insensitivity on this count: when she referred derisively to Porridge Island, a nook of London where some of its most wretched inhabitants went to eat, he jabbed back – 'Let's have no sneering at what is serious to so many' – and pointed out that many people who passed in that direction felt they must turn away, for even the modest offerings of Porridge Island were luxuries they could not afford.

In *Rambler* 166 he piercingly observed that 'The eye of wealth . . . seldom descends to examine the actions of those who are placed below the level of its notice'. The good qualities of the underprivileged, not 'brightened by elegance of manners', are 'cast aside like unpolished gems', and most of the time we simply overlook the most forlorn members of society. Our gaze skates past them; we are wrapped up in our own anxieties or submerged in conversation. Hester Thrale reported his saying that 'Every one in this world has as much as they can do in caring for themselves, and few have leisure really to *think* of their neighbours' distresses, however they may delight their tongues with *talking* of them.'

Of course, he had some experience of what it felt like to be poor, as well as of the contempt with which the rich often treated both destitute people and the very idea of destitution.He knew the difference between true poverty – lacking life's necessities – and what many perceive to be poverty – lacking its pleasant superfluities. He had seen, too, the way the most needy were peppered with insult by those only a little removed from penury. Consequently he was appalled by writers who romanticized poverty, producing not a true portrait of 'meanness, distress, complaint, anxiety and dependence', but instead a false image of the pauper's life as one of 'innocence and cheerfulness' or 'tranquillity and freedom'.

Altogether more real was the urge to maintain an impression of cheer and tranquillity when in fact one was gnawed by want. In *Adventurer* 120 he observed that 'great numbers are pressed by real necessities which it is their chief ambition to conceal, and are forced to purchase the appearance of competence and cheerfulness at the expense of many comforts and conveniences of life'. He understood the particular dread of poverty that afflicts the old, and was alive to the distinction between poor debtors and rich ones – witness his observation that 'Small debts are like small shot; they are rattling on every side, and can scarcely be escaped without a wound: great debts are like cannon; of loud noise, but of little danger.' I'm reminded here of the old joke 'If you owe the bank £100, that's your problem. If you owe the bank £100 million, that's the bank's problem.' Used to having mean little debts that nagged at him constantly, he knew all about their capacity to injure pride, friendships, work and well-being. When Boswell was slipping into financial difficulties, Sam pointed out to him that debt is a calamity rather than simply an inconvenience, because it 'produces so much inability to resist evil' and 'takes away so many means of doing good'.

His experiences led him to think a lot about charity. He reflected that 'no sooner is a new species of misery brought to view, and a design of relieving it professed, than every hand is open to contribute', and that when this happens 'every art . . . is employed *for a time* in the interest of virtue' (the emphasis is mine). People can and do come together for the purpose of philanthropy – but fashion plays a part, for today's dominant issue is tomorrow's forgotten cause. True charity requires a sustained commitment, not a temporary focus on a particular problem.

Say the word 'charity' today and there's a good chance

that it will call to mind chuggers in brightly coloured tab-
ards, eager to commit you to a monthly direct debit, or
mailshots staring up from the doormat, highlighting the
plight of others and the apparently modest sums that could
improve their lives. A word that once signified God's gift
of love to humankind and was one of the three Christian
graces described by St Paul has become a term for a type of
institution and its benign but often sterile endeavours.
What's more, although such institutions exist to benefit the
disadvantaged, they're mostly encumbered with expensive
bureaucracy, and actions meant to give succour can instead
seem like attempts to injure pride. In *Rambler* 162, a discussion of the afflictions of old age, Sam wrote that 'There is
no state more contrary to the dignity of wisdom than
perpetual and unlimited dependence'. The phrase 'cold as
charity', more than 300 years old, is a revealing one; it
speaks of how dismal it can feel to rely on others' largesse,
and of the class-bound condescension that can cause a
helping hand to seem instead like a gesture of reproof.

For Sam, every day offered opportunities for charity. He
did not necessarily have gifts of money in mind; as he says
in one of his sermons, 'He that cannot relieve the poor may
instruct the ignorant; and he that cannot attend the sick
may reclaim the vicious.' Contemporary ideas of spiritual
charity were shaped by the teachings of the seventeenth-
century theologian Edward Stillingfleet, who identified
seven forms it could take, which included comforting those
lost in sorrow and advising those mired in doubt. But in the
end it was practical support that mattered most. Strikingly,
in the first edition of the *Dictionary*, Sam's opening definition
of *relief* was 'the prominence of a figure in stone or metal;
the seeming prominence of a picture', but when he revised
the entry in the 1770s this sense was relegated and he gave

as its primary definition 'alleviation of calamity; mitigation of pain or sorrow'. The means of relieving suffering were uppermost in his mind.[1]

The practical bent of Sam's thoughts about poverty is apparent in his attitude to the death penalty. He considered it a disproportionate punishment for theft, and in *Rambler* 114 wondered, 'who can congratulate himself upon a life passed without some act more mischievous to the peace or prosperity of others, than the theft of a piece of money?' Hanging thieves was ineffective as a deterrent. Severe public punishment failed to produce the awe it was supposed to. Worse, it caused criminals to think not that theft was as serious as murder, but that murder was no more grave an offence than theft – and that killing the people they robbed would bring no harsher penalty than merely robbing them. His radical solution, with a nod to More's *Utopia*, was 'invigorating the laws by relaxation'. This, he knew, was something his readers would find strange.

This same spirit of reform was also apparent in his discussion of debtors' prisons. In these squalid, rotting mansions of misery one person in three hundred was confined – 'a loss to the nation, and no gain to the creditor'. Sam was impressed by arguments about the need for better ventilation in prisons and for a general improvement in conditions. But he saw the jailing of debtors as a symptom of a wider social problem, the abundance of easy credit. Could it be that a person who lends money is a participant in the crimes of the debtor and 'shares the guilt of improper trust'? The problem that needed resolving was the recklessness and greed of lenders who disregarded the circumstances of those to whom they lent. 'We have now imprisoned one generation of debtors after another,' he wrote in *Idler* 22, 'but we do not find that their numbers lessen. We have now learned, that rashness and imprudence will not be deterred from taking credit; let us try whether fraud and avarice may be more easily restrained from giving it.'

Such an overhaul of attitudes to debt and credit required an unlikely moral and economic jubilee. At least in its absence one could always give alms. When Sam heard a complaint that handing money to beggars was irresponsible, since they would use it to buy gin or tobacco, he countered that it was cruel to deny them 'such sweeteners of their existence'. 'Life is a pill which none of us can bear to swallow without gilding,' he argued, 'yet for the poor we delight in stripping it still barer.' That 'none of us' is worth pausing over. The vices we condemn are ones we practise too, except in more socially acceptable ways; a chic diner's good bottle of wine performs many of the same functions as a kerbside drinker's can of cheap cider.

In a sermon on the subject of charity, he questioned the tendency to draw a distinction between the deserving poor and undeserving. It was common to suppose that some paupers were too steeped in vice to be worth helping; there was a risk that assisting them would simply make it easier for them to drag others down to their level. Sam was unconvinced, though, and argued that 'we do not always encourage vice when we relieve the vicious. It is sufficient that our brother is in want; by which way he brought his want upon him, let us not too curiously enquire.' Besides, 'if a bad man be suffered to perish, how shall he repent?'

Struck by the specious piety of people keen to trumpet their virtue, he saw how often charity was hollow. When told of a woman of large fortune who did good for others and blushed with delight at the fame of her kindness, Sam argued that this was the norm: 'Human benevolence is mingled with vanity, interest, or some other motive.' There was, he believed, no such thing as *pure* benevolence. What he did not foresee was a world in which the large-scale relief of poverty and hunger could be an instrument of governments' foreign policy, and in which the benevolence of charitable giving would sometimes be transmuted into humanitarian projects whose main purpose is not to provide aid, but to legitimize their own expansion.

He did notice, though, that spurious patriotism could impinge on charity. During the Seven Years' War, public funds were used to clothe French soldiers taken prisoner. The argument against this was – in his paraphrase – 'that charity may be improperly and unseasonably exerted; that while we are relieving Frenchmen, there remain many Englishmen unrelieved'. But, he countered, 'the relief of enemies has a tendency to unite mankind in fraternal affection' and 'takes away something from the miseries of war'. Conflict already did enough to fill the world with horror: 'let it not then be unnecessarily extended . . . and no man be longer deemed an enemy than while his sword is drawn against us'.

✦ 34 ✦

A chapter about Boredom, which may serve to remind us
that there are no truly uninteresting things

SAM'S ACTS OF CHARITY compensated for what he thought
were oversights and omissions. He chastised himself for
neglecting religion, study and work. 'I have done nothing,'
he wrote in a prayer he composed on the eve of his fifty-fifth
birthday (which he called his fifty-sixth, as he included the
day on which he was born). 'I have now spent fifty-five years
in resolving, having from the earliest time almost that I can
remember been forming schemes of a better life.' Now
'the need of doing is . . . pressing, since the time of doing
is short'.

This is the sort of thing he says a lot. In his earliest surviving diary entry, from October 1729, there is a Latin phrase
that Boswell translates as 'I bid farewell to Sloth, being
resolved henceforth not to listen to her siren strains'. But
those siren strains were never blocked out, and the diaries
abound with his complaints of having 'trifled away' days and
weeks, of months drifting by as if in a dream. In September
1768 he writes, 'How the last year has passed I am unwilling
to terrify myself with thinking.' In April 1778 he reviews the
previous twelve months and finds 'a very melancholy and
shameful blank'. In April 1779 he carries out the same review,
which reveals 'little but dismal vacuity'. He is continually
making resolutions, and every New Year there are new
promises of reform: he will get up early, conduct himself

better, 'redeem the time I have spent in sloth', read the Bible in Greek, fast on Good Friday, worship at church more often and more regularly. He must manage his mind, combat doubts, conquer 'useless scruples' about his minor short-comings as a Christian. When he reflects on this pattern of behaviour, after years of broken commitments, he concludes that despite all his defeats he must resolve himself again, 'because reformation is necessary and despair is criminal'.

The dial of his watch, bought when he was fifty-nine, bore an inscription from St John's gospel, in the original Greek. 'For the night cometh,' it read. Sir Walter Scott would choose the same phrase as a motto to be inscribed on the sundial in his garden. That's gently amusing, but think of seeing it every time you looked at your watch. After three years, Sam decided to get a new dial-plate, and it's not hard to imagine why. He told Boswell that he'd concluded it made him appear ostentatious. But who looks at a watch more – other people, or its owner? I'm inclined to believe that he felt oppressed by the darkness of the sentiment, which must have seemed an admonition – yet another self-reproach. We can be sure that Sam, with his close knowledge of the New Testament, was continually reminded by this Greek snippet of the phrase's original context. In full, the quotation is 'For the night cometh, when no man can work.' The words are spoken by Jesus, who is healing a man born blind, and immediately before them is this: 'I must work the works of him that sent me, while it is day.'

The truth is that, despite periods of inertia, his career was fertile. Yet his statements about his lack of productivity were not a pose; they were formed in private, in the hope of goading himself into better working practices. Even when making headway with a task, he always thought that he could do more, and, like most people with a great capacity for work, dwelled on the blankness of his less fruitful days, believing himself a failure.

Writing to Boswell in the summer of 1775, he reports a recent trip to the Midlands and says that he was glad to get away for a while but then glad to return to London. This, surely, is the experience of anyone who takes a holiday: we exchange one set of anxieties for another, and, even though the second set may be trifling, leaving more space than usual for our minds and bodies to uncoil, we can soon become nostalgic for the first. Sam continues, 'I was, I am afraid, weary of being at home, and weary of being abroad. Is not this the state of life?' The pattern is familiar: we make up for the staleness or flatness of one experience by throwing ourselves into another, which promises some new flavour and may indeed deliver it – but soon comes to seem stale and flat.

Sam sees that boredom is natural. In the *Rambler* he refers to our need to 'relieve the vacuities of our being' and recognizes that they are an inevitable feature of life. The world is under no obligation to entertain us. To complain of boredom is to voice a misguided sense of entitlement. Yet he doesn't refer to boredom or being bored. The verb *to bore*, in the sense 'To weary by tedious conversation or simply by the failure to be interesting' (*OED*), emerged around 1750 and does not appear in his *Dictionary* of 1755. The *OED* dates the appearance of *boredom* and *boring* to midway through the following century. What we would call 'boring', Sam would have labelled 'irking' or 'wearisome'; what we call 'boredom' he would have known by half a dozen names, including 'tedium' and 'languor'. He would have balked at the then-fashionable 'ennui', as he was suspicious of the vogue for importing words from French, believing it a form of social pretentiousness that threatened to weaken the language. But ennui was something he knew deeply.

Boredom has a bad reputation. This is hardly a surprise. Often it is portrayed as the root of evil – a chasm in which dark thoughts breed, a form of despair that we visit upon ourselves, a poison eating away our capacity for movement. To be bored, we've been told, is to be weak and to lay one-self open to the lure of depravity. It's a sickness, easily and discreetly transmitted. It is an insult to the gift of being alive. The words 'I'm bored' have become a catch-all for many shades of unhappiness, and the adjective *boring* is a put-down that's at once criminally vague and devastatingly effective: 'He was boring in bed', 'It was such a boring lunch.' We're bombarded with suggestions about ways of keeping boredom from engulfing us, and parents are urged to fill their children's days with improving activities – karate, ballet, soccer skills, conversational Chinese – lest the kids discover ennui and get into bad habits like, say, drug-taking or reading.

Of all the statements on the subject that I've seen, my favourite is in *Cool Memories*, a collection of aphorisms by Jean Baudrillard. 'Boredom,' says the eternally provocative French thinker, 'is like a pitiless zooming in on the epidermis of time. Every instant is dilated and magnified like the pores of the face.'[1] These two sentences capture the relationship between boredom and self-inspection: when we are bored, we are agonizingly aware of the textures of the present moment and our place in it.

Yet we can think of boredom in less negative ways. As a corridor along which we are passing, slowly, rather than as a cell in which we are stuck. As part of the process of finding something that piques our interest, or a lingering period of looking before a giant leap. As a mark of our freedom, a privilege even, and an opportunity to think about our relationship with time – or just to think, period. Patricia

Meyer Spacks, in a history of this state of mind, observes that 'All endeavour of every kind takes place in the context of boredom impending or boredom repudiated and can be understood as impelled by the effort to withstand boredom's threat.'[2] *All* endeavour? Surely not. But Spacks's account usefully promotes the idea of boredom as a great engine of creativity. When we are bored, we escape into ourselves: we push at the limits of the internal world precisely because the external one seems so suffocating and stale. Craving something to desire, we in the end invent that *something*. Or perhaps it's not like that: rather, the value of boredom is that it allows life's tensions to slacken, and this release from excitement and anxiety makes it possible for the imagination to dilate.

In an essay called 'The Storyteller', published in 1936, the German philosopher Walter Benjamin pondered the modern obsession with speedy delivery of information. This in an age before emails, Google and the digital gratification of every impulse. For Benjamin, this fixation with satisfying immediate needs – a cult of relevance and 'verifiability' – was linked to a decline in storytelling. The virtue of storytellers, he believed, is that they don't force messages on their audience. A story is an activity rather than a product, and its rewards aren't immediate or consistent. The desire to tell stories originates in a certain weariness or tedium – we use them to fill up life's empty spaces – and our appreciation of stories depends on our having what he calls a 'gift for listening', which is also a product of boredom, for when we are bored we relax, becoming receptive to fresh insights. Benjamin concludes that 'Boredom is the dream bird that hatches the egg of experience. A rustling in the leaves drives him away.'

Walter Benjamin, an exponent of Marxism and Jewish

mysticism, is an unlikely bedfellow for Sam. Yet they have some things in common that are pertinent here: bitter memories of childhood sickness, the wish to awaken from the torpor of their parents, a delight in city life and its diversions, a penchant for intractable projects, the inclination to read and read until they have got to the very kernel of a subject, the belief that an orderly library is not automatically a good one, a strange relationship to solitude (part addiction, part revulsion), and the sense that, in Benjamin's phrase, 'Counsel woven into the fabric of real life is wisdom.' Sam certainly shared the understanding that dry spells are part of creativity. To daydream, remember past hurts, survey the conflict within oneself, dally in introspection, refine one's sense of the truth by butting up against untruths: these are not necessarily illuminating experiences in themselves, but they can bear fruit. The idle hour, the blind alley and the numb afternoon when ideas ferment in the unconscious are the elements of genius's apprenticeship, and it is when we rid ourselves of the manic urge to be productive that we finally manage to be creative.

ℳ 35 ℛ

Of Johnson among the Bluestockings – though it behoves us
to remark that he did not refer to them thus, and that
we might now be wise to forswear this somewhat
disdainous appellation

BOREDOM, INERTIA, frustration and repetition, punctuated
by moments of self-loathing and occasional flights of
euphoria: this, for Sam, was the truth about a life of writing
and the epitome of every artist's existence. But he was surrounded by idealized visions of that life, in which writers
and artists were represented as public figures, instructive
and exemplary. Among these, one that is now very striking
is the group portrait known as The Nine Living Muses of
Great Britain. A celebration of women's creative talents and
the national importance of their attainments, it indirectly
testifies to Johnson's centrality in the literary activity of the
period. Originally drawn in 1777, it by pleasant coincidence
appeared as an engraving in *Johnson's Ladies New and Polite
Pocket Memorandum for 1778*, and was exhibited at the Royal
Academy, as a finished painting, in 1779.[1] The Nine Living
Muses was the work of Richard Samuel, who was young
and ambitious and knew that this was the kind of picture
that could boost his career; showing contemporary writers
in classical garb, it affords a glamorous image of cultural
harmony, in which the subjects' silk gowns are perhaps
better differentiated than their faces. We can think of it as a
forerunner of those splashy colour-supplement tableaux that

corral writers or artists with only a superficial connection and identify them as a new wave.

Sam was intimate with five of the women depicted. He keenly supported Elizabeth Carter, the translator of Epictetus, and the novelist Charlotte Lennox, and he was especially helpful to Hannah More when she chose to revise her poem *Sir Eldred of the Bower*, the much-tweaked second edition of which appeared in 1778. He ultimately fell out with the other two – the historian and political pamphleteer Catharine Macaulay, and Elizabeth Montagu, who attacked what she thought was his failure to do justice to Shakespeare's dramatic genius. But it pleased him to witness the ascent of a new generation of women writers, and he encouraged them by suggesting projects, assisting with the revision of their work, and making useful introductions, not least to his many contacts among the booksellers.[2]

Though he believed that women's lot had improved since the late seventeenth century, he saw the limits of 'the female world' and wrote with feeling about the ill effects of the marriage market and tyrannical parenting. Convinced that young women continued to be stifled by lack of rights and opportunities, he argued that girls needed better education, with an emphasis on intellectual development. Hester Thrale records his telling Boswell, who wondered how much education his daughters should receive, 'Let them learn all they can – it is a paltry trick indeed to deny women the cultivation of their mental powers, and I think it is partly a proof we are afraid of them.' In his relationships with women he often revealed a sensitivity and fragility that male friends did not get to see. A character in *Rasselas* complains of having missed the 'endearing elegance of female friendship', and Sam found the company of women elegant – in the sense that it was on the whole harmonious, free from awkwardness and coarse talk. 'The regard of the female world,' he wrote in the *Rambler*, produces 'a particular pleasure'.

For a while, his greatest source of delight among the living muses was Charlotte Lennox (*née* Ramsay). The daughter of a Scottish soldier, she had spent her formative years in America before moving to Essex in her teens; still a teenager, she had in 1747 married Alexander Lennox, a rather shiftless figure. She met Sam through either William Strahan, the printer of his *Dictionary* and Mr Lennox's sometime employer, or Garrick, in whose company she briefly acted. Having made a poor impression on the stage (Horace Walpole pronounced her a 'deplorable actress'), she turned to writing fiction, and Sam threw an all-night party, at which he drank only lemonade, to celebrate the publication of her first novel *Harriot Stuart* (1750). He insisted on a special hot apple pie being baked to mark the occasion, and honoured her with a crown of laurel leaves. It has been suggested that he contributed some material to her next novel *The Female Quixote* (1752), but though he told Boswell that he was responsible for its dedication, to the extravagant and opera-loving Earl of Middlesex, it is doubtful that he wrote any other part of it.[3] Although *The Female Quixote* was a success and made her a much more saleable author, Lennox was often short of money, and Sam continued to champion her through the 1760s and into the 1770s. When, in 1778, she and her daughter appeared in court, pleading not guilty to an assault on a woman who seems to have been their maid, he arranged for one of his neighbours to bail them out.

By this time he was busy championing Fanny Burney. Whereas others thought she was hopelessly meek, he noticed her shrewd intelligence and joked that she was a 'rogue' and a 'spy'. They shared short-sightedness (literally, not figuratively) as well as prodigious powers of memory, and he was struck by the acuteness of her observation, both of others and of herself. In January 1778, the twenty-five-year-old Burney published, anonymously, her first novel. This was *Evelina*, one of the decade's most sensationally popular books, a perceptive satire of fashionable society, which centres on a young woman from the country who has to pilot a course through the squally waters of city life. Sam admired the novel's humour and style; Burney recorded that his approval 'almost crazed me with agreeable surprise – it gave me such a flight of spirits that I danced a jig'. She had another guide, Samuel Crisp, a collector of art and instruments who was widely travelled and passionate about music. He influenced her tastes, but his forays into poetry and drama were feeble; to become confident in her own writing, she needed the encouragement of an important, established literary figure. Johnson gave her this, urging her to publish under her own name, speak her mind in company, and pay no attention to the negative remarks occasioned by her success. He treated her as his literary equal, and when the anti-Catholic Gordon Riots flared in the summer of 1780, wrecking property in the original Grub Street, he proposed that the two of them survey the damage together – 'we have a very good right to go, so we'll visit the mansions of our progenitors, and take up our freedom together'.

Yet for all his support of the living muses, there is a different image of Dr Johnson that stubbornly endures – summed up in a British newspaper item from 2009 by Boris Johnson, then the mayor of London, which portrayed him as a 'sexist' and alleged, 'It wasn't just that he was opposed to women having jobs. He thought it was a bit off for them even to paint or draw.'[4] This assessment, like others of its kind, spotlights a comment Sam supposedly made on hearing from

Boswell about a Quaker meeting at which there was a female preacher: 'A woman's preaching is like a dog's walking on his hind legs. It is not done well; but you are surprised to find it done at all.' The quotation even pops up in Hillary Clinton's memoir *Living History*, cited as a precedent for men being taken aback that a woman could speak convincingly about the ins and outs of the American healthcare system.[5]

Aggrieved responses to this quotation tend to treat *preaching* as if it's a synonym for *speaking* or *thinking*. Hence a statement such as this, in the *Norton Anthology of Literature by Women*: 'when Dr Johnson compared a woman preacher to a dancing dog . . . he was assuming that creativity and femininity were contradictory terms'.[6] The person doing the 'assuming' here isn't Samuel Johnson. However firmly one may disagree with his opinion about who should be permitted to preach, that's what it is: a specific criticism, not a wholesale assault on women's reason, creativity or powers of argument.

Besides, the line may be apocryphal. Boswell originally recorded it in his journal without any context, and it's possible that he picked it up in London literary circles and chose to add to his stock of Johnsonian aphorisms. Perhaps it was a popular wisecrack of the day – an interpretation favoured by some of Sam's defenders. Others accept the words as his, but treat them as a blip. They note his enthusiasm for adopting a female persona in his essays, to talk about issues such as domestic violence, and highlight his responsiveness to female readers, as well as the appeal his ideas had for many women writers. Among these was the pioneering feminist Mary Wollstonecraft, who met him in the final year of his life, admired his essays (especially the *Rambler*), invoked him in her own writing, and included five pieces by him in her 1789 anthology *The Female Reader*, which was 'principally intended for the improvement of females', and made telling use of an extract from his play *Irene* to encapsulate the 'true end of life' (namely virtue).[7] Evidence of a less conspicuous kind can be found in the *Dictionary*, where, despite claiming to 'admit no testimony of living authors', he chooses quotations from contemporary women writers such as Jane Collier and Charlotte Lennox. His use of women's writings is not extensive, but unlike his precursors in lexicography, he thought that examples from their works were valuable and that they could be presented alongside citations from male authors, with equal weight.

What's for sure is that frequent repetition has allowed the statement about the dog walking on its hind legs to overshadow Sam's deep interest in the problems women faced. It eclipses awareness of his generosity to female authors, his desire to share in their intellectual pursuits, and his distaste for the patronizing language many of his male contemporaries used of them.

His role as a source of inspiration and advice for women writers is interesting in light of his negative comments on patronage. The most famous of these occurs in the great letter he wrote to Lord Chesterfield in 1755, but even before that he was under no illusions. He knew that patrons liked their beneficiaries to treat them with stooping servility; it was usual for patronage to compromise an author's artistic, political and psychological independence. Yet it didn't have to be like this. In his most substantial work of biography, the *Lives of the Poets*, it's apparent that he is hostile not to patronage *per se*, but to the many failures of patrons. As we've seen, in the *Dictionary* he defines *patron* as 'One who countenances, supports or protects. Commonly a wretch who supports with insolence, and is paid with flattery.' *Commonly*, not *always*. Sam was happy, in his own conduct, to kick against the norm: supporting (without insolence) and protecting were his preferred modes of patronage. The meaning of *countenances* may not immediately be clear, but it is the equivalent of 'encourages' or 'backs up'. This is Sam's forte, and it is worth noting that, besides the famous definition of *patron*, he offers others – including 'A guardian saint' and 'Advocate; defender; vindicator', all of which he was ready to be, when needed.

It is more useful to think of Sam as a mentor than as a patron. The word *mentor*, uncommon in his lifetime, does not appear in his *Dictionary*, and he appears never to have used it in any of his published writings; according to the *OED* the first author to adopt it was none other than Chesterfield, in 1750. But the term, now widely used, conveys the two essential characteristics of what Sam gave to Hannah More, Charlotte Lennox and Fanny Burney: practical assistance and psychological nurture. The latter must be confidential, and, precisely because of this, mentoring can be potent without leaving a visible imprint; for the recipient, its legacy may be lasting, and for the mentor too the rewards can abide, but, when most sincere, it is a relationship with a low profile. As a result it invites speculation and misreading, with overestimate perhaps as likely as underestimate. But even if we have to be wary of making specific claims about the extent of Sam's mentorship, the fact of its recurrence is impressive: he is paying back the generosity that was once shown to him by others, and illustrating the 'familial' character of the literary world, its potential to be a culture of sponsorship, advocacy and devotion.

✺ 36 ✺

One of our longer chapters, directed with no little
incongruity to the matter of life's brevity

SAM'S INVOLVEMENT in the careers of writers such as Charlotte Lennox and Fanny Burney strengthened an already
significant interest in the politics of literary reputation. The
subject occupied him in several essays, such as *Rambler* 127,
where he noted that 'It is not uncommon for those who at
their first entrance into the world were distinguished for
attainments or abilities, to disappoint the hopes which they
had raised, and to end in neglect and obscurity that life
which they began in honour.' 'To the long catalogue of the
inconveniences of old age,' he added, 'may be often added
the loss of fame.' A few months later, in *Rambler* 203, he
described such fame as 'a meteor which blazes a while and
disappears for ever', observing that 'if we except a few tran-
scendent and invincible names, which no revolution of
opinion or length of time is able to suppress, all those that
engage our thoughts, or diversify our conversation, are
every moment hasting to obscurity'.

Today, popular wisdom relating to such matters has
ossified in the elegant and endlessly repeated '*Ars longa, vita
brevis*'. I tend to think '*ars longa*' means 'It takes a long time
to master technique', yet it can be interpreted as a comment
on art's durability – 'Art lasts, but you don't have much time
in which to make it.' Often, though, the *ars* Sam pictures
isn't *longa* and it's the brevity of reputation that strikes him.

In *Rambler* 106 he writes that 'There are, indeed, few kinds of composition from which an author, however learned or ingenious, can hope a long continuance of fame' and 'Among those whose reputation is exhausted in a short time by its own luxuriance are the writers who take advantage of present incidents or characters which strongly interest the passions.' In the short term these writers command attention – 'It is not difficult to obtain readers, when we discuss a question which every one is desirous to understand, which is debated in every assembly, and has divided the nation into parties; or when we display the faults or virtues of him whose public conduct has made almost every man his enemy or his friend.' But the world moves on, and yesterday's indispensable bestsellers are tomorrow's charity shop rejectamenta.

It is with something like this in mind that Sam wonders in the preface to his edition of Shakespeare 'by what peculiarities of excellence . . . [he] has gained and kept the favour of his countrymen'. 'The reverence due to writings that have long subsisted arises,' he reflects, 'not from any credulous confidence in the superior wisdom of past ages, or gloomy persuasion of the degeneracy of mankind, but is the consequence of acknowledged and indubitable positions, that what has been longest known has been most considered, and what is most considered is best understood.' 'The irregular combinations of fanciful invention may delight a-while,' he argues, 'by that novelty of which the common satiety of life sends us all in quest; but the pleasures of sudden wonder are soon exhausted, and the mind can only repose on the stability of truth.' The greatest literature, in this view, grounds us. Its truth, even if delicately or ethereally expressed, is earthy.

One of his best-remembered comments on the subject,

fleetingly mentioned in an earlier chapter, is the terse 'Nothing odd will do long. *Tristram Shandy* did not last.' He said this while discussing with Boswell the fortunes of the more ludicrous sorts of literature. In the long term he was wrong; although Laurence Sterne's reputation dropped off when he died (and Sam was speaking eight years after his death), his novel has gone on to influence countless other writers and has established itself as a requisite of grad-school lit biz. But what's interesting here is that Sam is thinking about art's impermanence, and the attribute he holds responsible for *Tristram Shandy*'s lack of longevity is its being 'odd' – a prankish parody, a morally irresponsible trifle. Oddness means several different things to him: 'the state of not being even', uncouthness and impropriety, a peculiarity 'not to be numbered among any class' (i.e. a failure to belong to any recognized genre). It was, of course, a quality of which he had direct experience, and, while he can hardly have thought of *Tristram Shandy* as being much like him, he knew intimately how judgemental society could be about strangeness, whether of appearance or behaviour.

Besides being odd, *Tristram Shandy* was a comedy, and Sam was aware that comedy tends to have a short shelf life. We can all name comedies that have aged well, yet there are far more that haven't, and it is a genre that doesn't travel freely. After a while, or beyond their original milieu, jokes require explanatory notes, and such explanation is the death of humour. As Sam comments, of the fiddlier bits of Shakespeare, 'Notes are often necessary, but they are necessary evils', and 'the mind is refrigerated by interruption'. Sterne's brand of comedy, so determinedly eye-catching and experimental, struck Sam as the very opposite of durable, and its popularity seemed to rest on its author's relentless pursuit of fame – the decision of a country vicar to convert his existence into what we would now call performance art. In the National Portrait Gallery in London there's a fine Reynolds portrait of Sterne, which shows him with his finger pressed to the side of his head, appearing to point to his brain. It is a calculated and arrogant pose, a forerunner of today's glossy, knowing and artfully uninformative close-ups of celebrity. Sam knew the painting and its subject's half-smile; the one time they met was at Reynolds's house, in 1761, and Sterne caused offence by showing off a pornographic picture.

More prosaically, Sam doubted the appetite of either posterity or publishers for a work so in love with typographical experiment. *Tristram Shandy* prominently featured an assortment of squiggles, a black page, and another page that was curiously marbled (and made the book seem almost inside-out). It projected an air of incompleteness.[1] Understandably, Sam failed to picture a future in which readers would delight in the very aspects of Sterne's novel that unsettled his contemporaries – its indecency, noisiness and disruptiveness, its apparent plagiarism, its playful sense of itself as an *objet d'art*, and its hospitality to different modes of criticism (which would also have a role in the longevity of some of Sam's own writings). Besides, people making predictions about the mainstream always forget that there's another way of staying in the swim: you can slosh down the gutter of time.

Whereas an artwork's chance of lasting is a subject for critical debate, the truth of *vita brevis* is incontrovertible. Sam noted in the *Rambler* that one might hear the complaint several times a day: *Life is short*. This was banality itself. When someone says that life is short, it's evidence not of wisdom or worldly experience, but of their soul having become like a pipe, an organ through which sounds pass smoothly and complacently. In short, 'no ideas are annexed to the words'. He concluded that 'So far are we generally from thinking what we often say of the shortness of life, that at the time when it is necessarily shortest, we form projects which we delay to execute . . . and suffer those passions to gain upon us, which are only excusable in the prime of life.'

But these words, written when Sam was forty-one, were really self-censure. His consciousness of the passage of time was acute; in *The Vanity of Human Wishes*, 'Time hovers o'er, impatient to destroy, / And shuts up all the passages of joy', and in his life of Alexander Pope he comments, 'He that runs against Time has an antagonist not subject to casualties.' In prayers dating from 1752 and 1753 he writes of the 'residue of my life' (which is shrinking), and in the *Rambler* he argues that a defining quality of 'the state of man' is the 'thoughtlessness with which he floats along the stream of time' – a stream that, as he observes elsewhere, is 'continually washing' the 'dissoluble fabrics' of reputation and fashion.[2] The image of death that most impressed him was in *Paradise Lost*, where the fallen angel Belial speaks of it as like being 'swallowed up and lost / In the wide womb of uncreated night'.

In *Idler* 88 he writes that 'neither our friends nor our enemies wonder that we live and die like the rest of mankind'; it is a marvel only to us, but when we confront it 'we find at last that we have suffered our purposes to sleep till the time of action is past'. When we think of death, we reproach ourselves:

He that compares what he has done with what he has left undone, will feel the effect which must always follow the comparison of imagination with reality; he will look with contempt on his own unimportance, and wonder

to what purpose he came into the world; he will repine
that he shall leave behind him no evidence of his having
been, that he has added nothing to the system of life,
but has glided from youth to age among the crowd,
without any effort for distinction.

Death is a subject that never quite recedes from view, and
as he grows older it nags at him more and more. He understands its levelling effect, for he has seen, more times than
he can bear, its power to extinguish all that makes a person
notable. Whereas in his early works he pictured heroic figures tussling with the forces of destruction, he would come
to regard death as a confirmation of our shared humanity
and its fragility. Thinking about death means thinking about
what might come after death. It also means thinking about
how we might die – where, and with whom – and what we
ought to do before we die, and what we might fail to do. For
Sam, it was natural and painful to recall the projects he had
at some point contemplated but never got round to. Among
these were an edition of Chaucer, a collection of proverbs,
a sequel to *Rasselas*, a set of lives of the great philosophers,
a history of war, and an account of the 'revival of learning'
(which we now call the Renaissance). In the 1740s he wrote,
in one of the many prefaces with which he furnished other
writers' books, that 'The only way to preserve knowledge is
to increase it', and in his final decades he appalled himself
with the thought that he not done this enough.

In his later works he often appears either elegiac or on
the verge of launching into elegy, and in his letters he
repeatedly touches on mortality. Thus in September 1773 he
writes from Scotland to Hester Thrale that 'The return of
my birthday, if I remember it, fills me with thoughts which
it seems to be the general care of humanity to escape.' We

should be dubious about the words 'if I remember it', for surely no one forgets their own birthday, even if they prefer not to be reminded of it, and, as we have seen, this particular one was important to him. But it is true that, past forty, birthdays make us think about our impermanence. As he continues, his self-assessment is bleak: 'I can now look back upon threescore and four years, in which little has been done, and little has been enjoyed, a life diversified by misery, spent part in the sluggishness of penury, and part under the violence of pain.' He tries to content himself with the thought that 'perhaps I am better than I should have been, if I had been less afflicted'. This last remark feels throwaway, but it is a powerful idea. A life of perfect ease sounds delectable when you are struggling with countless tasks and trials. But easy living saps the mind's energy. Affliction is hideous, yet when we are in its midst we can try to see it as a test rather than a punishment.

His reflections on death were given extra impetus by an incident that occurred in 1777. In May of that year, a clergyman called William Dodd, noted for his emotional style of preaching, was sentenced to death for forging a bond with a value of £4,200. For more than twenty years Dodd had cultivated an image as a man of fashion and substance, pious but also well-connected. To sustain the fiction, he had borrowed heavily, and eventually, under pressure from his many creditors, he resorted to forgery. When the sentence was passed, he made an indirect approach to Sam, whom he had briefly met many years earlier, to speak up on his behalf. Sam condemned Dodd's crime and his extravagant habits, but thought the punishment too harsh. The offence, he wrote, 'has no very deep dye of turpitude' and 'involves only a temporary and reparable injury'. Besides, he recalled that Dodd had done useful work in promoting the Magdalen Hospital for penitent ex-prostitutes and the rather clunkily named Society for the Relief and Discharge of Persons Imprisoned for Small Debts. The man had erred, but his philanthropic efforts surely showed that his being allowed to live would add something to society, not endanger it.

Sam channelled a lot of effort into Dodd's cause. He was not alone in campaigning for clemency, but despite several petitions, one of which had 23,000 signatures, no mercy was shown. Lord Mansfield, lord chief justice and the subject of Sam's joke about the success of Scots who were 'caught young', argued that yielding to public opinion would create an unsafe precedent. Three weeks before the date set for his execution, Dodd preached a potent sermon that he presented as his own handiwork. In fact, most of it came from the pen of Sam – though it would be several years before he revealed that it was his. When he reflected on the episode, he was annoyed that Dodd had taken credit for the sermon, believing that in his final days he should have been more particular about such matters. 'Depend upon it,' he told Boswell, 'when a man knows he is to be hanged in a fortnight, it concentrates his mind wonderfully.'

If we turn to the sermon itself, we can see why Dodd might have supposed he would get away with claiming it as his own, for the language is characteristically emotive: he admits 'the justice of my sentence, while I am sinking under its severity', speaks to his fellow prisoners of the need to 'call upon God night and day', and insists it is essential that 'when we lament our sins, we are really humbled in self-abhorrence'. But there is a Johnsonian ring in the statement that 'on the dreadful day, when the sentence of the law has its full force, some will be found to have affected a shameless bravery': this is 'not the proper behaviour of a convicted criminal', for 'to meet death with intrepidity is the right only of innocence, if in any human being innocence could be found'. The last duties of the criminal, he declares, 'are humility and self-abasement'. Dodd may have enjoyed saying this, but it was not in his nature to enjoy thinking it.

Unlike Dodd, who to the very end thought he would be spared, Sam was constantly aware of his own mortality. He was influenced in this partly by his reading of William Law, who advised that one should think each day of death, and partly by his early experience of illness. The body doesn't lie, and it repeatedly found new ways to make him hear the rumblings of death's drumbeat. Writing to Hester Thrale in September 1777, he reflected that 'I have loitered, and what is worse, loitered with very little pleasure. The time has run away, as most time runs, without account, without use, and without memorial.' A few days later, he wrote to her again. Once more it was his birthday, and he commented that the occasion now seemed to come round more quickly. I think all of us, as we age, develop the impression that time moves faster, but it's worth adding that people with Tourette's syndrome appear to have a particularly keen perception of time intervals, which is possibly related to the efforts they are used to making in order to suppress their tics.[3]

The tone of self-rebuke is familiar, and in truth he did plenty over this period, not least firing off letters of good counsel to friends. Indeed, the day after writing to Hester Thrale that 'Age is a very stubborn disease', he went with Boswell to Kedleston Hall in Derbyshire, and some of his remarks on that occasion suggest mischief and gaiety. 'If I had no duties,' he said, 'I would spend my life in driving briskly in a post-chaise with a pretty woman; but she would be one who could understand me.' Over the next few days he took delight in explaining the myriad different methods of shaving, in pointing out the deficiencies of his friend John Taylor's pet bulldog, and in arguing that Garrick, reputed now to have a fortune of £100,000, was for all the acclaim he had received no more praiseworthy than a rope-walker or a ballad-singer (and perhaps less so).

While Boswell liked to have details of this kind to note down, he wanted Sam to discourse on important subjects, and one evening in April 1778, with the Dodd case still fresh in the mind, he initiated another discussion of death. Sam's companions on this occasion included Anna Seward, a poet nicknamed the Swan of Lichfield. A friend of Lucy Porter's and the granddaughter of the schoolmaster John Hunter, she would turn out to be one of Sam's harshest critics, enraged by the memory of his colossal status and by what she felt was Boswell's craven idolatry. That evening she was less vigorously opinionated than she would later prove, but asserted that annihilation was nothing to be afraid of, since it 'is only a pleasing sleep without a dream'. Sam objected: 'It is neither pleasing, nor sleep . . . The lady confounds annihilation, which is nothing, with the apprehension of it, which is dreadful. It is in the apprehension of it that the horror of annihilation consists.' These were among the lines that most impressed Samuel Beckett, and in a copy I have of Boswell's *Life of Johnson* a previous owner has written alongside them 'Dr J confronts The Void.'

Over the next few years he often looked into it. To Lucy Porter he wrote on 5 July 1783 that 'The world passes away, and we are passing with it'. The same day he told Hester Thrale that 'My organs are yet feeble.' The spectres of friends' deaths were crowding in on him. In July the next year he wrote to Joshua Reynolds that he hoped to go to Derbyshire for some fresher air; once there, he felt no better, and in August, hearing that the painter Allan Ramsay had died at Dover after a grim Channel crossing, he reflected that 'On which side soever I turn, Mortality presents its formidable frown.' Old friends had passed into oblivion: 'That we must all die, we always knew', but 'I wish I had sooner remembered it'.

He had never, of course, forgotten about death. He lived in an age in which attitudes to it became noticeably more dramatic; where previously there had been what the historian Philippe Ariès calls a 'familiar resignation to the collective destiny of the species', an understanding of death as something 'tamed' by the rituals of piety and as a result 'banal', there was now a newly stark sense of death 'as a transgression which tears man from his daily life, from rational society', and increasingly the very idea of it was enough to stir extreme emotion.[4] Close to his end, Sam was with Hawkins when he spoke of his dread of the ultimate judgement. Hawkins records that 'with a look that cut me to the heart' he revealed his fears and finally wondered, 'Shall I, who have been a teacher of others, myself be a castaway?'

Sam was quoting St Paul, from his first letter to the Corinthians: 'But I keep under my body, and bring it into subjection: lest that by any means, when I have preached to others, I myself should be a castaway.' Right to the end the body seemed to pose a threat; he believed that its needs and impulses would lead him into temptation. What we know of Sam's body makes this anxiety more upsetting, for it is clear that in his final months the world of the flesh was a source of excruciating pain to him, not of any kind of reward, and that he treated his own person with mortifying strictness. Near the end of his life one of his testicles became so swollen that he took it upon himself to stab it with a lancet under the bedclothes. His autopsy would reveal that one of his kidneys had been destroyed by water pressure and two of the valves in his aorta had calcified; some of the cells in his lungs were so dilated by emphysema that they were the size of gooseberries, and he had a stone in his gall bladder described as being the size of a pigeon's egg – the last detail uncanny, as in the *Dictionary* he had referred to bezoar, a stone found in the stomach of a goat, sometimes attaining precisely those dimensions.

The overriding impression here is of pain. In *Rambler* 32, Sam refers to 'the armies of pain' that 'send their arrows against us on every side'; he comments that 'the strongest armour . . . will only blunt their points'. His choice of language emphasizes that pain is an event. We might usefully think of that event as the output of a biological alarm system; it causes us to pay attention to some part of ourselves where sensory receptors – nociceptors – are detecting harm. The sensation of pain is not merely something we register, but something we evaluate and communicate: if it's not immediately obvious, we consider what may have caused it, how we can ease it, what makes it worse, and we also think about how we should comport ourselves, remembering what we have heard about the virtues of endurance yet worrying that too stoical a manner may cause people to think our suffering is only trivial. As we enlist others' assistance we fight against their incomprehension, their failure to appreciate our pain's particularity or indeed its diffuseness. We may even reflect on how, when the pain is gone, we will embark on a fresh scheme of physical and spiritual self-improvement. Awful physical pain causes us existential pain, since it seems to belong to death; we will do almost anything to relieve it, and part of this is the need to drive away the idea of our certain mortality. In the *Idler*, Sam observed that 'The mind is seldom quickened to very vigorous operations but by pain, or the dread of pain'; he wrote these words in August 1758, when not yet fifty, and we can already sense his experience of agony. In his declining years, its intensity and frequency grew. At the same time his attentiveness to himself increased, and it was in seeking to be a reliable witness to his many afflictions that he became so adept at parsing life's discontents.

Others could admire this aptitude and still be glad that they lacked it. A remarkable instance of this occurred when Sam was in his late sixties; it was a social encounter of a kind that we've all had, in which someone we've forgotten turns out never to have forgotten us, and their generous assessment of what we have accomplished is touching – but also ruffles us, because it allows us to recognize how people see us, to perceive for a moment what they think we have left undone and how we may be remembered. It came in April 1778, when Sam was accosted in the street, after the Good Friday service at St Clement Danes, by Oliver Edwards, who had been at university with him nearly half a century earlier and had not clapped eyes on him since. The two men talked eagerly, and Edwards mentioned that he had made a lot of money as a lawyer, but had given a large part of it to needy relatives. 'It is better to *live* rich than to *die* rich,' responded Sam, echoing a line in Sir Thomas Browne's *Christian Morals*. A few moments later Edwards came back with the deathless comment 'You are a philosopher, Dr Johnson. I have tried too in my time to be a philosopher; but, I don't know how, cheerfulness was always breaking in.'

❧ 37 ❧

Some thoughts upon the business of Cultural Legislation,
which is less atrocious than it sounds

BY THE TIME Sam had his chance meeting with Oliver
Edwards, he was busy with his last great work. Now known
as the *Lives of the Poets*, it began as a series of prefaces and
its origins lay in commercial rivalry. In 1776, a young Scot
called John Bell started to issue cheap reprints of the works
of the major English poets (eventually 109 volumes). Piqued,
a consortium of forty-two London booksellers and six printers swiftly planned a response. They approached Sam to
lend his authority to an edition that they promised would be
'elegantly printed . . . on a fine writing paper' – a classier
undertaking than Bell's, with more scholarly weight behind
it. The idea was that he would contribute a sketch of each
poet.

Sam, who felt that to date there had been scarcely any
good accounts of the lives of English writers, played only a
small part in deciding which ones to include. The four he
managed to add to the booksellers' list are now obscure:
some of Isaac Watts's hymns are still sung ('When I survey
the wondrous cross', 'Jesus shall reign where'er the sun'), but
who reads Luton-born love poet John Pomfret, or innocuous
clergyman Thomas Yalden, or pious Sir Richard Blackmore? Of these, it's the last whose inclusion tells us most.
To a modern eye, Blackmore's achievements don't look all
that wondrous: epics about King Arthur, a poem about the

effects on the brain of exposure to the sun, opposition to a scheme to provide free medicine for London's poor. In his lifetime he was relentlessly attacked. But Sam is sympathetic to him, noting his abilities as a physician. 'Contempt,' he writes, 'is a kind of gangrene, which, if it seizes one part of a character, corrupts all the rest by degrees.' Besides, the sheer volume of vitriol that his critics had rained down on him made the details of his existence worth recording. Failing all else, Blackmore had been canny enough to invent a character called Mr Johnson, who was the hero of a club that from time to time retreated to a country house 'to enjoy philosophical leisure'. Sam quotes Blackmore's reference to this Mr Johnson as 'a critic of the first rank' whose taste is 'distinguishing, just, and delicate' and whose judgements 'result from the nature and reason of things'. Understandably, he is rather taken with this figure and is clear that 'his character shall not be suppressed'.

Despite his modest editorial contribution, when the first volumes came out in 1779, the public referred to 'Dr Johnson's edition of the English poets' or simply 'Johnson's Poets'. The latter was the wording that appeared on the spines of bound sets. Sam objected, declaring in a letter to an unidentified correspondent that 'This is indecent.' Had the edition truly been his, its contents would have been different. But his name was crucial to the venture, ensuring publicity, and it has been hard to shake the idea that the *Lives of the Poets* is his map of what matters. In hindsight, it takes a place alongside several other large projects begun in the 1760s and 1770s that presented an overview of an art form and its practitioners. Chief among these were Sir Joshua Reynolds's *Discourses on Art* and Charles Burney's *General History of Music*. These were surveys, designed to fulfil more than one purpose; in his study of the genre, Lawrence

Lipking writes that they 'woo connoisseurs and antiquarians and common readers' and at the same time 'serve patriotism and taste and scholarship and tradition and romance', but 'stretched and buckled with the fatigue of responding to too many demands'.[1] Most of the significant endeavours in this vein were by members of Sam's circle: besides the efforts of Burney and Reynolds, there were Sir John Hawkins's *History of Music* and Thomas Warton's *History of English Poetry*.

Sam's particular contribution was a panoramic work that drew on sixty years of reading. In the end much more substantial than the concise prefaces the booksellers had in mind, the *Lives of the Poets* was simultaneously a work of literary history, a collection of closely focused critical studies and an important component of an immense literary anthology. It was also, like the *Dictionary*, designed to promote a sense of cultural heritage. 'This,' it appeared to say, 'is English poetry.' It made a substantial body of work accessible. For some, that body of work wasn't broad enough; it didn't include Chaucer or even Shakespeare, beginning instead with Abraham Cowley (1618–1667). Hence Elizabeth Barrett Browning's complaint that 'Johnson . . . wrote the lives of the poets and left out the poets.'[2] That wasn't quite the truth of the matter, and it's in any case interesting that he starts with Cowley, who was a professional poet rather than a polite amateur, set out a theory of what it meant to be an author (especially in time of war), and worried that our failure to name things condemned much that was of value to be forgotten.

In the light of the last of these details, it is striking that when Sam wrote about Cowley he referred – as no one had quite done before, though Dryden and Pope came close – to the 'metaphysical poets'. This 'race of writers' practised a form of freakish, precious 'wit': 'The most heterogeneous ideas are yoked by violence together.' In other words, these poets make strange comparisons in order to surprise us and project an air of ingenuity, as well as to explore afresh the contours of experience. Thus John Donne likens his soul and his lover's to a pair of compasses – hers is the fixed foot, and 'when the other far doth roam, / It leans and hearkens after it'. Or he points out to his mistress, who's reluctant to have sex with him, that they are already conjoined: a flea has bitten them both, and in its body their bloods are mingled. 'Metaphysical poetry' has stuck as a way of labelling the works of Donne and Cowley, along with Andrew Marvell, Richard Crashaw and George Herbert. The term draws attention to the potential for poetry to make us *feel* thoughts and *think* feelings; Sam believes these poets' particular ways of doing this are likely to alienate most readers, and it is of course this very quality, an audacious cleverness verging sometimes on ecstasy and sometimes on inscrutability, that later generations have prized.

Sam knew the importance of giving a phenomenon a name. Doing so helps us care for it – in the sense that we are able to discuss it, conveniently and with conviction, and also, of course, in the sense that we can make our relationship with it purposeful. Often that purposefulness takes the form of curation; we are the advocates or gallerists of what we have named. But in this case, the act of naming made it easier for Sam to disparage a style of poetry he found self-indulgent. The name marked a boundary, keeping a certain kind of unhealthy conceitedness in quarantine. When people today refer to metaphysical poetry, it is rarely with this intention. Yet we see here that labelling a problem is a way of turning it into a discussion point. An aversion to labels, and especially to being labelled, is an aversion to the schematic and reductive, to the obsession with brands and transactions, to the notion that the menu is the meal, but it is because labels are schematic and reductive that we find them so useful.

Besides functioning as criticism and history, the fifty-two parts of the *Lives of the Poets* are also, of course, works of biography – Sam's favourite thing to read, and certainly one of his favourite genres in which to write. He thinks of it as both morally and psychologically interesting. In *Rambler* 60 he articulates a theory of the form, which can instruct us about 'every diversity of condition'. The business of the biographer is 'to lead the thoughts into domestic privacies, and display the minute details of daily life'. Not for him the high strains of panegyric; he looks at his subjects and imagines being in their shoes. How do their works relate to their circumstances? What choices have shaped their careers? How do they think? What disturbs or excites them? What are their motives, and are there ways of reading these besides the merely obvious?

This is what we now expect of biography, but it wasn't what his contemporaries expected. For them, the business of the biographer was to select and arrange incidents from a person's life; for him, it was essential to add both authorial energy and philosophical inquisitiveness, to assess the value of sources and enlist readers' powers of sympathy and judgement. He is interested in locating his poets' early moments of frustration, naming the places they were educated and the people who did most to shape their minds, and understanding their professional relationships (especially those with their publishers). He wants to draw attention to literature's means of production and reproduction. All of this promises to be illuminating – and if it's grubby, so be it. Before the *Lives of the Poets*, it was usual for biographers to omit details of their subjects' drinking, but Sam sees a weakness for drink as revealing and chooses to be candid about it.[3] To write a biography was to access another person's psyche, the truth of their private self, and this meant having to unearth truths about one's own self. And to read a biography was, he saw, to compare our lives to the lives of others and learn from them, to make better sense of our existence. The attraction of the form lay in its 'giving us what comes near to ourselves, what we can turn to use'. 'We are all prompted by the same motives, all deceived by the same fallacies, all animated by hope, obstructed by danger, entangled by desire, and seduced by pleasure.'

'We know somewhat, and we imagine the rest,' he writes in his life of Wentworth Dillon, Earl of Roscommon, who had written about the need for a 'sympathetic bond' between authors and their translators. This was in *An Essay on Translated Verse*, a poem published in 1684, which Sam admired more than anything else Roscommon wrote. It's easy to see why. For Roscommon, the goal in translating another person's work was to be 'No longer his interpreter, but he': a translator should choose a project where it was possible to identify strongly with the original author. Yet Sam, precisely because he recognizes the imaginative element of biography, is a sceptical life-writer. He is careful not to exaggerate the connections between life and art. Where there is uncertainty about a detail of a writer's life, he usually evaluates the possibilities rather than plumping for the one he likes the most and sweeping all others aside. He's dubious about popular anecdotes, about attempts to attribute a single clear-cut meaning to a person's experiences, and about the claims of previous biographers, especially the authors of those fawning acts of hagiography he called 'honeysuckle lives'. This last category sickened him: when we write a life, we 'must represent it as it really was' and should not 'hide the man' in order to 'produce a hero'.

He sees how much a well-chosen detail can achieve. It opens a shaft of light on the truth of a person's character. Thus he tells us that Alexander Pope wore three pairs of stockings in order to bulk up his slender legs, and that they had to be drawn on and off by a maid. From this we get the impression of Pope as a refined and vulnerable man who must perform an awkward ritual of robustness to keep the chilly world at bay. His other physical deficiencies confirm this – whether it's his needing a stiff canvas bodice to hold himself upright, or his use of a fur doublet under his shirt to shut out the cold. When we read that his death 'was imputed by some of his friends to a silver saucepan, in which it was his delight to heat potted lampreys', the tragic relationship between performance and frailty is underscored. In reality, Pope died as a result of his lungs slowly weakening, which was the effect of kyphoscoliosis. But the silver saucepan and the medieval delicacy he cooked in it are the stuff of bathos; although Pope had written about heroes, felled by the sword or the javelin, his own death had been wholly unheroic. As Sam comments, 'The death of great men is not always proportioned to their lives', and lurking inside this statement is a suspicion that the deaths of the great are in fact never proportionate to their lives.

In other lives, there's the same evocative succinctness. We learn that James Thomson, author of *The Seasons*, was late to a dinner with friends after the premiere of a play he had written because he'd sweated so much in his anxiety that his wig had become messy and required an emergency trip to the barber. Perennially skint, Thomson at last found a degree of financial security when appointed surveyor general of customs for the Leeward Islands. Yet soon afterwards he caught a chill while travelling on the Thames from Hammer-smith to Kew, underestimated its seriousness, went out again too soon, developed a fever and expired. The playwright Thomas Otway was even more hapless. Reduced by debt to starvation, he stumbled naked and delirious into a coffee house, where a gentleman generously gave him a guinea; Otway used some of this to buy a roll and choked to death on his first mouthful.

In these snippets, there is a suggestion of the character of the project as a whole. Sam wrote the *Lives* as his health was failing, and their colour is autumnal. But there are glints of comedy in his portraits of writers' frailties. Chief among these is self-delusion. Even the greatest can't escape vanity, petty rivalry and small-mindedness. Sometimes writers are crippled by the sense that their every act is under surveil-lance. A case in point is Jonathan Swift, who had a rule that he would give only one coin to a beggar – 'and therefore always stored his pocket with coins of different value', to make sure he had the right piece of change for each suppli-cant. Sometimes the problem is the inattention of the world, or of that section of the world whose attention the writer most desires. Sam understands that writers are disposed to crave the approval of the very people who are least likely to give it. In this vein he repeats the story of how Samuel Butler, acclaimed for his satire *Hudibras*, failed in a bid to attract the patronage of the rakish Duke of Buckingham, because, just as they were about to meet, the Duke spotted 'a pimp of his acquaintance . . . trip by with a brace of ladies' and 'immediately quitted his engagement to follow another kind of business'.

The poets he depicts expend their energy and talent on trifling business. The competitiveness of authors is espe-cially costly, as the efforts they channel into keeping ahead of their rivals (or keeping them down) convert ardour into malice and tend to have only a brief effect. Yet he understands the psychology of this. An author is 'a kind of general challenger', who invites judgement, hopes for applause, risks rebuke, and inevitably feels beleaguered. Every challenge the author mounts is a call for comparison with others and their achievements, and authors can't avoid picturing how they measure up against their peers.

'Let no man dream of influence beyond his life,' he writes, in the context of Alexander Pope's ambitions of lasting fame, and Pope emerges as a textbook case of the writer's self-excruciation. He delights in his own importance, but can't stop looking for evidence to the contrary. Publicly claiming to be laid-back about attacks on his work and his person ('these things are my diversion'), he in fact writhes in agony as he reads ever crueller barbs about his 'warped carcass', 'harmless quill', 'little-tiny manhood' and 'poor thingless body'. Again and again the poets are masochists, ravenous for celebrity and deeply anxious about its effects. Few seem to have enough money; most are aware of the transience of reputation. It is no accident that, when the *Lives* became available as four free-standing volumes in 1781, Sam arranged them not by their subjects' date of birth, but by the dates of their deaths. Theirs are to a large degree stories of doubt and stymied ambition. Doomed to be disappointed, they are weak and capricious, or they pickle in the juices of resentment. He can discuss these failings with painful candour, for he has either experienced them or seen them close up. But they are not the ingredients of congenial personality. As he wrote in the *Rambler*, a writer's fans, 'tempted to a nearer knowledge' of the person behind the works they cherish, 'have indeed had frequent reason to repent their curiosity'.

In the *Lives*, his frankness about his subjects' works can be disarming. For instance, he remarks that *Paradise Lost*, despite its author's 'peculiar power to astonish', suffers from a 'want of human interest' and 'None ever wished it longer than it is'. Dryden 'delighted to tread upon the brink of meaning', and of a less distinguished poet, James Hammond, Sam avers, 'It would be hard to find in all his productions three stanzas that deserve to be remembered.' When he turns his attention to the plays of William Congreve, he admits he 'cannot speak distinctly, for since I inspected them many years have passed', but this doesn't stop him declaring that Congreve's characters are 'artificial, with very little of nature, and not much of life', and that 'He formed a peculiar idea of comic excellence, which he supposed to consist in gay remarks and unexpected answers' – with the result that 'His scenes exhibit not much of humour, imagery, or passion'. Congreve's briefer poems get short shrift: they are 'seldom worth the cost of criticism'. Yet even Congreve has his moments. Sam singles out a passage in his play *The Mourning Bride*, in which a young woman enters a mausoleum, where 'the tombs / And monumental caves of death look cold, / And shoot a chillness to my trembling heart'. Here, he believes, the reader discovers a new way of looking at something familiar – 'he feels what he remembers to have felt before, but he feels it with great increase of sensibility'.

The most famous moment in the *Lives* is Sam's almost breezy declaration 'I rejoice to concur with the common reader'. This comes in his assessment of Thomas Gray's extraordinarily popular 'Elegy Written in a Country Churchyard', and the statement is all the more significant because he generally thought Gray's poems lacked either grace or intelligence. He condemned a weak bit of his 'Ode on a Distant Prospect of Eton College' as 'useless and puerile', and felt that when Gray's poetry reached its greatest heights, it was mostly 'by walking on tiptoe'. But in the case of Gray's 'Elegy', he could agree with the prevailing taste, and that pleased him, as he believed that 'by the common sense of readers . . . must be finally decided all claim to poetical honours'.

Sam's 'common reader' is a member of the reading public, a person who buys books and has opinions that are, in his phrase, 'uncorrupted by literary prejudices'. One might counter this by saying that everyone has prejudices, but he was thinking of those that are held by critics and scholars – the sort of readers who don't sit by a fire caught up in a story, but instead cultivate rarefied theories. For Sam, the duty of the creative writer isn't to beget literary criticism or sustain radical arguments, but consists of 'engaging attention and alluring curiosity'; anyone who fails to do these things is wasting readers' time. This isn't a case of being crassly entertaining or juicily provocative. Readers 'uncorrupted by literary prejudices' may prefer Dan Brown to Dante, or Virginia Andrews to Virginia Woolf, yet won't necessarily do so; the point is not that they have simple tastes, or what the literati might regard as low ones, but rather that they have their own tastes, undisturbed by the intellectual fashion of the day.

In his life of Swift, Sam speaks of England as a 'nation of readers'. One of the triumphs of his age, it seemed, was that learning could at last be 'universally diffused', rather than remaining the preserve of a small, self-perpetuating elite. Besides being a champion of the reading public, a growing sphere, he was alive to the ideas and interests of the booksellers who catered for its needs and desires – and whom he called 'the patrons of literature'. In cartoons of

the period, such as Thomas Rowlandson's *Bookseller &*
Author, the bookseller was well-nourished and prosperous,
while the author appeared cringing, scrawny and desperate.
Sam knew better. After all, in his own words, 'I was bred
a bookseller, and have not forgotten my trade.' The truth
was that many of those in the business were patient and
charitable, and their decisions about what to publish were
driven by political inclination or cultural interest rather than
simply by the desire to make a fat profit. Sam saw them as
collaborators.

Sure in his grasp of the economics of their trade, he
recognized its precariousness. A 'nation of readers' was one
consisting of people who possessed the skill rather than
those determined to exercise it. The proliferation of reading
matter, in his age and even more so in ours, is no guarantee
that reading itself will thrive. 'It is strange,' he reflected,
with a certain wryness, 'that there should be so little reading
in the world, and so much writing.' He said this near the end
of his life, on an evening when he was visited by Boswell and
by Edmund Burke's son Richard, and he added, even more
dispiritingly, that 'People in general do not willingly read, if
they can have anything else to amuse them.' It would be an
oddball publisher who printed these remarks and pinned
them up in the office, but Sam's insight is typical in being
realistic – about the place of reading in the world, and
about the challenges people in the book business must face.

It is ironic that the *Lives of the Poets*, which have lasted so
well, began as a kind of garnish for what was in essence a
defensive commercial venture. But it's also instructive. It
tells us something about Sam: his curiosity and intellectual
vigour meant that he did far more than the commission
required, seeing in it an opportunity to celebrate literature,
its practitioners' 'sudden elevations of mind' and readers'

experience of those sudden elevations. It tells us something bigger, too: that in embracing a project initiated by others, who perhaps have no higher purpose than earning money or staking out a patch of ground, one is not obliged to be servile, and that the business of literature – making money out of it – doesn't have to involve cheapening culture and ideas.

❧ 38 ❧

In which this account of the great Johnson is concluded,
with a Farewell to the reader

AFTER HE COMPLETED the *Lives of the Poets*, the main events
of Sam's life were social and domestic. While Henry Thrale
was alive he spent a great deal of time at Streatham Park,
as well as the Thrales' new property in Grosvenor Square,
but often he was at home, among his books on the third
storey of his house in Bolt Court. Then the highlight of his
day was usually dinner; among his favourite companions
were Reynolds, Baretti and the Corsican patriot Pasquale
Paoli. Poor health troubled him increasingly, and there were
days when he could think of nothing else; Boswell feels able
to say, of 1782, that 'the history of his life this year is little
more than a mournful recital of the variations of his illness'.
He rose late, wrote letters, went to church, received visitors,
was bled, and studied Dutch. He made a few trips, to Brigh-
ton and Salisbury and Rochester; he boated on the Medway
and inspected Stonehenge. His mental powers remained, yet
when friends saw him they were moved to comment on his
sharp physical decline.

In the bitter winter of 1784 his health worsened, and as
news spread that he was near death, there was keen public
interest in what kind of end he might have. For a couple of
decades he had seemed one of those rare figures whose
posterity begins in their lifetime. What would his last words
be? Would there be some final, decisive articulation of his

wisdom? The fascination with last words was not new, but it had recently become a contentious subject, much discussed in print. Sam would have recalled John of Gaunt's lines in Shakespeare's *Richard II*: 'They say the tongues of dying men / Enforce attention like deep harmony'. Among his contemporaries, it was usual to think that a person's final utterance was likely to be particularly clear-sighted, an irrevocable expression of beliefs or values. When people said dull things at the end, their dullness was conveniently forgotten, but when they spoke movingly, the words' finality seemed sacred. They served as a key to understanding an entire life; the exit line unlocked the mystery of everything that had preceded it. This cult of last words continues, though it's not as pronounced as it was in the eighteenth and nineteenth centuries. It speaks of – and to – our desire for meaning, closure and completeness. We crave a definitive statement about the truth of a life. About, for that matter, the truth of life in general.

According to whose account you accept, Sam's dying utterance was a conventional 'God bless you', the Latin '*Iam moriturus*' ('I who am about to die'), or something about a cup of warm milk not being handed to him in the way he would have liked. We can be sure, though, that his life ended on the evening of 13 December 1784, a Monday, at Bolt Court. Several details stand out in the copious newspaper coverage: a preoccupation with his legacy to Francis Barber, a concern about where he should be buried – Westminster Abbey and St Paul's are recommended – and disappointment that in his final days he destroyed manuscripts that included valuable notes on his own life. The *Morning Chronicle* pronounced him 'a saint' and urged a period of national mourning. Other publications certified that he had already attained mythic status. The *Public Advertiser* deplored the circulation of vast numbers of anecdotes about him (most of them, inevitably, rubbish), and on Christmas Eve the *Edinburgh Advertiser* reported that eleven writers were separately at work on biographies of him.[1]

'How many maggots,' remarked Edmund Burke, 'have crawled out of that great body!' The image conveyed his disgust, and Burke, who had previously used maggots as a symbol of falsehood, clearly had low expectations of most of the biographers. Perhaps he recalled Shakespeare's reference to 'maggot ostentation' – in a speech from *Love's Labour's Lost* that Sam had quoted in his *Dictionary* entry for *maggot*. The character who utters these words, Berowne, speaks of the 'taffeta phrases' that bloat the language of praise, and, although he is thinking about the verbal games favoured by suitors, his words apply to the effusiveness and pedantry of literary parasites who've got something to sell.

From the moment Sam's death was known, there emerged a pattern with which we are now well acquainted: everyone who had associated with him, no matter how fleetingly, had a story of sorts, and while many of those who had never met him expressed disappointment that they would now not get the chance to do so, dissenters insisted that he had been overrated. There were valuable glimpses of the authentic Johnson, but also a surfeit of far-fetched, self-promoting yarns. Writers aspiring to topical seriousness took him as their subject. Thomas Percy's *Verses on the Death of Dr Samuel Johnson* (1785) praised his success in freeing the English language from 'the mad grasp of fashion's wild decree' and issued the rather clunky instruction 'Ye sons of Britain, venerate a name / That fix'd the channels of your country's fame.' In the same year, Thomas Hobhouse's *Elegy to the Memory of Dr Samuel Johnson* included the apt couplet

'His last dread precepts ever shall survive / And Johnson's death shall teach the world to live'.[2]

Boswell would write in the *Life* that he could not express all that he felt upon the loss of his great guide and friend. Instead he quoted William Gerard Hamilton, an Irish politician Sam had admired: 'No man can be said to put you in mind of Johnson', and his death 'has made a chasm, which not only nothing can fill up, but which nothing has a tendency to fill up'. Plenty of people have tried to occupy the space he vacated – self-anointed polymaths and linguistic savants, princes of apophthegm and titans of literary London – and plenty have done their bit to recreate his immensity – biographers and critics, idolaters and cock-eyed champions of misquotation. A sense of his distinctive powers and irreplaceable authority has endured.

In Alan Bennett's play *The History Boys*, the more than faintly Johnsonian teacher Hector tells his charges that 'The best moments in reading are when you come across something . . . which you had thought special and particular to you.' There it is: a thought, a phrase, an attitude, written down by someone you have never met – 'And it is as if a hand has come out and taken yours.' Sam's hand reaches down the ages in just this manner. He speaks of familiar subjects in unfamiliar ways, and it can seem as if he has a wise word for every occasion.

Isaiah Berlin drew a distinction between those writers and thinkers who are foxes and those who are hedgehogs. Or rather, he popularized a distinction originally drawn by the Greek poet Archilochus, nearly 2,700 years ago. Archilochus wasn't thinking about writers, but his words seem peculiarly applicable to them: the fox knows many things, but the hedgehog knows one big thing. According to Berlin, among writers and thinkers there is a 'great chasm between those, on one side, who relate everything to a single central vision . . . and, on the other side, those who pursue many ends, often unrelated and even contradictory'.[3] Sam, I'd argue, was a fox who could do a good impression of being a hedgehog.

It's not entirely satisfactory to speak of him in such terms, because he was physically most unlike either creature. Still, it is the fox-like Samuel Johnson who can enter into a discussion of beekeeping or kelp-gathering as readily as he can write a biography or a political tract, and whose intellect inclines, in the words of the critic Jean Hagstrum, 'towards reducing, revising, displacing, or altering mental structures too easily established'.[4] It is the fox-like Johnson, too, who can write in *Adventurer* 126 of the perils of being someone who 'never compares his notions with those of others, readily acquiesces in his first thoughts, and very seldom discovers the objections which may be raised against his opinions'. A person unappreciative of the 'advantages of society' and 'general converse' has failed to get to grips with the sheer 'multiplicity of objects' and 'thinks himself in possession of truth, when he is only fondling an error long since exploded'. Deep intelligence, according to this view, comes from being responsive to a breadth of stimuli.

But what of the one big thing, the hedgehog's singular notion? It is a principle summed up in *Rasselas*, almost in passing, by Princess Nekayah. In conversation with her brother, Nekayah comments that 'We differ from ourselves just as we differ from each other'. She is thinking of how, when we reflect on questions to do with politics and morality, we can never have a fully rounded understanding of what's at stake – what one might today call a 360-degree view. Her words echo Montaigne's assertion that 'We are entirely made up of bits and pieces, woven together so diversely and shapelessly that each one of them pulls its own way at every moment. And there is as much difference between us and ourselves as there is between us and other people.'[5]

Nekayah's statement has a broad significance. It affirms two principles that we're on the whole not very willing to acknowledge. The first is simple and unsettling: we are inconsistent. This is an uncomfortable notion – we have been programmed to think that consistency is a great virtue – yet it has some salutary effects. When we notice our inconsistencies, we are discovering complexity, not inadequacy. The worst of ourselves is part of who we are and, rather than denying this, we should accept it, for suffering and error can be translated into wisdom. This is how we earn our truth, and we grow from truth to truth. Then there is the second principle, more familiar but easily neglected: differing from others is normal, and our disagreements, animosities and tensions don't always need to be actively (and forcefully) resolved, because over time they may resolve themselves or prove bearable (even interesting or rewarding), like the discrepancies within ourselves. These two principles merge into a single principle: when our tolerance fails, it is not only for the obvious reason that we cannot stomach, let alone welcome, other people's difference from us, but also because we have not managed to understand our own contradictions.

Sam points up the need for such perspective. Near the end of *Rasselas*, Imlac emphasizes that 'You are only one atom of the mass of humanity, and have neither such virtue or vice . . . that you should be singled out for supernatural favours or afflictions.' Reading this, it feels natural to rush towards the end of the sentence, but the most important part is the first. We are significant to ourselves and to the people that love us, but each of us is *only one atom of the mass of human-ity*. This isn't simply a statement about the paltriness of the individual, or a reminder not to get big ideas about how consequential we are; it's also a declaration about equality.

Acknowledgements

An acknowledgement, according to Samuel Johnson's *Dictionary*, can be 'confession of a benefit received' and also 'confession of a fault'.

By 'benefit' he meant 'a kindness; a favour conferred; an act of love'. I am grateful for favours done me by James Basker, Robert Macfarlane and Michael Proffitt; for the larger kindnesses of Alexandra Harris, Gesche Ipsen and Leo Robson; and for the unstinting generosity of Jessica Edwards and Paul Hitchings.

Thanks are also due to my judicious editor, Georgina Morley, her colleague Chloe May, my copy-editor Fraser Crichton, my agent Peter Straus and his assistant Matthew Turner.

Finally, I would like to take this opportunity to acknowledge two people who shaped my interest in Samuel Johnson: John Mullan and the late Tony Nuttall.

Such faults as this book contains are mine.

Bibliography

I have used the following editions of works by Johnson and his biographers:

The Yale Edition of the Works of Samuel Johnson, 23 vols (New Haven,
   Connecticut: Yale University Press, 1959–)
Johnsonian Miscellanies, ed. George Birkbeck Hill, 2 vols (Oxford:
   Clarendon Press, 1897)
The Early Biographies of Samuel Johnson, ed. O M Brack, Jr and Robert
   E. Kelley (Iowa City: University of Iowa Press, 1974)
Samuel Johnson, *The Lives of the Poets*, ed. Roger Lonsdale, 4 vols
   (Oxford: Clarendon Press, 2006)
The Letters of Samuel Johnson, ed. Bruce Redford, 5 vols (Oxford:
   Clarendon Press, 1992–94)

James Boswell, *The Life of Samuel Johnson, LL.D.*, ed. George Birkbeck
   Hill, revised and enlarged by L. F. Powell, 6 vols (Oxford:
   Clarendon Press, 1934–64)
James Boswell, *The Life of Samuel Johnson*, ed. David Womersley
   (London: Penguin, 2008)
Sir John Hawkins, *The Life of Samuel Johnson, LL.D.*, ed. O M Brack, Jr
   (Athens, Georgia: University of Georgia Press, 2009)

Other works consulted:

M. D. Aeschliman, 'The Good Man Speaking Well', *National Review* 37
   (11 January 1985), 49–52
Paul Kent Alkon, *Samuel Johnson and Moral Discipline* (Evanston, Illinois:
   Northwestern University Press, 1967)
David R. Anderson and Gwin J. Kolb (eds), *Approaches to Teaching the
   Works of Samuel Johnson* (New York: Modern Language
   Association of America, 1993)

Julia Annas, 'Epictetus on Moral Perspectives', in Theodore Scaltsas
     and Andrew S. Mason (eds), *The Philosophy of Epictetus* (Oxford:
     Oxford University Press, 2007), 140–152

Philippe Ariès, *Western Attitudes Towards Death: From the Middle Ages to the
     Present*, trans. Patricia M. Ranum (Baltimore, Maryland: Johns
     Hopkins University Press, 1974)

Deirdre Bair, *Samuel Beckett: A Biography* (New York: Touchstone, 1993)

Sarah Bakewell, *How To Live: or A Life of Montaigne in One Question and
     Twenty Attempts at an Answer* (London: Vintage, 2011)

Katharine Balderston (ed.), *Thraliana: The Diary of Mrs Hester Lynch
     Thrale (Later Mrs Piozzi) 1776–1809*, 2nd ed., 2 vols (Oxford:
     Clarendon Press, 1951)

Barry Baldwin, 'The Mysterious Letter "M" in Johnson's Diaries',
     The Age of Johnson: A Scholarly Annual 6 (1994), 131–145

Louise K. Barnett, 'Dr Johnson's Mother: Maternal Ideology and the
     Life of Savage', *Studies on Voltaire and the Eighteenth Century* 304
     (1992), 856–859

Philip Edward Baruth, 'Recognizing the Author-Function: Alternatives
     to Greene's Black-and-Red Book of Johnson *Logia*', *The Age of
     Johnson: A Scholarly Annual* 5 (1992), 35–59

James G. Basker, 'Dancing Dogs, Women Preachers and the Myth of
     Johnson's Misogyny', *The Age of Johnson: A Scholarly Annual* 3
     (1990), 63–90

—————, *Samuel Johnson in the Mind of Thomas Jefferson*
     (Charlottesville, Virginia: privately printed for the Johnsonians,
     1999)

John Batchelor (ed.), *The Art of Literary Biography* (Oxford: Clarendon
     Press, 1995)

Jonathan Bate, *The Genius of Shakespeare* (London: Picador, 1997)

Walter Jackson Bate, *The Achievement of Samuel Johnson* (New York:
     Oxford University Press, 1955)

—————, *Samuel Johnson* (London: Hogarth Press, 1984)

Gavin de Becker, *The Gift of Fear: Survival Signals That Protect Us from
     Violence* (London: Bloomsbury, 2000)

Wendy Laura Belcher, *Abyssinia's Samuel Johnson: Ethiopian Thought in the
     Making of an English Author* (New York: Oxford University Press,
     2012)

Maxine Berg, *Luxury and Pleasure in Eighteenth-Century Britain* (Oxford:
     Oxford University Press, 2005)

Isaiah Berlin, *The Hedgehog and the Fox: An Essay on Tolstoy's View of
     History* (London: Weidenfeld and Nicolson, 1953)

Tom Bingham, *Dr Johnson and the Law, and Other Essays on Johnson* (London: Inner Temple, 2010)

Harold Bloom, *Where Shall Wisdom Be Found?* (New York: Riverhead Books, 2004)

Margaret A. Boden, *Creativity and Art: Three Roads to Surprise* (Oxford: Oxford University Press, 2010)

Sissela Bok, *Exploring Happiness: From Aristotle to Brain Science* (New Haven, Connecticut: Yale University Press, 2010)

James T. Boulton (ed.), *Johnson: The Critical Heritage* (London: Routledge & Kegan Paul, 1971)

Joanna Bourke, *Fear: A Cultural History* (London: Virago, 2005)
_____, *The Story of Pain: From Prayer to Painkillers* (Oxford: Oxford University Press, 2014)

Toni O'Shaughnessy Bowers, 'Critical Complicities: *Savage* Mothers, Johnson's Mother, and the Containment of Maternal Difference', *The Age of Johnson: A Scholarly Annual* 5 (1992), 115–146

Gay W. Brack, 'Tetty and Samuel Johnson: The Romance and the Reality', *The Age of Johnson: A Scholarly Annual* 5 (1992), 147–178

O M Brack, Jr, 'Samuel Johnson and the Epitaph on a Duckling', *Books at Iowa* 45 (1986), 62–79
_____ and Robert DeMaria, Jr, '"Some Remarks on the Progress of Learning": A New Preface by Samuel Johnson', *New Rambler* E:6 (2002–3), 61–74
_____ and Susan Carlile, 'Samuel Johnson's Contributions to Charlotte Lennox's *The Female Quixote*', *Yale University Library Gazette* 77, No. 3/4 (2003), 166–173

Frank Brady, *James Boswell: The Later Years 1769–1795* (London: Heinemann, 1984)

John Brewer, *The Pleasures of the Imagination: English Culture in the Eighteenth Century* (London: HarperCollins, 1997)

Bertrand H. Bronson, *Johnson Agonistes and Other Essays* (Cambridge: Cambridge University Press, 1946)

John Russell Brown (ed.), *The Oxford Illustrated History of Theatre* (Oxford: Oxford University Press, 1995)

Morris R. Brownell, *Samuel Johnson's Attitude to the Arts* (Oxford: Clarendon Press, 1989)

Michael Bundock, 'Johnson and Women in Boswell's *Life of Johnson*', *The Age of Johnson: A Scholarly Annual* 16 (2005), 81–109
_____, *The Fortunes of Francis Barber* (London: Yale University Press, 2015)

John J. Burke, Jr and Donald Kay (eds), *The Unknown Samuel Johnson*
(Madison: University of Wisconsin Press, 1983)

Annette Wheeler Cafarelli, 'Johnson and Women: Demasculinizing
Literary History', *The Age of Johnson: A Scholarly Annual* 5 (1992),
61–114

Michael Caines, *Shakespeare and the Eighteenth Century* (Oxford: Oxford
University Press, 2013)

John Cannon, *Samuel Johnson and the Politics of Hanoverian England*
(Oxford: Clarendon Press, 1994)

Chester F. Chapin, *The Religious Thought of Samuel Johnson* (Ann Arbor:
University of Michigan Press, 1968)

_____, 'Samuel Johnson, Anthropologist', *Eighteenth-Century Life*
19 (November 1995), 22–37

Kate Chisholm, *Wits and Wives: Dr Johnson in the Company of Women*
(London: Chatto & Windus, 2011)

Jonathan Clark, *Samuel Johnson: Literature, Religion and English Cultural
Politics from the Restoration to Romanticism* (Cambridge: Cambridge
University Press, 1994)

_____, *The Politics of Samuel Johnson* (Basingstoke: Palgrave
Macmillan, 2012)

_____, *The Interpretation of Samuel Johnson* (Basingstoke: Palgrave
Macmillan, 2012)

_____ and Howard Erskine-Hill (eds), *Samuel Johnson in Historical
Context* (Basingstoke: Palgrave, 2002)

Norma Clarke, *Dr Johnson's Women* (London: Hambledon & London,
2000)

James L. Clifford, *Young Samuel Johnson* (London: William Heinemann,
1957)

_____, *Hester Lynch Piozzi (Mrs Thrale)*, 2nd ed. with corrections
(Oxford: Clarendon Press, 1968)

_____, *Dictionary Johnson: Samuel Johnson's Middle Years* (London:
Heinemann, 1979)

Greg Clingham, (ed.), *The Cambridge Companion to Samuel Johnson*
(Cambridge: Cambridge University Press, 1997)

_____, *Johnson, Writing, and Memory* (Cambridge: Cambridge
University Press, 2002)

_____ and Philip Smallwood (eds), *Samuel Johnson After 300 Years*
(Cambridge: Cambridge University Press, 2012)

Ruby Cohn, *Just Play: Beckett's Theatre* (Princeton, New Jersey:
Princeton University Press, 1980)

Peter Conrad, *The Everyman History of English Literature* (London: J. M. Dent, 1985)

John Cresswell, 'The Streatham Johnson Knew', *New Rambler* E:3 (1999–2000), 22–28

Mihaly Csikszentmihalyi, *The Systems Model of Creativity: The Collected Works of Mihaly Csikszentmihalyi* (Dordrecht: Springer, 2014)

Thomas M. Curley, *Samuel Johnson and the Age of Travel* (Athens, Georgia: University of Georgia Press, 1976)

_____, *Sir Robert Chambers: Law, Literature, and Empire in the Age of Johnson* (Madison: University of Wisconsin Press, 1998)

_____, *Samuel Johnson, the Ossian Fraud, and the Celtic Revival in Great Britain and Ireland* (Cambridge: Cambridge University Press, 2009)

Leopold Damrosch, Jr, *Samuel Johnson and the Tragic Sense* (Princeton, New Jersey: Princeton University Press, 1972)

_____, *The Uses of Johnson's Criticism* (Charlottesville: University Press of Virginia, 1976)

Matthew M. Davis, 'Oxford Oath-Taking: The Evidence from Thomas Hearne's Diaries', *The Age of Johnson: A Scholarly Annual* 22 (2012), 169–189

Philip Davis, *In Mind of Johnson: A Study of Johnson the Rambler* (London: Athlone Press, 1989)

Robert DeMaria, Jr, *Johnson's Dictionary and the Language of Learning* (Oxford: Clarendon Press, 1986)

_____, *The Life of Samuel Johnson: A Critical Biography* (Oxford: Blackwell, 1993)

_____, *Samuel Johnson and the Life of Reading* (Baltimore, Maryland: Johns Hopkins University Press, 1997)

Helen Deutsch, *Loving Dr Johnson* (Chicago: University of Chicago Press, 2005)

Donald D. Eddy and J. D. Fleeman, *A Preliminary Handlist of Books to Which Dr Samuel Johnson Subscribed* (Charlottesville: Bibliographical Society of the University of Virginia, 1993)

Elizabeth L. Eisenstein, *The Printing Revolution in Early Modern Europe*, 2nd ed. (Cambridge: Cambridge University Press, 2005)

James Engell (ed.), *Johnson and His Age* (Cambridge, Massachusetts: Harvard University Press, 1984)

Patricia Fara and Karalyn Patterson (eds), *Memory* (Cambridge: Cambridge University Press, 1998)

Julia H. Fawcett, *Spectacular Disappearances: Celebrity and Privacy, 1696–1801* (Ann Arbor: University of Michigan Press, 2016)

J. D. Fleeman, *A Preliminary Handlist of Copies of Books Associated with Dr Samuel Johnson* (Oxford: Bodleian Library, 1984)

_____, *A Bibliography of the Works of Samuel Johnson*, prepared for publication by James McLaverty, 2 vols (Oxford: Clarendon Press, 2000)

Robert Folkenflik, *Samuel Johnson, Biographer* (Ithaca, New York: Cornell University Press, 1978)

Sigmund Freud, *Introductory Lectures on Psychoanalysis*, trans. Joan Riviere, 2nd ed. (London: George Allen & Unwin, 1943)

Robert Friedel, 'Serendipity is No Accident', *Kenyon Review* 23, No. 2 (2001), 36–47

Paul Fussell, *The Rhetorical World of Augustan Humanism: Ethics and Imagery from Swift to Burke* (Oxford: Clarendon Press, 1965)

_____, *Samuel Johnson and the Life of Writing* (London: Chatto & Windus, 1972)

John Glendening, 'Young Fanny Burney and the Mentor', *The Age of Johnson: A Scholarly Annual* 4 (1991), 281–312

_____, *The High Road: Romantic Tourism, Scotland, and Literature, 1720–1820* (Basingstoke: Macmillan, 1997)

Graham Good, *The Observing Self: Rediscovering the Essay* (London: Routledge, 1988)

Adam Gopnik, 'Man of Fetters', *New Yorker*, 8 December 2008, 90–96

James Gray, *Johnson's Sermons: A Study* (Oxford: Clarendon Press, 1972)

Donald Greene (ed.), *Samuel Johnson: A Collection of Critical Essays* (Englewood Cliffs, New Jersey: Prentice-Hall, 1965)

_____, *Samuel Johnson*, updated edition (Boston: Twayne Publishers, 1989)

_____, *The Politics of Samuel Johnson*, 2nd ed. (Athens, Georgia: University of Georgia Press, 1990)

_____, 'The *Logia* of Samuel Johnson and the Quest for the Historical Johnson', *The Age of Johnson: A Scholarly Annual* 3 (1990), 1–33

_____, '"A Secret Far Dearer to Him than His Life": Johnson's "Vile Melancholy" Reconsidered', *The Age of Johnson: A Scholarly Annual* 4 (1991), 1–40

_____, 'The Myth of Johnson's Misogyny: Some Addenda', *South Central Review* 9, No. 4 (1992), 6–17

Gloria Sybil Gross, *This Invisible Riot of the Mind: Samuel Johnson's Psychological Theory* (Philadelphia: University of Pennsylvania Press, 1992)

Isobel Grundy (ed.), *Samuel Johnson: New Critical Essays* (London: Vision Press, 1984)

_____, 'Samuel Johnson: A Writer of Lives Looks at Death', *Modern Language Review* 79, No. 2 (1984), 257–265

_____, *Samuel Johnson and the Scale of Greatness* (Leicester: Leicester University Press, 1986)

_____, 'Samuel Johnson as Patron of Women', *The Age of Johnson: A Scholarly Annual* 1 (1987), 59–77

Anita Guerrini, *Obesity and Depression in the Enlightenment* (Norman: University of Oklahoma Press, 2000)

Karl S. Guthke, *Last Words: Variations on a Theme in Cultural History* (Princeton, New Jersey: Princeton University Press, 1992)

Jean H. Hagstrum, *Samuel Johnson's Literary Criticism* (Chicago: University of Chicago Press, 1967)

H. F. Hallett, 'Dr Johnson's Refutation of Bishop Berkeley', *Mind* 56 (1947), 132–147

Sasha Handley, *Visions of an Unseen World: Ghost Beliefs and Ghost Stories in Eighteenth-Century England* (London: Pickering & Chatto, 2007)

Clare Harman, *Fanny Burney: A Biography* (London: HarperCollins, 2000)

Kevin Hart, *Samuel Johnson and the Culture of Property* (Cambridge: Cambridge University Press, 1999)

Erica Harth, 'The Virtue of Love: Lord Hardwicke's Marriage Act', *Cultural Critique* 9 (1988), 123–154

Allen T. Hazen, *Samuel Johnson's Prefaces & Dedications* (New Haven, Connecticut: Yale University Press, 1937)

Frederick W. Hilles (ed.), *The Age of Johnson: Essays Presented to Chauncey Brewster Tinker* (New Haven, Connecticut: Yale University Press, 1949)

_____, *New Light on Dr Johnson: Essays on the Occasion of his 250th Birthday* (New Haven, Connecticut: Yale University Press, 1959)

Charles H. Hinnant, *'Steel for the Mind': Samuel Johnson and Critical Discourse* (Newark: University of Delaware Press, 1994)

Henry Hitchings, *Defining the World: The Extraordinary Story of Dr Johnson's Dictionary* (New York: Farrar, Straus & Giroux, 2005)

Richard Holmes, *Dr Johnson and Mr Savage* (London: Flamingo, 1994)

Thomas A. Horrocks and Howard D. Weinbrot (eds), *Johnson After Three Centuries: New Light on Texts and Contexts* (Cambridge, Massachusetts: Harvard University Press, 2011)

Nicholas Hudson, *Samuel Johnson and Eighteenth-Century Thought*, revised ed. with corrections (Oxford: Clarendon Press, 1990)

_____, *Samuel Johnson and the Making of Modern England* (Cambridge: Cambridge University Press, 2003)

_____, *A Political Biography of Samuel Johnson* (London: Pickering & Chatto, 2013)

Mary Jane Hurst, 'Samuel Johnson's Dying Words', *English Language Notes* 23, No. 2 (1985), 45–53

Lewis Hyde, 'Two Accidents: Reflections on Chance and Creativity', *Kenyon Review* 18, No. 3/4 (1996), 19–35

George Irwin, *Samuel Johnson: A Personality in Conflict* (Auckland: Auckland University Press, 1971)

Iona Italia, 'Johnson as Moralist in *The Rambler*', *The Age of Johnson: A Scholarly Annual* 14 (2003), 51–76

Nalini Jain (ed.), *Re-Viewing Samuel Johnson* (London: Sangam, 1991)

Freya Johnston, *Samuel Johnson and the Art of Sinking 1709–1791* (Oxford: Oxford University Press, 2005)

_____ and Lynda Mugglestone (eds), *Samuel Johnson: The Arc of the Pendulum* (Oxford: Oxford University Press, 2012)

Sarah Jordan, 'Samuel Johnson and Idleness', *The Age of Johnson: A Scholarly Annual* 11 (2000), 145–176

Jacob Sider Jost, 'The *Gentleman's Magazine*, Samuel Johnson, and the Symbolic Economy of Eighteenth-Century Poetry', *Review of English Studies* 66 (2015), 915–935

Thomas Kaminski, *The Early Career of Samuel Johnson* (New York: Oxford University Press, 1987)

W. R. Keast, 'The Theoretical Foundations of Johnson's Criticism', in *Critics and Criticism*, ed. Ronald S. Crane (Chicago: Chicago University Press, 1952), 389–407

_____, 'The Two *Clarissa*s in Johnson's *Dictionary*', *Studies in Philology* 54, No. 3 (1957), 429–439

Kathleen Nulton Kemmerer, *'A Neutral Being Between the Sexes': Samuel Johnson's Sexual Politics* (Lewisburg, Pennsylvania: Bucknell University Press, 1998)

Alvin Kernan, *Samuel Johnson and the Impact of Print* (Princeton, New Jersey: Princeton University Press, 1989)

Thomas Keymer and Jon Mee (eds), *The Cambridge Companion to English Literature from 1740 to 1830* (Cambridge: Cambridge University Press, 2004)

Peter Kivy, 'Genius and the Creative Imagination', in *The Oxford Handbook of British Philosophy in the Eighteenth Century*, ed. James A. Harris (Oxford: Oxford University Press, 2013), 468–487

Paul J. Korshin (ed.), *Johnson After Two Hundred Years* (Philadelphia: University of Pennsylvania Press, 1986)

_____, '"Extensive View": Johnson and Boswell as Travelers and Observers', in *All Before Them*, ed. John McVeagh (London: Ashfield, 1990), 233–245

_____, 'Samuel Johnson's Life Experience with Poverty', *The Age of Johnson: A Scholarly Annual* 11 (2000), 3–20

_____ and Robert R. Allen (eds), *Greene Centennial Studies: Essays Presented to Donald Greene in the Centennial Year of the University of Southern California* (Charlottesville: University Press of Virginia, 1984)

Craig Koslofsky, *Evening's Empire: A History of the Night in Early Modern Europe* (Cambridge: Cambridge University Press, 2011)

Beth Kowaleski-Wallace, 'Tea, Gender, and Domesticity in Eighteenth-Century England', *Studies in Eighteenth-Century Culture* 23 (1994), 131–145

Joseph Wood Krutch, *Samuel Johnson* (London: Cassell, 1948)

Olivia Laing, *The Lonely City: Adventures in the Art of Being Alone* (Edinburgh: Canongate, 2016)

John Lanchester, 'You Are the Product', *London Review of Books*, 17 August 2017, 3–10

Paul Langford, *A Polite and Commercial People: England 1727–1783* (Oxford: Clarendon Press, 1989)

Herman W. Liebert, 'A Constellation of Genius; Being a Full Account of the Trial of Joseph Baretti' (New Haven, Connecticut: privately printed for the Johnsonians, 1958)

Lawrence Lipking, *The Ordering of the Arts in Eighteenth-Century England* (Princeton, New Jersey: Princeton University Press, 1970)

_____, 'What Was It Like To Be Johnson?', *The Age of Johnson: A Scholarly Annual* 1 (1987), 35–57

_____, *Samuel Johnson: The Life of an Author* (Cambridge, Massachusetts: Harvard University Press, 1998)

Donald M. Lockhart, '"The Fourth Son of the Mighty Emperor": The Ethiopian Background of Johnson's *Rasselas*', *PMLA* 78, No. 5 (1963), 516–528

Jack Lynch, 'Samuel Johnson's "Love of Truth" and Literary Fraud', *Studies in English Literature 1500–1900* 42, No. 3 (2002), 601–618

_____, *The Age of Elizabeth in the Age of Johnson* (Cambridge: Cambridge University Press, 2003)

_____ (ed.), *Samuel Johnson in Context* (Cambridge: Cambridge University Press, 2012)

_____, 'Generous Liberal-Minded Men: Booksellers and Poetic
    Careers in Johnson's *Lives of the Poets*', *Yearbook of English Studies*
    45 (2015), 93–108
_____ and Anne McDermott (eds), *Anniversary Essays on Johnson's*
    Dictionary (Cambridge: Cambridge University Press, 2005)
Steven Lynn, *Samuel Johnson After Deconstruction: Rhetoric and the* Rambler
    (Carbondale: Southern Illinois University Press, 1992)
Robert Macfarlane, *Original Copy: Plagiarism and Originality in Nineteenth-*
    Century Literature (Oxford: Oxford University Press, 2007)
Iain McGilchrist, *Against Criticism* (London: Faber, 1982)
Helen Louise McGuffie, *Samuel Johnson in the British Press, 1749–1784:*
    A Chronological Checklist (New York: Garland, 1976)
Carey McIntosh, *The Choice of Life: Samuel Johnson and the World of*
    Fiction (New Haven, Connecticut: Yale University Press, 1973)
Ian McIntyre, *Garrick* (London: Allen Lane, 1999)
_____, *Joshua Reynolds: The Life and Times of the First President of*
    the Royal Academy (London: Allen Lane, 2003)
_____, *Hester: The Remarkable Life of Dr Johnson's 'Dear Mistress'*
    (London: Constable, 2008)
Andrew McKendry, 'The Haphazard Journey of a Mind: Experience
    and Reflection in Samuel Johnson's *Journey to the Western Islands*
    of Scotland', *The Age of Johnson: A Scholarly Annual* 20 (2010), 11–34
Jennifer A. McMahon, *Art and Ethics in a Material World: Kant's Pragmatist*
    Legacy (New York: Routledge, 2014)
Martin Maner, *The Philosophical Biographer: Doubt and Dialectic in Johnson's*
    Lives of the Poets (Athens, Georgia: University of Georgia
    Press, 1988)
Rosalind K. Marshall, *Columba's Iona: A New History* (Dingwall:
    Sandstone Press, 2013)
Peter Martin, *Samuel Johnson: A Biography* (Cambridge, Massachusetts:
    Belknap Press, 2008)
Jeffrey Meyers, *Samuel Johnson: The Struggle* (New York: Basic Books,
    2008)
Stephen Miller, *Conversation: A History of a Declining Art* (New Haven,
    Connecticut: Yale University Press, 2006)
Sarah R. Morrison, 'Samuel Johnson, Mr Rambler, and Women',
    The Age of Johnson: A Scholarly Annual 14 (2003), 23–50
Tom Morton, *Dr Johnson's Dictionary of Modern Life* (London: Square
    Peg, 2010)
Lynda Mugglestone, *Samuel Johnson and the Journey into Words* (Oxford:
    Oxford University Press, 2015)

Ghazi Q. Nassir, *Samuel Johnson's Attitude Towards Islam: A Study of His Oriental Readings and Writings* (Lampeter: Edwin Mellen Press, 2012)

Prem Nath (ed.), *Fresh Reflections on Samuel Johnson: Essays in Criticism* (Troy, New York: Whitston, 1987)

David Nokes, *Jonathan Swift, A Hypocrite Reversed: A Critical Biography* (Oxford: Oxford University Press, 1985)

_____, *Samuel Johnson: A Life* (London: Faber, 2009)

Patrick O'Flaherty, 'Johnson's *Idler*: The Equipment of a Satirist', *English Literary History* 37, No. 2 (1970), 211–225

_____, 'Towards an Understanding of Johnson's *Rambler*', *Studies in English Literature, 1500–1900* 18, No. 3 (1978), 523–536

David Olusoga, *Black and British: A Forgotten History* (London: Macmillan, 2016)

Norman Page, *A Dr Johnson Chronology* (Basingstoke: Macmillan, 1990)

Catherine N. Parke, *Samuel Johnson and Biographical Thinking* (Columbia: University of Missouri Press, 1991)

Fred Parker, *Johnson's Shakespeare* (Oxford: Clarendon Press, 1989)

_____, *Scepticism in Literature: An Essay on Pope, Hume, Sterne, and Johnson* (Oxford: Oxford University Press, 2003)

Douglas Lane Patey, 'Johnson's Refutation of Berkeley: Kicking the Stone Again', *Journal of the History of Ideas* 47, No. 1 (1986), 139–145

Adam Phillips, *On Kissing, Tickling and Being Bored: Psychoanalytic Essays on the Unexamined Life* (London: Faber, 1993)

_____, *Going Sane* (London: Hamish Hamilton, 2005)

Liza Picard, *Dr Johnson's London* (London: Weidenfeld & Nicolson, 2000)

Charles E. Pierce, Jr, *The Religious Life of Samuel Johnson* (London: Athlone Press, 1983)

Roy Porter, *London: A Social History* (London: Hamish Hamilton, 1994)

_____, *Flesh in the Age of Reason* (London: Allen Lane, 2003)

Adam Potkay, *The Passion for Happiness: Samuel Johnson and David Hume* (Ithaca, New York: Cornell University Press, 2000)

Frederick A. Pottle, *Pride and Negligence: The History of the Boswell Papers* (New York: McGraw-Hill, 1982)

Michael Puett and Christine Gross-Loh, *The Path: A New Way to Think About Everything* (London: Penguin, 2017)

Maurice J. Quinlan, *Samuel Johnson: A Layman's Religion* (Madison: University of Wisconsin Press, 1964)

Laura Quinney, *Literary Power and the Criteria of Truth* (Gainesville: University Press of Florida, 1995)

_____, *The Poetics of Disappointment* (Charlottesville: University Press of Virginia, 1999)

John B. Radner, *Johnson and Boswell: A Biography of Friendship* (New Haven, Connecticut: Yale University Press, 2012)

Walter Raleigh, *Six Essays on Johnson* (Oxford: Clarendon Press, 1910)

Claude Rawson, *Swift and Others* (Cambridge: Cambridge University Press, 2015)

Aleyn Lyell Reade, *Johnsonian Gleanings*, 11 vols (privately printed, 1909–1952)

Allen Reddick, *The Making of Johnson's Dictionary, 1746–1773*, 2nd ed. (Cambridge: Cambridge University Press, 1996)

Bruce Redford, *The Converse of the Pen: Acts of Intimacy in the Eighteenth-Century Familiar Letter* (Chicago: University of Chicago Press, 1986)

Hugo M. Reichard, 'Boswell's Johnson, the Hero Made by a Committee', *PMLA* 95, No. 2 (1980), 225–233

Fiona Ritchie and Peter Sabor (eds), *Shakespeare in the Eighteenth Century* (Cambridge: Cambridge University Press, 2012)

Stefka Ritchie, *The Reformist Ideas of Samuel Johnson* (Newcastle upon Tyne: Cambridge Scholars, 2017)

Donald O. Rogers, 'Samuel Johnson's Concept of the Imagination', *South Central Bulletin* 33, No. 4 (1973), 213–218

Pat Rogers, *Grub Street: Studies in a Subculture* (London: Methuen, 1972)

_____, *Johnson* (Oxford: Oxford University Press, 1993)

_____, *Johnson and Boswell: The Transit of Caledonia* (Oxford: Clarendon Press, 1995)

_____, *The Samuel Johnson Encyclopedia* (Westport, Connecticut: Greenwood Press, 1996)

Trevor Ross, *The Making of the English Literary Canon: From the Middle Ages to the Late Eighteenth Century* (Montreal & Kingston: McGill-Queen's University Press, 1998)

Arieh Sachs, *Passionate Intelligence: Imagination and Reason in the Work of Samuel Johnson* (Baltimore, Maryland: Johns Hopkins Press, 1967)

Renata Salecl, *Choice* (London: Profile, 2010)

Daniel L. Schacter, *Searching for Memory: The Brain, the Mind, and the Past* (New York: Basic Books, 1996)

Richard B. Schwartz, *Samuel Johnson and the New Science* (Madison: University of Wisconsin Press, 1971)

_____, *Samuel Johnson and the Problem of Evil* (Madison: University of Wisconsin Press, 1975)

Adam B. Seligman, Robert P. Weller, Michael J. Puett and Bennett Simon, *Ritual and Its Consequences: An Essay on the Limits of Sincerity* (Oxford: Oxford University Press, 2008)

Arthur Sherbo, *Samuel Johnson, Editor of Shakespeare* (Urbana: University of Illinois Press, 1956)

Stuart Sherman, *Telling Time: Clocks, Diaries and English Diurnal Form, 1660–1785* (Chicago: University of Chicago Press, 1996)

Bruce Silver, 'Boswell on Johnson's Refutation of Berkeley: Revisiting the Stone', *Journal of the History of Ideas* 54, No. 3 (1993), 437–448

Philip Smallwood (ed.), *Johnson Re-Visioned: Looking Before and After* (Lewisburg, Pennsylvania: Bucknell University Press, 2001)

Frederik N. Smith, *Beckett's Eighteenth Century* (Basingstoke: Palgrave, 2002)

Patricia Meyer Spacks, *Boredom: The Literary History of a State of Mind* (Chicago: University of Chicago Press, 1995)

Robert D. Spector, *Samuel Johnson and the Essay* (Westport, Connecticut: Greenwood Press, 1997)

Tom Standage, *Writing on the Wall: Social Media – The First 2,000 Years* (London: Bloomsbury, 2013)

Donald A. Stauffer, *The Art of Biography in Eighteenth Century England* (Princeton, New Jersey: Princeton University Press, 1941)

Aaron Stavisky, 'Johnson's "Vile Melancholy" Reconsidered Once More', *The Age of Johnson: A Scholarly Annual* 9 (1998), 1–24

_____, 'Johnson's Poverty: The Uses of Adversity', *The Age of Johnson: A Scholarly Annual* 14 (2003), 131–143

Leslie Stephen, *Samuel Johnson* (London: Macmillan, 1878)

John Allen Stevenson, 'Sterne: Comedian and Experimental Novelist', in John Richetti (ed.), *The Columbia History of the British Novel* (New York: Columbia University Press, 1994), 154–180

Thomas Szasz, *Pain and Pleasure: A Study of Bodily Feelings*, 2nd ed. (Syracuse, New York: Syracuse University Press, 1988)

Paul Tankard, 'A Petty Writer: Johnson and the *Rambler* Pamphlets', *The Age of Johnson: A Scholarly Annual* 10 (1999), 67–87

_____, '"That Great Literary Projector": Samuel Johnson's Designs, or Catalogue of Projected Works', *The Age of Johnson: A Scholarly Annual* 13 (2002), 103–180

_____, 'Nineteen More Johnsonian Designs: A Supplement to

"That Great Literary Projector"', *The Age of Johnson: A Scholarly Annual* 23 (2015), 141–157

Edward Tomarken, *Johnson, Rasselas, and the Choice of Criticism* (Lexington: University Press of Kentucky, 1989)

Robert Tombs, *The English and Their History* (London: Allen Lane, 2014)

Clarence Tracy, *The Artificial Bastard: A Biography of Richard Savage* (Toronto: University of Toronto Press, 1953)

Fan Tsen-Chung, *Dr Johnson and Chinese Culture* (London: The China Society, 1945)

A. S. Turberville (ed.), *Johnson's England: An Account of the Life and Manners of his Age*, 2 vols (Oxford: Clarendon Press, 1933)

Gordon Turnbull, 'Not a woman in sight', *Times Literary Supplement*, 18 December 2009, 19–21

E. S. Turner, *The Shocking History of Advertising* (London: Michael Joseph, 1952)

John A. Vance, *Samuel Johnson and the Sense of History* (Athens, Georgia: University of Georgia Press, 1984)

_____ (ed.), *Boswell's* Life of Johnson: *New Questions, New Answers* (Athens, Georgia: University of Georgia Press, 1985)

David F. Venturo, *Johnson the Poet: The Poetic Career of Samuel Johnson* (London: Associated University Presses, 1999)

Ernst Verbeek, *The Measure and the Choice: A Pathographic Essay on Samuel Johnson* (Ghent: E. Story Scientia, 1971)

Robert Voitle, *Samuel Johnson the Moralist* (Cambridge, Massachusetts: Harvard University Press, 1961)

Magdi Wahba (ed.), *Johnsonian Studies* (Cairo: Société Orientale de Publicité, 1962)

John Wain, *Samuel Johnson* (London: Macmillan, 1974)

Mary Warnock, *Memory* (London: Faber, 1987)

W. B. C. Watkins, *Perilous Balance: The Tragic Genius of Swift, Johnson, and Sterne* (Princeton, New Jersey: Princeton University Press, 1939)

Martin Wechselblatt, *Bad Behavior: Samuel Johnson and Modern Cultural Authority* (Lewisburg, Pennsylvania: Bucknell University Press, 1998)

Howard D. Weinbrot, *Aspects of Samuel Johnson: Essays on His Arts, Mind, Afterlife, and Politics* (Newark: University of Delaware Press, 2005)

_____ (ed.), *Samuel Johnson: New Contexts for a New Century* (San Marino, California: Huntington Library, 2014)

_____, 'Samuel Johnson's Practical Sermon on Marriage in

Context: Spousal Whiggery and the Book of Common Prayer',
Modern Philology 114, No. 2 (2016), 310–336

T. F. Wharton, *Samuel Johnson and the Theme of Hope* (London:
Macmillan, 1984)

David Wheeler (ed.), *Domestick Privacies: Samuel Johnson and the Art of
Biography* (Lexington: University Press of Kentucky, 1987)

James Boyd White, *When Words Lose Their Meaning: Constitutions and
Reconstitutions of Language, Character, and Community* (Chicago:
University of Chicago Press, 1984)

Jerry White, *London in the Eighteenth Century: A Great and Monstrous Thing*
(London: Bodley Head, 2012)

Lance Wilcox, 'Healing the Lacerated Mind: Samuel Johnson's
Strategies of Consolation', *1650–1850: Ideas, Æsthetics, and
Inquiries in the Early Modern Era* 7 (2002), 193–208

Gillian Williamson, *British Masculinity in the* Gentleman's Magazine,
1731 to 1815 (Basingstoke: Palgrave Macmillan, 2016)

John Wiltshire, *Samuel Johnson in the Medical World* (Cambridge:
Cambridge University Press, 1991)

_____, *The Making of Dr Johnson: Icon of Modern Culture* (Hastings:
Helm, 2009)

W. K. Wimsatt, Jr, *The Prose Style of Samuel Johnson* (New Haven,
Connecticut: Yale University Press, 1941)

_____, *Philosophic Words: A Study of Style and Meaning in the
Rambler and* Dictionary (New Haven, Connecticut: Yale
University Press, 1948)

Calhoun Winton, *John Gay and the London Theatre* (Lexington: University
Press of Kentucky, 1993)

Alun Withey, *Technology, Self-Fashioning and Politeness in Eighteenth-Century
Britain: Refined Bodies* (Basingstoke: Palgrave Macmillan, 2016)

Tim Wu, *The Attention Merchants: From the Daily Newspaper to Social Media,
How Our Time and Attention is Harvested and Sold* (London:
Atlantic, 2017)

James Yeowell, *A Literary Antiquary: Memoir of William Oldys* (London:
Spottiswoode, 1862)

Robert Zaretsky, *Boswell's Enlightenment* (Cambridge, Massachusetts:
Belknap Press, 2015)

Notes

I have not provided references to quotations from Samuel Johnson's works or the works of other members of his circle. Today it is easy to track down these quotations online, and to insert a reference for each of them would result in this book being glutted with notes.

I have modernized the spelling of eighteenth-century texts in cases where their meaning would otherwise be opaque for many readers.

2.

1. John Hawkesworth, *An Account of the Voyages Undertaken by the Order of his Present Majesty for Making Discoveries in the Southern Hemisphere*, 3 vols (London: Strahan & Cadell, 1773), III, 578.
2. The last five words are an allusion to John Donne's poem 'The Will': 'Then all your beauties will be no more worth / Than gold in mines, where none doth draw it forth; / And all your graces no more use shall have, / Than a sun-dial in a grave'.

3.

1. Virgil, *Georgics*, trans. Peter Fallon (Oxford: Oxford University Press, 2006), 33.
2. Several versions of the poem have circulated. This one was recorded by Johnson's friend Charlotte Lennox. For a full discussion of the poem, see O M Brack, Jr, 'Samuel Johnson and the Epitaph on a Duckling', *Books at Iowa* 45 (1986), 62–79.

4.

1. John Wain, *Samuel Johnson* (London: Macmillan, 1974), 40. James L. Clifford, *Young Samuel Johnson* (London: William Heinemann, 1957), 97.
2. Laura Quinney, *The Poetics of Disappointment* (Charlottesville: University Press of Virginia, 1999), ix, 1–4.
3. C. G. Jung, *Memories, Dreams, Reflections*, ed. Aniela Jaffé, trans. Richard and Clara Winston (London: Collins and Routledge & Kegan Paul, 1963), 172.
4. For the detail about Sam's name appearing on title pages, see J. D. Fleeman, *A Bibliography of the Works of Samuel Johnson*, prepared for publication by James McLaverty, 2 vols (Oxford: Clarendon Press, 2000), I, 32. For his inscription to Hector, see Fleeman, *A Preliminary Handlist of Copies of Books Associated with Dr Samuel Johnson* (Oxford: Bodleian Library, 1984), 24.
5. This is Adam Phillips's theory about Johnson, as set out in David Nokes, *Samuel Johnson: A Life* (London: Faber, 2009), 42.
6. Wendy Laura Belcher, *Abyssinia's Samuel Johnson: Ethiopian Thought in the Making of an English Author* (New York: Oxford University Press, 2012), 42–61, 88–96.

5.

1. Peter Martin, *Samuel Johnson: A Biography* (Cambridge, Massachusetts: Belknap Press, 2008), 60.
2. Robert DeMaria, Jr, *Samuel Johnson and the Life of Reading* (Baltimore, Maryland: Johns Hopkins University Press, 1997), 74.
3. Hugo M. Reichard, 'Boswell's Johnson, the Hero Made by a Committee', *PMLA* 95, No. 2 (1980), 225.
4. Lewis Hyde, 'Two Accidents: Reflections on Chance and Creativity', *Kenyon Review* 18, No. 3/4 (1996), 25–26.
5. Nassim Nicholas Taleb, *Antifragile: Things that Gain from Disorder* (London: Penguin, 2013), 6.
6. Robert Friedel, 'Serendipity is No Accident', *Kenyon Review* 23, No. 2 (2001), 39–40.
7. Among those to attribute this quotation to Einstein is George Saunders in *The Brain-Dead Megaphone* (London: Bloomsbury, 2008), 180.

6.

1. Leslie Stephen, *Samuel Johnson* (London: Macmillan, 1878), 12.
2. For a full discussion of the Marriage Act, see Erica Harth, 'The Virtue of Love: Lord Hardwicke's Marriage Act', *Cultural Critique* 9 (1988), 123–154.
3. James L. Clifford, *Hester Lynch Piozzi (Mrs Thrale)*, 2nd ed. with corrections (Oxford: Clarendon Press, 1968), 99–101.

7.

1. John Russell Brown (ed.), *The Oxford Illustrated History of Theatre* (Oxford: Oxford University Press, 1995), 261–263.
2. Ian McIntyre, *Garrick* (London: Penguin Allen Lane, 1999), 29.
3. Adam Gopnik, 'Man of Fetters', *New Yorker*, 8 December 2008.
4. The letter and observations relating to it appear in Aleyn Lyell Reade, *Johnsonian Gleanings*, 11 vols (privately printed, 1909–1952), I, 1–2; VI, 58–61.
5. This is discussed in detail in Gillian Williamson, *British Masculinity in the* Gentleman's Magazine, *1731 to 1815* (Basingstoke: Palgrave Macmillan, 2016), 33–70.
6. See Jacob Sider Jost, 'The *Gentleman's Magazine*, Samuel Johnson, and the Symbolic Economy of Eighteenth-Century Poetry', *Review of English Studies* 66 (2015), 915–935.
7. Liza Picard, *Dr Johnson's London* (London: Weidenfeld & Nicolson, 2000), 10–11, 13.
8. According to the historian Roy Porter, it was a place for 'families seeking country calm close to town'. Other such spots included Blackheath, Chiswick, Richmond and Chelsea. See Porter's *London: A Social History* (London: Hamish Hamilton, 1994), 120.
9. James Ralph, *A New Critical Review of the Publick Buildings, Statues and Ornaments, in and about London and Westminster*, 2nd ed. (London: J. Clarke, 1736), 75.
10. Oliver Goldsmith, *An Enquiry into the Present State of Polite Learning in Europe*, 2nd ed. (London: J. Dodsley, 1774), 103.
11. The image is used by the journalist Jasper Milvain in George Gissing's novel *New Grub Street* (1891) – but of the British Museum reading room.

8.

1. Pat Rogers, *Grub Street: Studies in a Subculture* (London: Methuen, 1972), 363–364.
2. Richard Holmes, *Dr Johnson and Mr Savage* (London: Flamingo, 1994), 39.
3. Ibid., xii.

10.

1. Jerry White, *London in the Eighteenth Century: A Great and Monstrous Thing* (London: Bodley Head, 2012), 87.
2. James Yeowell, *A Literary Antiquary: Memoir of William Oldys* (London: Spottiswoode, 1862), xxii.

11.

1. Richard Holmes, 'Inventing the Truth', in John Batchelor (ed.), *The Art of Literary Biography* (Oxford: Clarendon Press, 1995), 24.
2. It is *The Life of Samuel Johnson, LL.D., Comprehending an Account of His Studies and Numerous Works, in Chronological Order; a Series of his Epistolary Correspondence and Conversations with Many Eminent Persons; and Various Original Pieces of His Composition, Never Before Published: the Whole Exhibiting a View of Literature and Literary Men in Great Britain, for Near Half a Century, During Which He Flourished.*
3. These figures come from John B. Radner, *Johnson and Boswell: A Biography of Friendship* (New Haven, Connecticut: Yale University Press, 2012), 355–358.

12.

1. The subject is addressed at length by Morris R. Brownell in *Samuel Johnson's Attitude to the Arts* (Oxford: Clarendon Press, 1989).
2. *An Essay on Tragedy, with a Critical Examen of* Mahomet and Irene (London: Ralph Griffiths, 1749), 17, 19. The author is thought to have been an actor, John Hippisley.

13.

1. Olivia Laing, *The Lonely City: Adventures in the Art of Being Alone* (Edinburgh: Canongate, 2016), 3–4.
2. Ernst Verbeek, *The Measure and the Choice: A Pathographic Essay on Samuel Johnson* (Ghent: E. Story Scientia, 1971), 127–128.

14.

1. Max Porter, *Grief is the Thing with Feathers* (London: Faber, 2015), 4–5, 16, 20.
2. Michael Bundock, *The Fortunes of Francis Barber* (London: Yale University Press, 2015), 47–48. David Olusoga, *Black and British: A Forgotten History* (London: Macmillan, 2016), 100, 81–82, 85.
3. *The Letters of Samuel Johnson*, ed. Bruce Redford, 5 vols (Oxford: Clarendon Press, 1992–94), I, x–xi.

15.

1. DeMaria, *Samuel Johnson and the Life of Reading*, 4–15.

16.

1. Friedrich Nietzsche, *Ecce Homo*, trans. Duncan Large (Oxford: Oxford University Press, 2007), 9.

17.

1. Steven Lynn, *Samuel Johnson After Deconstruction: Rhetoric and the Rambler* (Carbondale: Southern Illinois University Press, 1992), 19–20.
2. This redeployment of scientific terminology is discussed in W. K. Wimsatt, Jr, *Philosophic Words: A Study of Style and Meaning in the* Rambler *and* Dictionary (New Haven, Connecticut: Yale University Press, 1948).
3. At the time of writing, he is the *OED*'s first cited user of all these words.
4. Walter Raleigh, *Six Essays on Johnson* (Oxford: Clarendon Press, 1910), 22.
5. The example comes from Wimsatt, *The Prose Style of Samuel Johnson* (New Haven, Connecticut: Yale University Press, 1941), 41.

18.

1. https://founders.archives.gov/documents/
   Jefferson/98-01-02-1459 Retrieved 13 March 2017.
2. James G. Basker, *Samuel Johnson in the Mind of Thomas Jefferson*
   (Charlottesville, Virginia: privately printed for the Johnsonians,
   1999), 6.

20.

1. Sigmund Freud, *Introductory Lectures on Psychoanalysis*, trans.
   Joan Riviere, 2nd ed. (London: George Allen & Unwin, 1943),
   329–332.
2. Joanna Bourke, *Fear: A Cultural History* (London: Virago, 2005),
   389–391.
3. Adam Phillips, *On Kissing, Tickling and Being Bored: Psychoanalytic
   Essays on the Unexamined Life* (London: Faber, 1993), 54–55.
4. Walter Jackson Bate, *The Achievement of Samuel Johnson* (New
   York: Oxford University Press, 1955), 93–94.
5. Adam Phillips, *Going Sane* (London: Hamish Hamilton, 2005),
   44–45, 48, 60.
6. Helen Macdonald, *H is for Hawk* (London: Jonathan Cape,
   2014), 195.

21.

1. Helen Louise McGuffie, *Samuel Johnson in the British Press,
   1749–1784: A Chronological Checklist* (New York: Garland, 1976),
   32–33, 35, 83, 203.
2. Ian McIntyre, *Joshua Reynolds: The Life and Times of the First
   President of the Royal Academy* (London: Allen Lane, 2003), 99.
3. On the question of the preface's indebtedness to the work of
   others, see Arthur Sherbo, *Samuel Johnson, Editor of Shakespeare*
   (Urbana: University of Illinois Press, 1956), 28–45.
4. Edgar says, 'Here in the sands / Thee I'll rake up', and the
   note reads: 'I'll "cover" thee. In Staffordshire, to "rake" the fire,
   is to cover it with fuel for the night.'
5. Fred Parker, *Johnson's Shakespeare* (Oxford: Clarendon Press,
   1989), 62.

22.

1. The best discussion of these changes is Alvin Kernan's *Samuel Johnson and the Impact of Print* (Princeton, New Jersey: Princeton University Press, 1989).
2. These examples are from E. S. Turner, *The Shocking History of Advertising* (London: Michael Joseph, 1952), 24–47.
3. Jack Lynch, 'Samuel Johnson's "Love of Truth" and Literary Fraud', *Studies in English Literature 1500–1900* 42, No. 3 (2002), 605, 616.
4. John Gilbert Cooper, *Letters Concerning Taste*, 3rd ed. (London: R. and J. Dodsley, 1755), 2–3.
5. John Lanchester, 'You Are the Product', *London Review of Books*, 17 August 2017.
6. Tim Wu, *The Attention Merchants: From the Daily Newspaper to Social Media, How Our Time and Attention is Harvested and Sold* (London: Atlantic, 2017), 72, 339, 344.

23.

1. See https://qmhistoryoftea.files.wordpress.com/2012/09/teatable.jpg Retrieved 23 January 2017.
2. Soame Jenyns, *The Modern Fine Gentleman* (London: M. Cooper, 1746), 4.
3. W. R. Keast, 'The Two *Clarissa*s in Johnson's *Dictionary*', *Studies in Philology* 54, No. 3 (1957), 436, 439.
4. Donald M. Lockhart, '"The Fourth Son of the Mighty Emperor": The Ethiopian Background of Johnson's *Rasselas*', *PMLA* 78, No. 5 (1963), 516–528.

24.

1. The subject is interestingly explored in Tom Standage's *Writing on the Wall: Social Media – The First 2,000 Years* (London: Bloomsbury, 2013).

25.

1. Edward Ward, *The Secret History of Clubs* (London, 1709), 48.
2. I explore the changing nature of nocturnal life in my book *Sorry! The English and their Manners* (London: John Murray, 2013).

My thinking about the character and consequences of nocturnal sociability draws on Craig Koslofsky, *Evening's Empire: A History of the Night in Early Modern Europe* (Cambridge: Cambridge University Press, 2011).

3. McGuffie, *Samuel Johnson in the British Press*, 45–46, 61, 64, 43.
4. Michel de Montaigne, *The Complete Essays*, ed. and trans. M. A. Screech (London: Penguin, 2003), 1045, 1051.
5. This idea is explored in detail in Adam B. Seligman, Robert P. Weller, Michael J. Puett and Bennett Simon, *Ritual and Its Consequences: An Essay on the Limits of Sincerity* (Oxford: Oxford University Press, 2008).

26.

1. Tom Bingham, *Dr Johnson and the Law, and Other Essays on Johnson* (London: Inner Temple, 2010), 12, 25.
2. For a detailed account of these two visits, see Robert Zaretsky, *Boswell's Enlightenment* (Cambridge, Mass.: Belknap Press, 2015), 148–182.

27.

1. *Monthly Review* 74 (1786), 379, 383.
2. Some of this detail comes from John Cresswell, 'The Streatham Johnson Knew', *New Rambler* E:3 (1999–2000), 22–28.
3. Walter Jackson Bate, *Samuel Johnson* (London: Hogarth Press, 1984), 434.
4. Quoted in Nokes, *Samuel Johnson: A Life*, 259.
5. Martin, *Samuel Johnson: A Biography*, 388; Jeffrey Meyers, *Samuel Johnson: The Struggle* (New York: Basic Books, 2008), 365.
6. A. Edward Newton, *Doctor Johnson: A Play* (London: J. M. Dent, 1924), 114.
7. The quotations are from Deirdre Bair, *Samuel Beckett: A Biography* (New York: Touchstone, 1993), 257–258.
8. See Ruby Cohn, *Just Play: Beckett's Theatre* (Princeton, New Jersey: Princeton University Press, 1980), 143–162, 295–305.
9. Frederik N. Smith, *Beckett's Eighteenth Century* (Basingstoke: Palgrave, 2002), 110–111, 118, 126, 130.
10. Quoted in Bair, *Samuel Beckett*, 253–254.
11. *Monthly Review* 78 (1788), 325–326.

28.

1. See Fred Parker, *Scepticism in Literature: An Essay on Pope, Hume, Sterne, and Johnson* (Oxford: Oxford University Press, 2003), 232–281.
2. For further detail of the story see Sasha Handley, *Visions of an Unseen World: Ghost Beliefs and Ghost Stories in Eighteenth-Century England* (London: Pickering & Chatto, 2007), 141–148.

29.

1. Bate, *The Achievement of Samuel Johnson*, 48.
2. On Jacobitism in Staffordshire, see Paul Monod, 'A Voyage out of Staffordshire; or, Samuel Johnson's Jacobite Journey', in Jonathan Clark and Howard Erskine-Hill (eds), *Samuel Johnson in Historical Context* (Basingstoke: Palgrave, 2002), 11–43.

30.

1. Martin Martin, *A Description of the Western Isles of Scotland* (London: Andrew Bell, 1703), Preface, 135.
2. For a full account of the dispute, see Thomas M. Curley, *Samuel Johnson, the Ossian Fraud, and the Celtic Revival in Great Britain and Ireland* (Cambridge: Cambridge University Press, 2009).
3. Pat Rogers, *The Samuel Johnson Encyclopedia* (Westport, Connecticut: Greenwood Press, 1996), 352.
4. Leigh Hunt, *Table-Talk* (London: Smith, Elder, 1851), 2.
5. Pat Rogers, *Johnson and Boswell: The Transit of Caledonia* (Oxford: Clarendon Press, 1995), 26.

31.

1. My thinking here is influenced by Adam Potkay's *The Passion for Happiness: Samuel Johnson and David Hume* (Ithaca, New York: Cornell University Press, 2000).

32.

1. George Cheyne, *The English Malady: Or, A Treatise of Nervous Diseases of All Kinds* (London: G. Strahan, 1733), 111, 125.
2. *All the Works of Epictetus, Which Are Now Extant*, 2nd ed. (London: Millar, Rivington, R. and J. Dodsley, 1759), xx, xxvi.

33.

1. Stefka Ritchie, *The Reformist Ideas of Samuel Johnson* (Newcastle upon Tyne: Cambridge Scholars, 2017), 47–48.

34.

1. Jean Baudrillard, *Cool Memories*, trans. Chris Turner (London: Verso, 1990), 100.
2. Patricia Meyer Spacks, *Boredom: The Literary History of a State of Mind* (Chicago: University of Chicago Press, 1995), 2.

35.

1. John Brewer, *The Pleasures of the Imagination: English Culture in the Eighteenth Century* (London: HarperCollins, 1997), 78.
2. The other four women in the picture are essayist Anna Letitia Barbauld, playwright Elizabeth Griffith, the painter Angelica Kauffman and the singer Elizabeth Sheridan.
3. The claim that he did so is efficiently debunked by O M Brack, Jr, and Susan Carlile in 'Samuel Johnson's Contributions to Charlotte Lennox's *The Female Quixote*', *Yale University Library Gazette* 77, No. 3/4 (2003), 166–173.
4. Boris Johnson, 'Dr Johnson was a slobbering, sexist xenophobe who understood human nature', *Daily Telegraph*, 14 September 2009. http://www.telegraph.co.uk/comment/columnists/borisjohnson/6186117/Dr-Johnson-was-a-slobbering-sexist-xenophobe-who-understood-human-nature.html Retrieved 2 June 2017.
5. Hillary Rodham Clinton, *Living History* (New York: Scribner, 2003), 190.
6. Quoted in James G. Basker, 'Multicultural Perspectives: Johnson, Race, and Gender', in Philip Smallwood (ed.), *Johnson Re-Visioned: Looking Before and After* (Lewisburg, Pennsylvania: Bucknell University Press, 2001), 65.
7. On the 'myth of Johnson's misogyny', see James G. Basker, 'Dancing Dogs, Women Preachers and the Myth of Johnson's Misogyny', *The Age of Johnson: A Scholarly Annual* 3 (1990), 63–90, and Donald Greene, 'The Myth of Johnson's Misogyny: Some Addenda', *South Central Review* 9, No. 4 (1992), 6–17. For broader discussion of the issue, see Kathleen Nulton

Kemmerer, *'A Neutral Being Between the Sexes': Samuel Johnson's Sexual Politics* (Lewisburg, Pennsylvania: Bucknell University Press, 1998).

36.

1. See John Allen Stevenson, 'Sterne: Comedian and Experimental Novelist', in John Richetti (ed.), *The Columbia History of the British Novel* (New York: Columbia University Press, 1994), 162, and also Julia H. Fawcett, *Spectacular Disappearances: Celebrity and Privacy, 1696–1801* (Ann Arbor: University of Michigan Press, 2016), 98–135.
2. Philip Smallwood, 'Johnson and Time', in *Samuel Johnson: The Arc of the Pendulum*, ed. Freya Johnston and Lynda Mugglestone (Oxford: Oxford University Press, 2012).
3. See, for instance, C. M. Vicario et al., 'Time processing in children with Tourette's syndrome', *Brain and Cognition* 73, No. 1 (2010), 28–34.
4. Philippe Ariès, *Western Attitudes Towards Death: From the Middle Ages to the Present*, trans. Patricia M. Ranum (Baltimore, Maryland: Johns Hopkins University Press, 1974), 55–60.

37.

1. Lawrence Lipking, *The Ordering of the Arts in Eighteenth-Century England* (Princeton, New Jersey: Princeton University Press, 1970), 18–19.
2. Elizabeth Barrett Browning, *The Greek Christian Poets and the English Poets* (London: Chapman & Hall, 1863), 191.
3. Robert Folkenflik, *Samuel Johnson, Biographer* (Ithaca, New York: Cornell University Press, 1978), 82–83.

38.

1. McGuffie, *Samuel Johnson in the British Press*, 335, 338, 341.
2. Thomas Percy, *Verses on the Death of Dr Samuel Johnson* (London: Charles Dilly, 1785), 14. Thomas Hobhouse, *Elegy to the Memory of Dr Samuel Johnson* (London: John Stockdale, 1785), 9.
3. Isaiah Berlin, *The Hedgehog and the Fox: An Essay on Tolstoy's View of History* (London: Weidenfeld and Nicolson, 1953), 1.

4. Jean H. Hagstrum, 'Samuel Johnson among the Deconstructionists', in Nalini Jain (ed.), *Re-Viewing Samuel Johnson* (London: Sangam, 1991), 116.
5. Montaigne, *The Complete Essays*, 380.